PENNY ARCADE™ 5

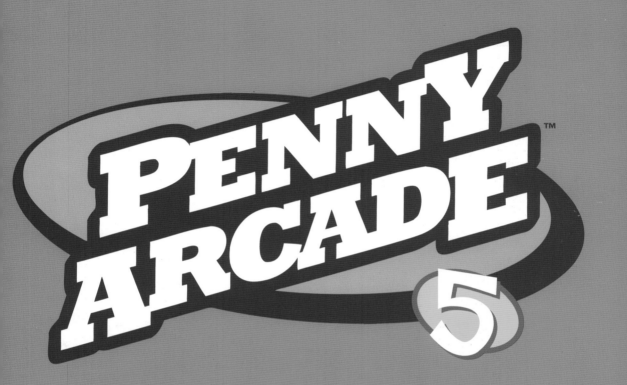

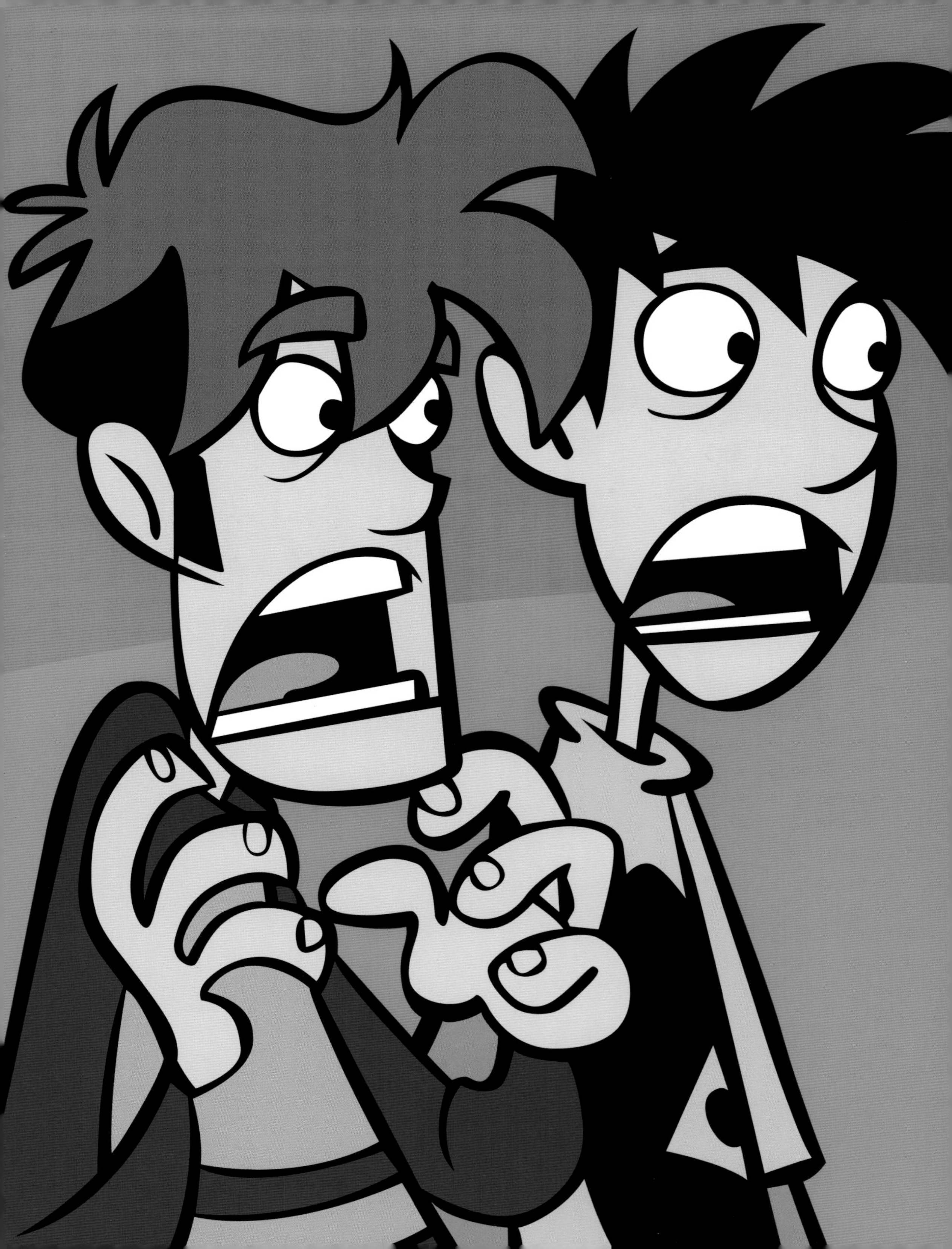

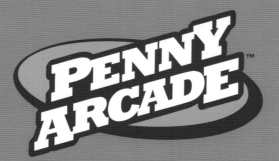

PENNY-ARCADE.COM

BY JERRY HOLKINS & MIKE KRAHULIK

dark horse books®

Publisher
MIKE RICHARDSON

Editors
SAMANTHA ROBERTSON
and **JEREMY BARLOW**

Designer
DAVID NESTELLE

Art Director
LIA RIBACCHI

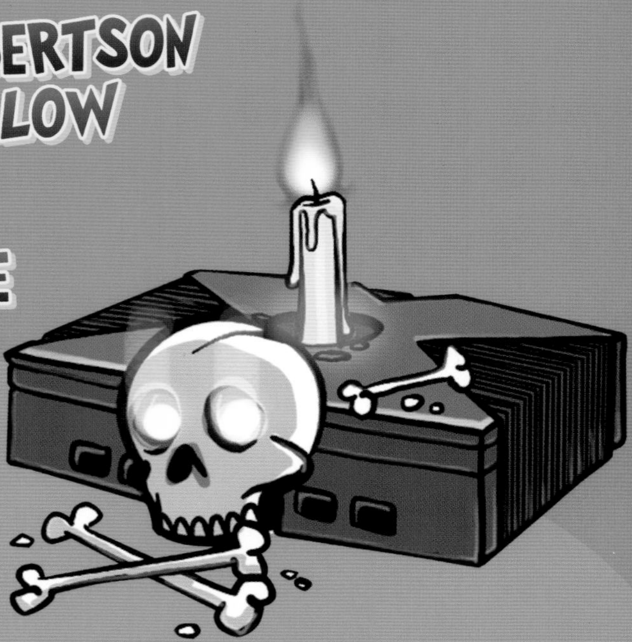

Very special thanks to ROBERT KHOO at Penny Arcade!

PENNY ARCADE Volume 5: The Case of the Mummy's Gold

This volume collects comic strips from the Penny Arcade website, originally published online from January 1, 2004 through December 31, 2004.

Published by
Dark Horse Books
A division of Dark Horse Comics, Inc.
10956 SE Main Street
Milwaukie, OR 97222

darkhorse.com

To find a comics shop in your area, call the Comic Shop Locator Service toll-free at 1-888-266-4226

First edition: July 2008
ISBN 978-1-59307-814-0

10 9 8 7 6 5 4 3 2 1
Printed in China

Foreword by Wil Wheaton

I can't recall the first time I saw *Penny Arcade*, but it's pretty safe to assume either Fark or one of my gamer friends shoved it in front of my face. I wish I had a great story about how the first *Penny Arcade* comic I read shone the bright light of a hopeful future onto my life, but I don't, because I've read and loved and shared with my friends nearly every comic they've published since 2001. That's a lot of comics, and in the last seven years, they've all kind of blurred together into a big pile of Fruit Fucker leavings.

However, I may have the distinction of being one of the only people to end up in a *Penny Arcade* comic within seventy-two hours of meeting Mike and Jerry. I probably share this distinction with at least one dickwad Gamestop employee, but I leave that little detail out when I'm trying to impress my friends by sharing this fun fact. And we're all friends, right?

Please say yes.

(And while I'm talking about impressing people, you know what would really impress my kids? If Mike and Jerry put me into another *Penny Arcade* strip. I'm just saying, it's for the children . . . not for drooling fanboy me.)

But enough about me. Let's talk about *Penny Arcade* for a minute, okay? You most likely own this book because you know how awesome it is, or because someone you know has impeccable taste in gifts. If you don't own it yet, the RIAA would like to have a word with you about reading words you haven't paid to enjoy, so go buy it already before they haul your ass off. Yes, the RIAA is so evil they will hunt down people reading books that have nothing to do with music.

If you're new to *Penny Arcade*, and you've chosen this book to take a walk through the archives, go ahead and flip through the book for a minute, then come back here and keep reading.

Go ahead, I'll wait.

Hey, quick, before the New Kid gets back: have any of you guys seen my Weighted Companion Cube? I think the New Kid may have taken it and—

Oh! Hey, you're back. We, uh, we totally weren't talking about you while you were gone.

So it's pretty cool, isn't it? I bet you'd like to know how these two guys from Seattle have been able to make a living publishing this comic, and how it's lasted for nearly ten years. Well, as someone who's been reading it for over half that decade, I'd like to tell you why I think *Penny Arcade* continues to be massively popular with one of the most critical, discerning audiences in history. (I say that as someone who is intimately—whoa, totally wrong word—acquainted with Trekkies, so I know from impossible-to-please fanboys.)

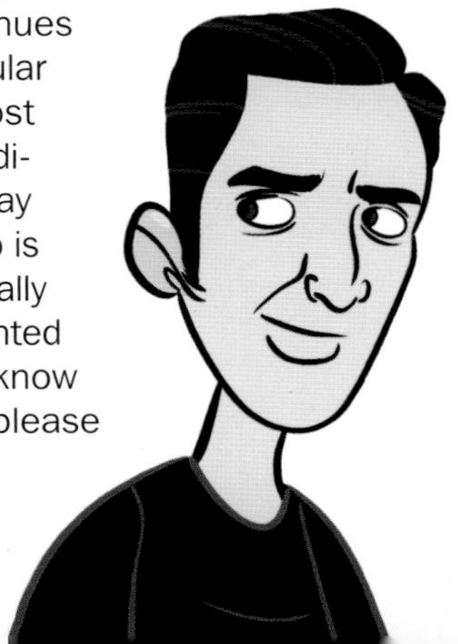

Gamers are intensely passionate. We're fiercely—dare we admit, irrationally?—loyal to our analog and electronic gaming systems. We're also some of the most cynical and fickle people on the planet. We're tough to fool, and if we get burned once, we never forget. A lifetime spent smashing buttons and running around corridors from consoles to arcades hasn't given us the best attention spans in the world.

We are also *Penny Arcade*'s target audience.

Game publishers have lots of money to spend on games—and on advertising at sites like Penny Arcade. It would be understandable if Jerry and Mike were, from time to time (roughly three times a week, by my count), nervous about writing something that might put their figurative dicks in the proverbial mashed potatoes.

How can they do it? How can they stare down that two-headed monster and still have such reckless bravado when they put *Penny Arcade* together? Just listen to Mike and Jerry's podcast, Downloadable Content, and sit with them while they open up their creative process. It only takes a few minutes to realize that these guys are having *fun*. They don't worry about taking creative risks (and thank jeebus they don't, because if they did, they wouldn't have created Twisp and Catsby) and they don't worry about pleasing everyone in the audience. They're not afraid to speak the truth to those in power, and they pointed out that Uwe Boll was an epic douche long before it was fashionable to do so.

Their total fearlessness lets Mike and Jerry lampoon slimy game publishers one day, make fun of profane gamers and their unintentionally hilarious message board polemics the next day, and then spend two weeks exploring feudal Japan with the Cardboard Tube Samurai.

Through it all, they have consistently defended and even advocated for gamers in a world that more and more frequently scapegoats us for everything from spoiled milk to terrorism. They've stood up to lawsuits from professional attention-whore Jack Thompson and beaten him at his own game. They started Child's Play, a charity that's raised over two million dollars to bring games, toys, and joy to sick kids in hospitals all over America, proving that at least some of us gamers are not the bloodthirsty psychopaths that pandering politicians and hysterical reporters would like you to believe we are. And when they noticed that the annual E3 trade show was a disastrous pile of leaky-seal suck, they started the Penny Arcade Expo to give us something to look forward to each August.

It wasn't always this way, though. Penny Arcade is more than a comic, now, it's a fucking *empire*, but the strips collected in this book hearken to a time before any of us—Mike and Jerry included—had any idea how bright the future would be, and how many pairs of Timbuk3-branded shades we'd need to face it. Many of these comics reflect a simpler time when online console-based multiplayer gaming was just getting started, when we were convinced that the physics in Half Life were as perfect as the texture mapping in Unreal Tournament, when WoW was still in closed beta, and when we still believed that, one day, we'd get to play Duke Nukem Forever.

It's an honor to introduce the fifth *Penny Arcade* collection, because it happens to contain some of my all-time favorite strips, including "Green Blackboards (and other Anomalies)," which introduced the world to John Gabriel's Greater Internet Fuckwad Theory, and "No Produce is Safe," which introduced us to Fruit Fucker Prime—whose poster adorns the wall in my home office, much to the chagrin of my wife.

Maybe she'll get me a Twisp and Catsby poster for my birthday this year.

See you at PAX!

—Author, Actor, Raconteur,
and Gamer For Fucking Life
Wil Wheaton
January 8, 2008
Pasadena, CA

V

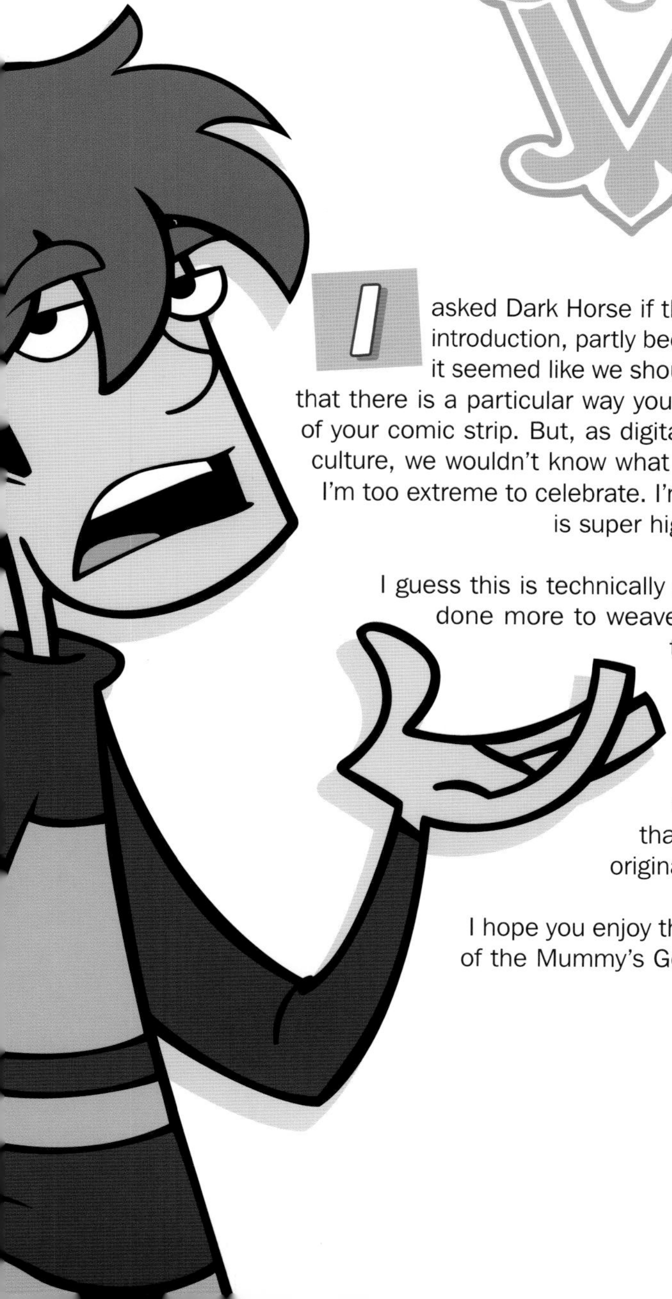

I asked Dark Horse if they could make me a cool "V" to go above the introduction, partly because I couldn't think of a title, but also because it seemed like we should turn things up for the fifth volume. It may be that there is a particular way you are *supposed* to celebrate the fifth collection of your comic strip. But, as digital renegades riding the jagged edge of comics culture, we wouldn't know what it is. And, as a hard-ass Internet provocateur, I'm too extreme to celebrate. I'm always fucking jumping off of something that is super high, or delivering hard chops to the midsection.

I guess this is technically a pentalogy now, and it makes me wish I had done more to weave an epic tale through each of them. I could try to establish one after the fact, I suppose. Let's say that the first book is about a Sword, second one . . . a Cup, and for the third one let's go the Bird route. Fourth book, I want to say Umbrella. That's something you can really use. Fifth book, Comb. It can be assumed that each of these objects is magical, although I originally typed *bagical*, which . . . might also be true.

I hope you enjoy this volume of *Penny Arcade*, entitled The Curse of the Mummy's Gold. Or, wait. Is it The "Case" of the Mummy's Gold? Hold on, let me look.

Okay, yeah. It's "Case."

—Tycho Brahe
December 24, 2007
Seattle, WA

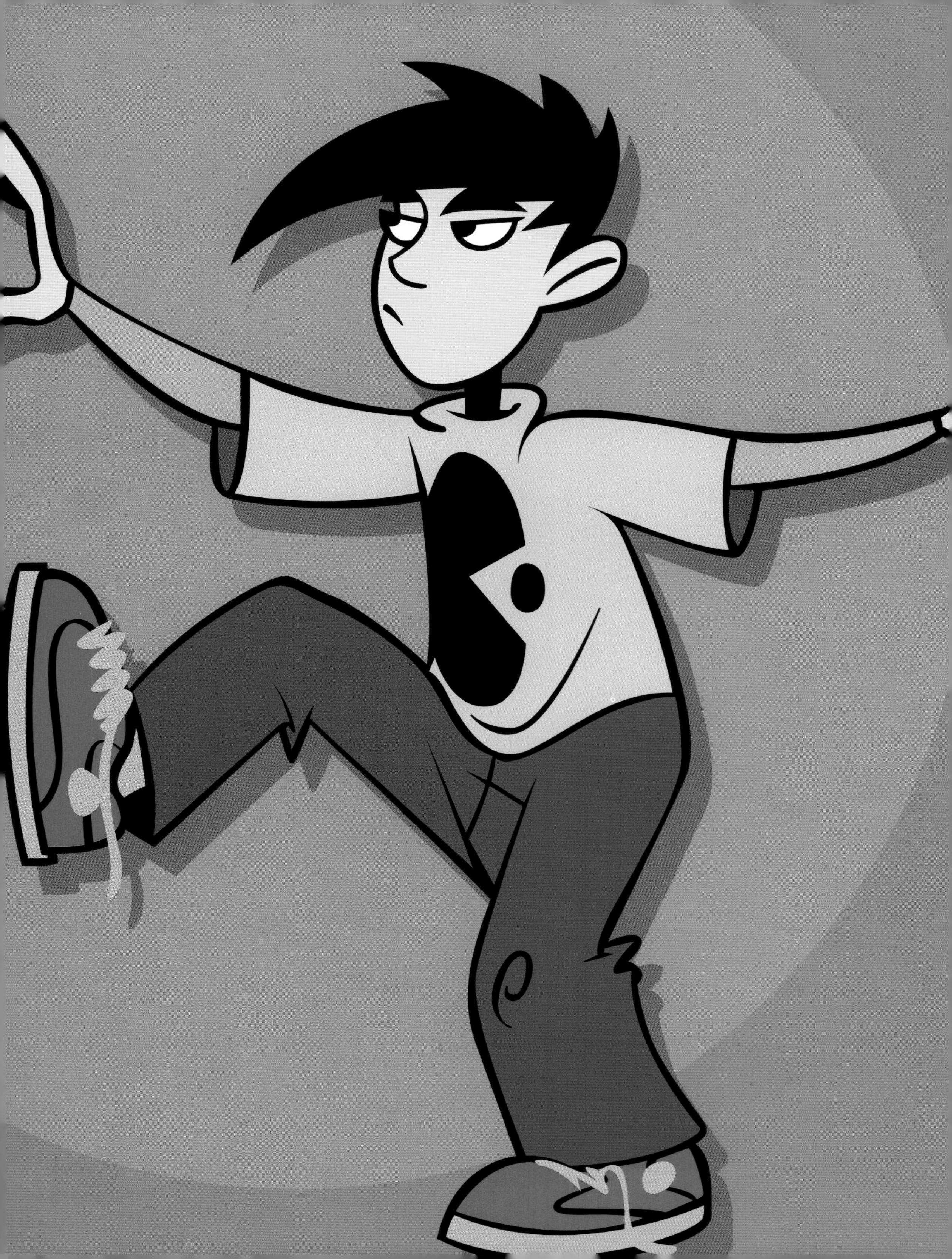

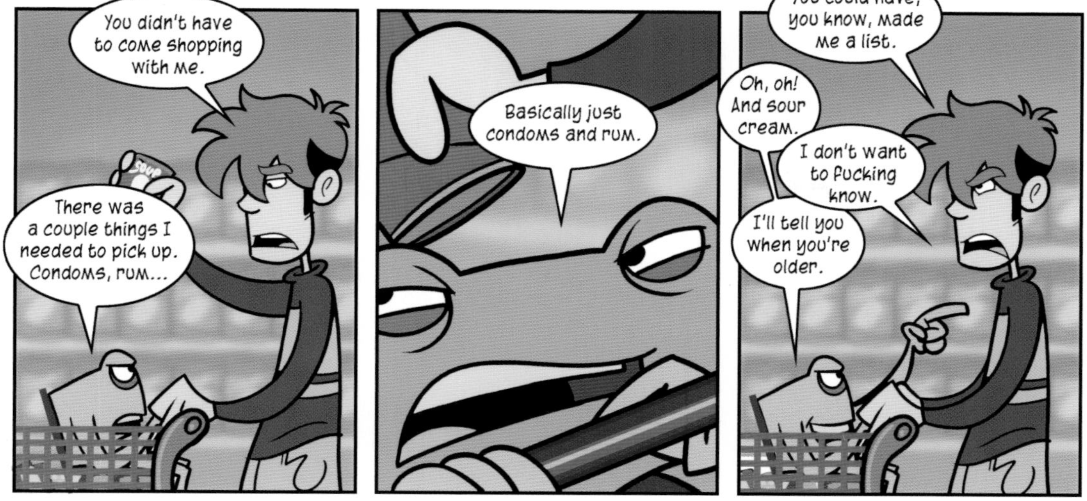
You didn't have to come shopping with me.
There was a couple things I needed to pick up. Condoms, rum...
SOUP
Basically just condoms and rum.
You could have, you know, made me a list.
Oh, oh! And sour cream.
I don't want to fucking know.
I'll tell you when you're older.

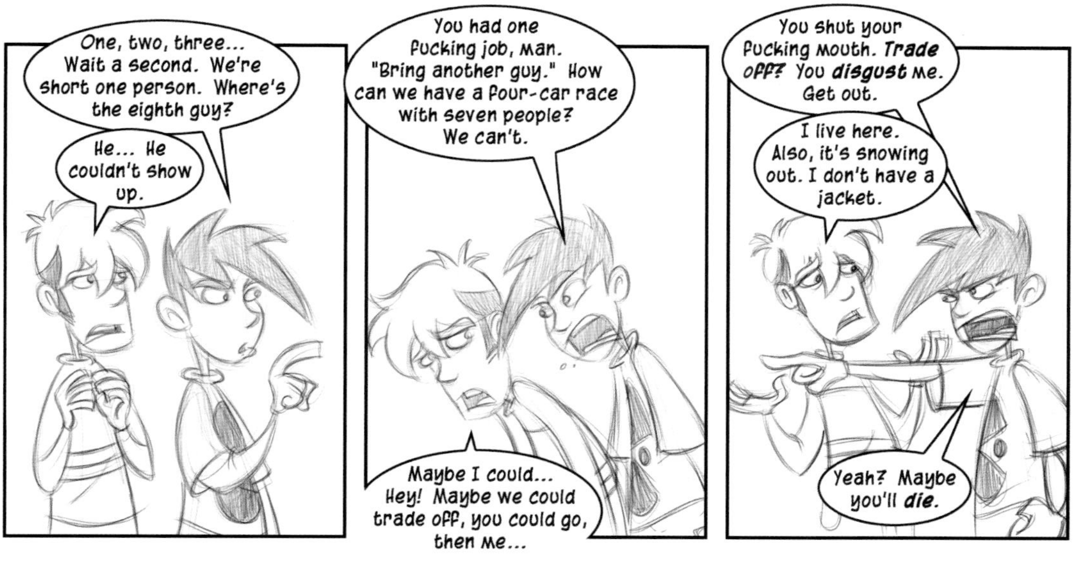
One, two, three... Wait a second. We're short one person. Where's the eighth guy?
He... He couldn't show up.
You had one fucking job, man. "Bring another guy." How can we have a four-car race with seven people? We can't.
Maybe I could... Hey! Maybe we could trade off, you could go, then me...
You shut your fucking mouth. *Trade off?* You *disgust* me. Get out.
I live here. Also, it's snowing out. I don't have a jacket.
Yeah? Maybe you'll *die.*

PERHAPS BEST UNSAID

January 2, 2004 Check out the post for this strip, seriously—I was incandescent with rage. Local news had just declared that the *one hundred and seventy-five thousand dollars* worth of toys and games readers had purchased for Child's Play weren't given by gamers, they were given by "a local Catholic School." Also, it was only *one* thousand dollars. I assumed they were idiots at first, but maybe they are simply allergic to *facts.*

IT IS SO VERY COLD

January 7, 2004 There's actually no explanation anywhere in our deep, goblin-infested archive as to why there would be no colors on this strip. So, it is *again* my task to beg your pardon for my hostile, careless cohort. I apologize from way, way down in my soul. Like, *way* down. He's like some stray animal I found, mangy and skeletal, and I must spend the better part of each day making sure he doesn't choke on something.

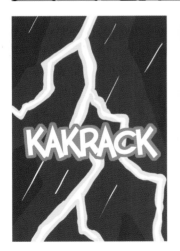

THE WANDERING AGE 2

January 5, 2004 This is my favorite CTS comic. If I said that about another one, I was wrong.

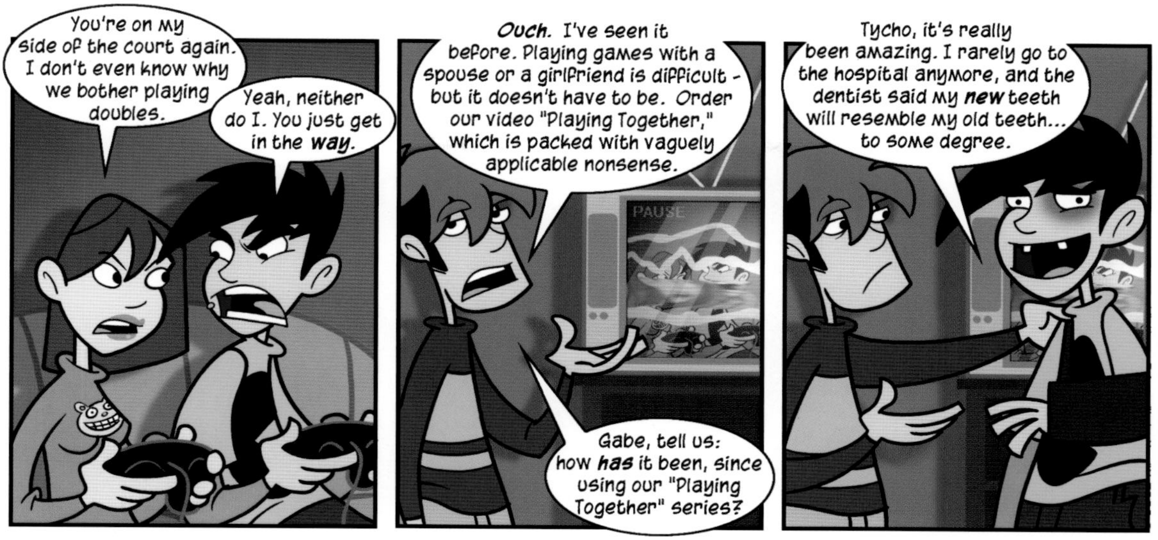
You're on my side of the court again. I don't even know why we bother playing doubles.
Yeah, neither do I. You just get in the *way*.
Ouch. I've seen it before. Playing games with a spouse or a girlfriend is difficult - but it doesn't have to be. Order our video "Playing Together," which is packed with vaguely applicable nonsense.
PAUSE
Gabe, tell us: how *has* it been, since using our "Playing Together" series?
Tycho, it's really been amazing. I rarely go to the hospital anymore, and the dentist said my *new* teeth will resemble my old teeth... to some degree.

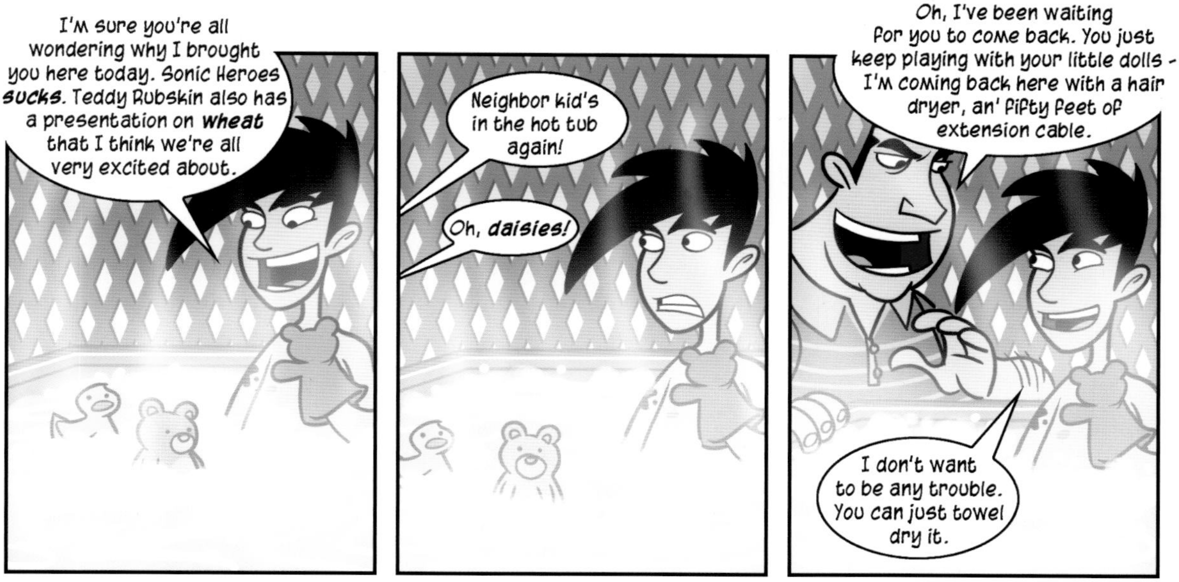
I'm sure you're all wondering why I brought you here today. Sonic Heroes *sucks*. Teddy Rubskin also has a presentation on *wheat* that I think we're all very excited about.
Neighbor kid's in the hot tub again!
Oh, *daisies!*
Oh, I've been waiting for you to come back. You just keep playing with your little dolls - I'm coming back here with a hair dryer, an' fifty feet of extension cable.
I don't want to be any trouble. You can just towel dry it.

THE COMIC THAT HEALS

January 9, 2004 I have heard many gamers complain about spouses (etc.) who aren't "down" with gaming, but two gamers wrasslin' over a single television is no better and is, in some ways, worse. And that's not just on account of the wrasslin', which reasonable people may have differing opinions on. At the most basic level: think about buying your games and systems *twice*. Be careful what you wish for.

GABRIEL AND FRIENDS

January 12, 2004 Having a board meeting with your bath toys in a neighbor's hot tub is a very, um . . . unique hook. Oh, hey, about that CTS strip on the other page. I just noticed that the assassin in the last panel there has her pinky extended, giving her the full five fingers. He must have really wanted that pinky, because Gabriel almost never draws the full five fingers. I could count the number of times he has drawn five fingers on one hand, provided the hand I was counting on *also* had five fingers.

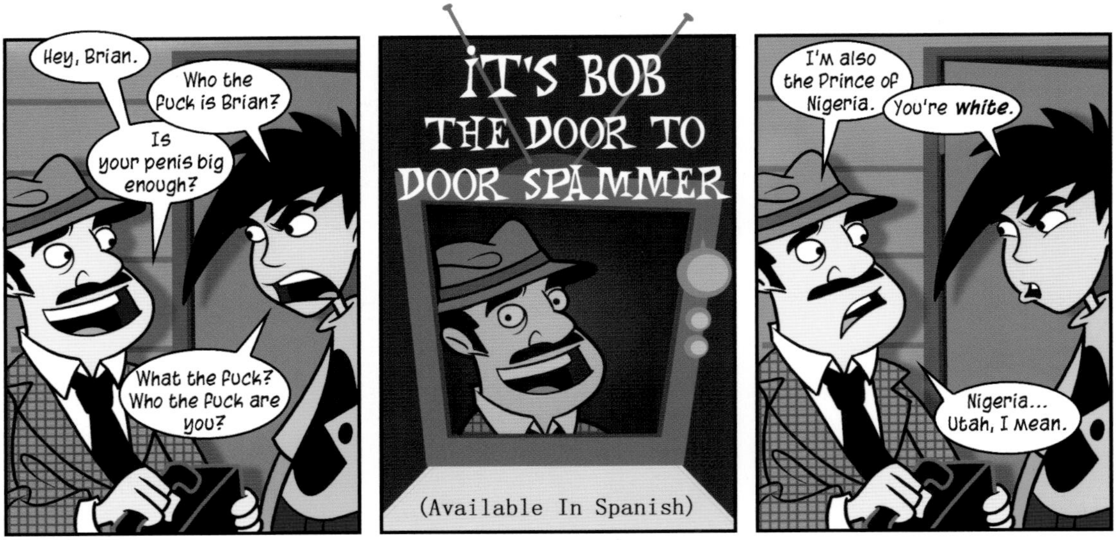
Hey, Brian.
Who the fuck is Brian?
Is your penis big enough?
What the fuck? Who the fuck are you?
IT'S BOB THE DOOR TO DOOR SPAMMER
(Available In Spanish)
I'm also the Prince of Nigeria.
You're white.
Nigeria... Utah, I mean.

COMING THURSDAYS ON UPN

January 14, 2004 Spam had become a political topic around this time, causing our nation's leaders to cobble together some kind of partial response while the cameras were still rolling on the issue. It was also around this time that I contributed a song about spam to a compilation called *Outside the Inbox*, put together by my friend Brad Sucks. I submitted it under the name "Verbose," which felt right. My cat figures on the song prominently.

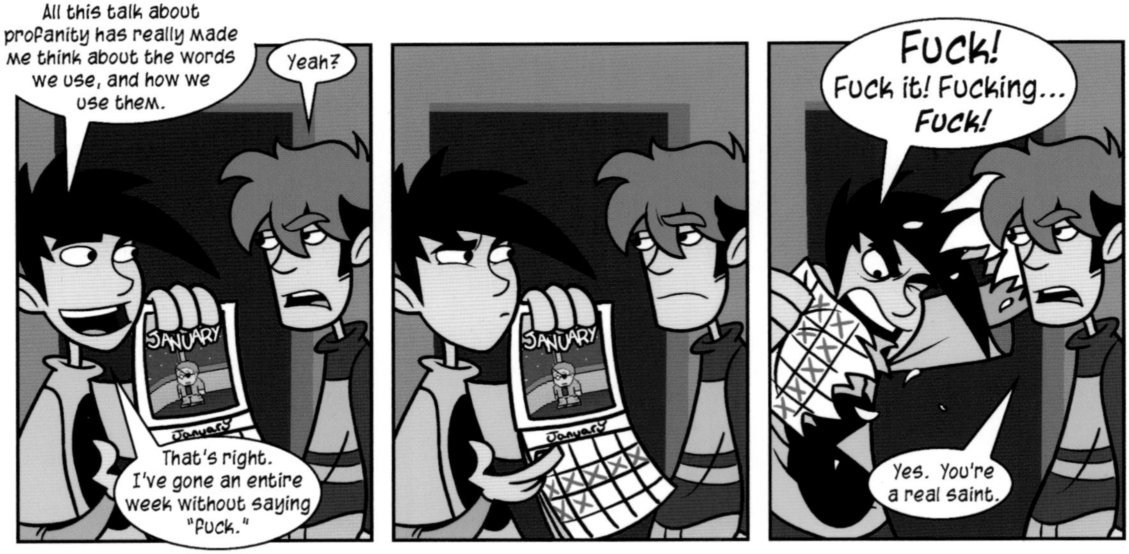
All this talk about profanity has really made me think about the words we use, and how we use them.
Yeah?
JANUARY
January
That's right. I've gone an entire week without saying "fuck."
Fuck! Fuck it! Fucking... Fuck!
Yes. You're a real saint.

I CAN SEE THE START OF A TINY HALO

January 16, 2004 The FCC was snarling at someone for this or that, bad words or some shit. *I'm* just glad that there is someone to worry about this grave matter professionally. No doubt they sit around a great, oaken table and rank words like "hump," "doody," and "pooper" in terms of their society-shredding potential. Their task is impossible, of course. Even the worst broadcast television is *pristine* compared to your average junior high cafeteria.

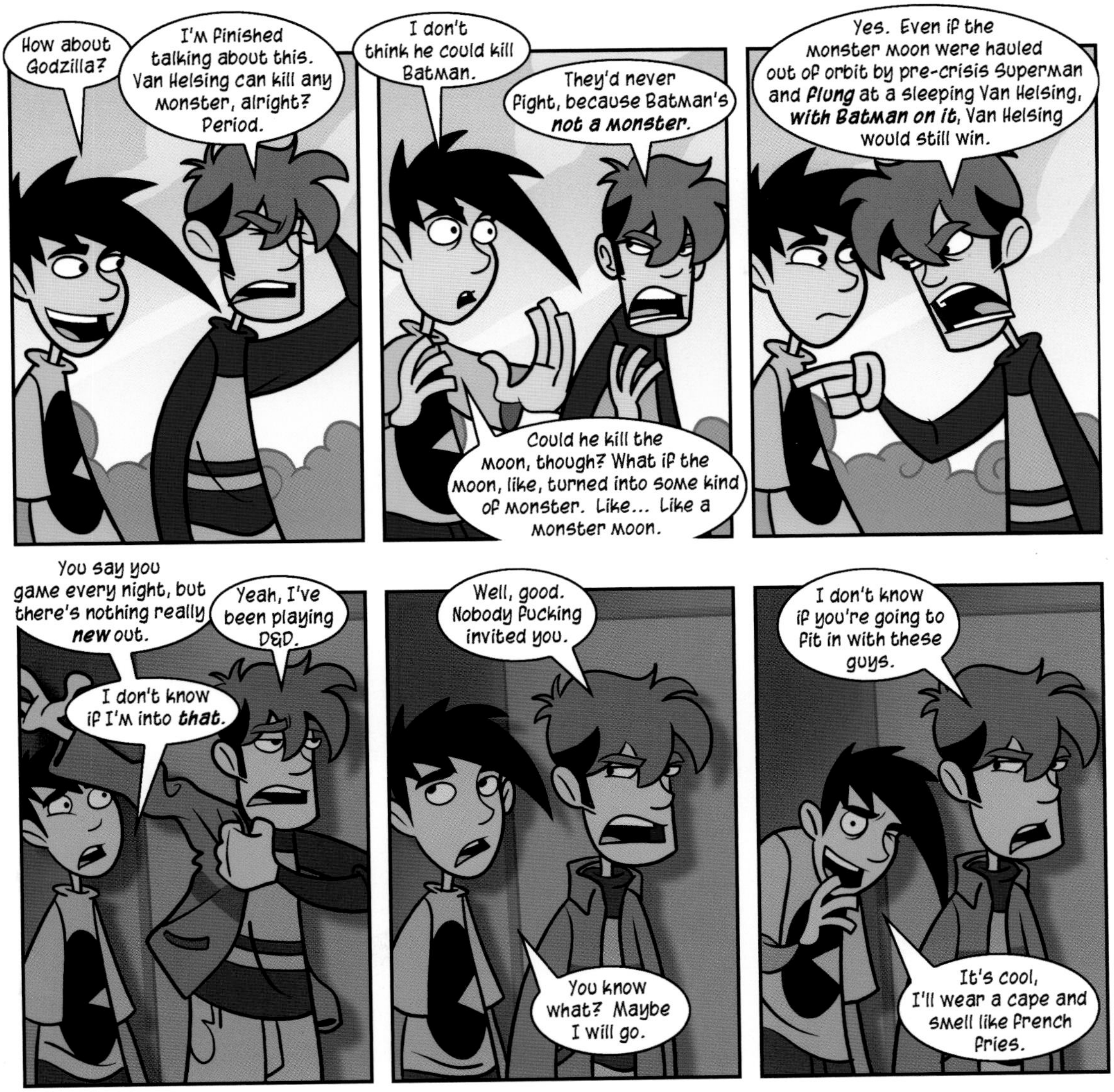
How about Godzilla?
I'm finished talking about this. Van Helsing can kill any monster, alright? Period.
I don't think he could kill Batman.
They'd never fight, because Batman's **not a monster**.
Could he kill the moon, though? What if the moon, like, turned into some kind of monster. Like... Like a monster moon.
Yes. Even if the monster moon were hauled out of orbit by pre-crisis Superman and **flung** at a sleeping Van Helsing, **with Batman on it**, Van Helsing would still win.
You say you game every night, but there's nothing really **new** out.
Yeah, I've been playing D&D.
I don't know if I'm into **that**.
Well, good. Nobody fucking invited you.
You know what? Maybe I will go.
I don't know if you're going to fit in with these guys.
It's cool, I'll wear a cape and smell like french fries.

CHANNELING KEVIN SMITH

January 19, 2004 You know, I never ended up seeing Van Helsing. I felt confident that—given the martial prowess expressed so completely above—he would best however many slavering beasts were set before him with guile slash brutality. Perhaps he would fall in love with someone above his station, or engage in gallows humor. Betting places the chances of a harrowing escape at somewhere near one hundred percent.

DUNGEONS AND SOMETHING ELSE, PART ONE

January 21, 2004 I haven't had an opportunity to "roll the bones" (as they say) for quite a while, although I plan to use the release of D&D Fourth Edition as an excuse to tap back in. I have a ridiculous set of pink glow-in-the-dark dice that I insist on using, even though the twenty-sider is actually lopsided—it seems to roll an inordinate amount of twenties and ones. Throwing that thing is a dangerous act, like playing Russian Roulette.

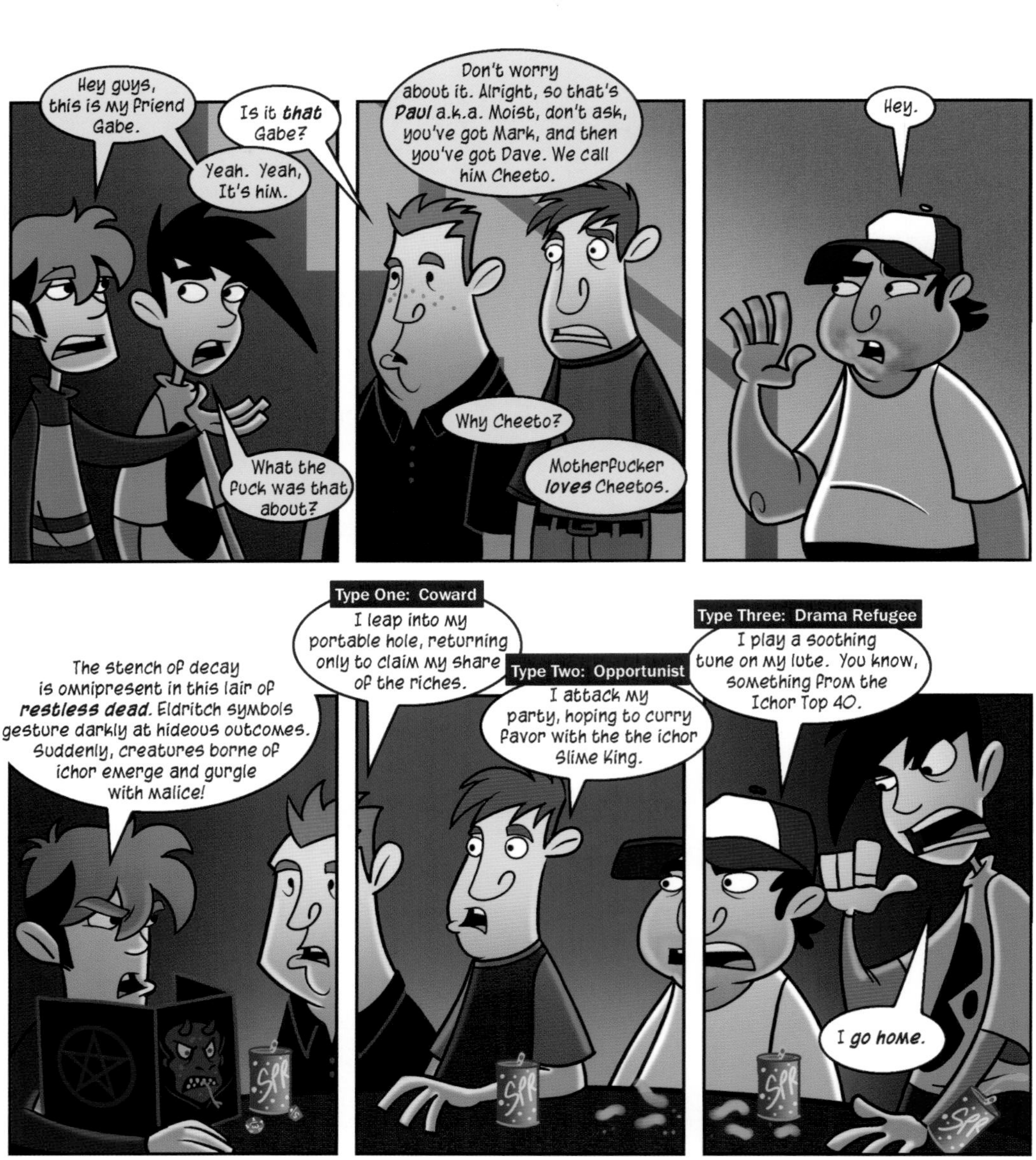
Hey guys, this is my friend Gabe.
Is it that Gabe?
Yeah. Yeah, It's him.
What the fuck was that about?
Don't worry about it. Alright, so that's Paul a.k.a. Moist, don't ask, you've got Mark, and then you've got Dave. We call him Cheeto.
Why Cheeto?
Motherfucker loves Cheetos.
Hey.
The stench of decay is omnipresent in this lair of restless dead. Eldritch symbols gesture darkly at hideous outcomes. Suddenly, creatures borne of ichor emerge and gurgle with malice!
Type One: Coward
I leap into my portable hole, returning only to claim my share of the riches.
Type Two: Opportunist
I attack my party, hoping to curry favor with the the ichor Slime King.
Type Three: Drama Refugee
I play a soothing tune on my lute. You know, something from the Ichor Top 40.
I go home.

DUNGEONS AND SOMETHING ELSE, PART TWO

January 23, 2004 I love that you've got someone named Moist, and then someone named Cheeto, and then you've just got Mark. Regular old, shelf-model Mark. Not Marky Mark, not Mark and Mindy. Not Mark Chocolate or even *Hunter's* Mark. You could even rock it J. K. Rowling style and take it all the way up to "Dark Mark." Not him! He's just Mark, and he seems to like it.

DUNGEONS AND SOMETHING ELSE, PART THREE

January 26, 2004 I have to say that I *do* love that Dungeon Master's screen. Most of my table hours were spent on the other side of such screens, poring over them to absorb their deep wisdom. I have a very clear image in my mind of a thief on one of these screens prying out the jeweled eye of some idol, a gem easily the size of a basketball. In my gaming career, I've probably stared at that thing for at least twenty hours. It put a name to some deep desire I never knew I had.

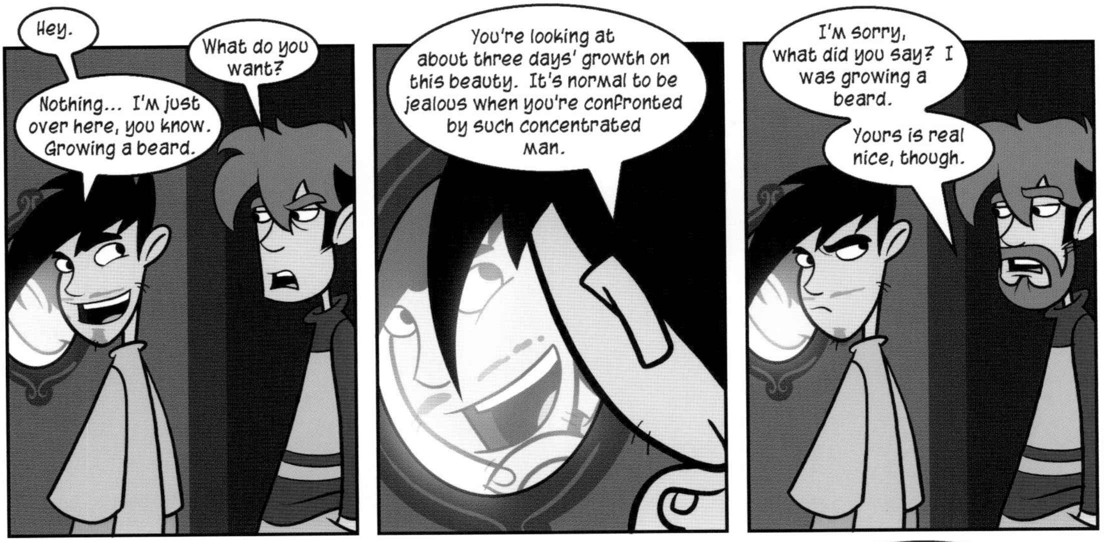
Hey.
What do you want?
Nothing... I'm just over here, you know. Growing a beard.
You're looking at about three days' growth on this beauty. It's normal to be jealous when you're confronted by such concentrated man.
I'm sorry, what did you say? I was growing a beard.
Yours is real nice, though.

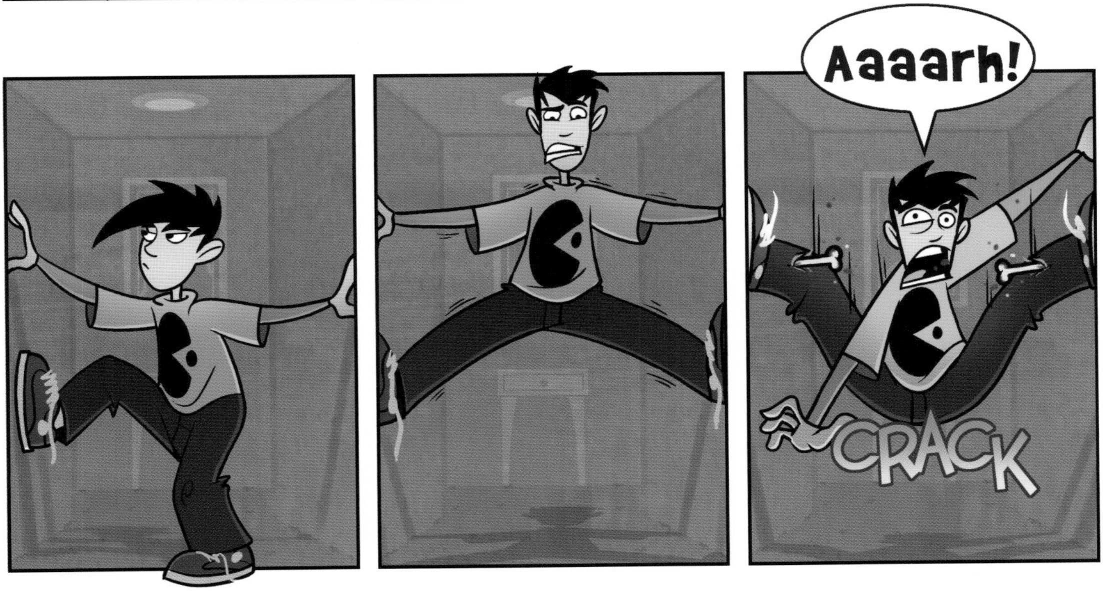
Aaaarh!
CRACK

SHAVING IS NOT DIFFICULT OR TIME CONSUMING

January 28, 2004 This comic is, to all outward appearances, a piece about how Gabriel can't grow hair. The sinister reality is that he is coated from head to toe in a rug of thick black hair. If he wants to see at all, his eyelids require *daily* shaving. It's healthy hair—lustrous, I'm saying—but it's dense. At PAX, we basically have to shear him each morning before we trot him out. The tender skin beneath is white and slightly translucent, like a grub.

THEM BONES

January 30, 2004 He actually does this, and his tibia *never* erupt from his legs when executing these Fisherian maneuvers. He can skitter straight up the wall and just *wait*, presumably to catch prey. He hissed at me once when I was on my way out to the car, and I was surprised to find him on the ceiling of the parkade, hanging there, *gibbous*, like some bad moon.

Let's go over there!
Hey, what's up there?
Look at that cave! Let's go into the *caaave.*
I'm sorry you didn't make it into the WoW beta. But this, what's going on here? This isn't working.
You're right. I should probably be at the keyboard.

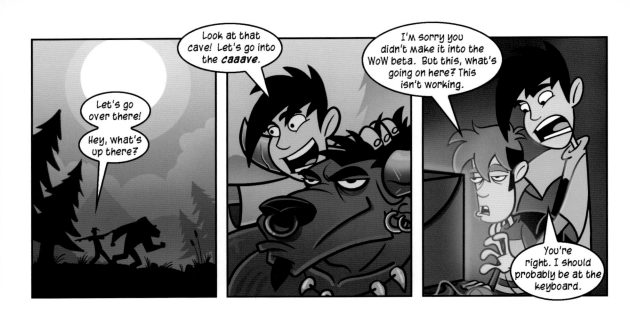

ONE NIGHT IN AZEROTH

February 2, 2004 It's hard to imagine a time in Earth's mysterious past where toons were not farming Molten Core, but here you are. Even in World of Warcraft's raw, rudimentary *Alpha* you could see that they had boiled it way, way down. They were friendly to players in ways developers had previously been brutal. Combat was—and this is crazy!—*semi-enjoyable*. We recently started playing again, and the hooks are in deep. I wonder if I'll be free by the time this book goes to print.

LOCK YOUR DOORS (facing page)

February 4, 2004 This was the first strip we wrote after we decided to get an office together. We wanted to work on bigger, more elaborate projects, and since I had to go to his house to work on things, it created a situation where I both worked from home *and* had a ridiculous commute. The irony weighs on a person. Once we had an office, we didn't really know what to do there. I'd certainly worked in an office before, and I know how to work as a general concept, but I couldn't tell if having an office for Penny Arcade was the right thing for the strip. This shared worry completely obliterated our ability to write, causing this bizarre thing to be created.

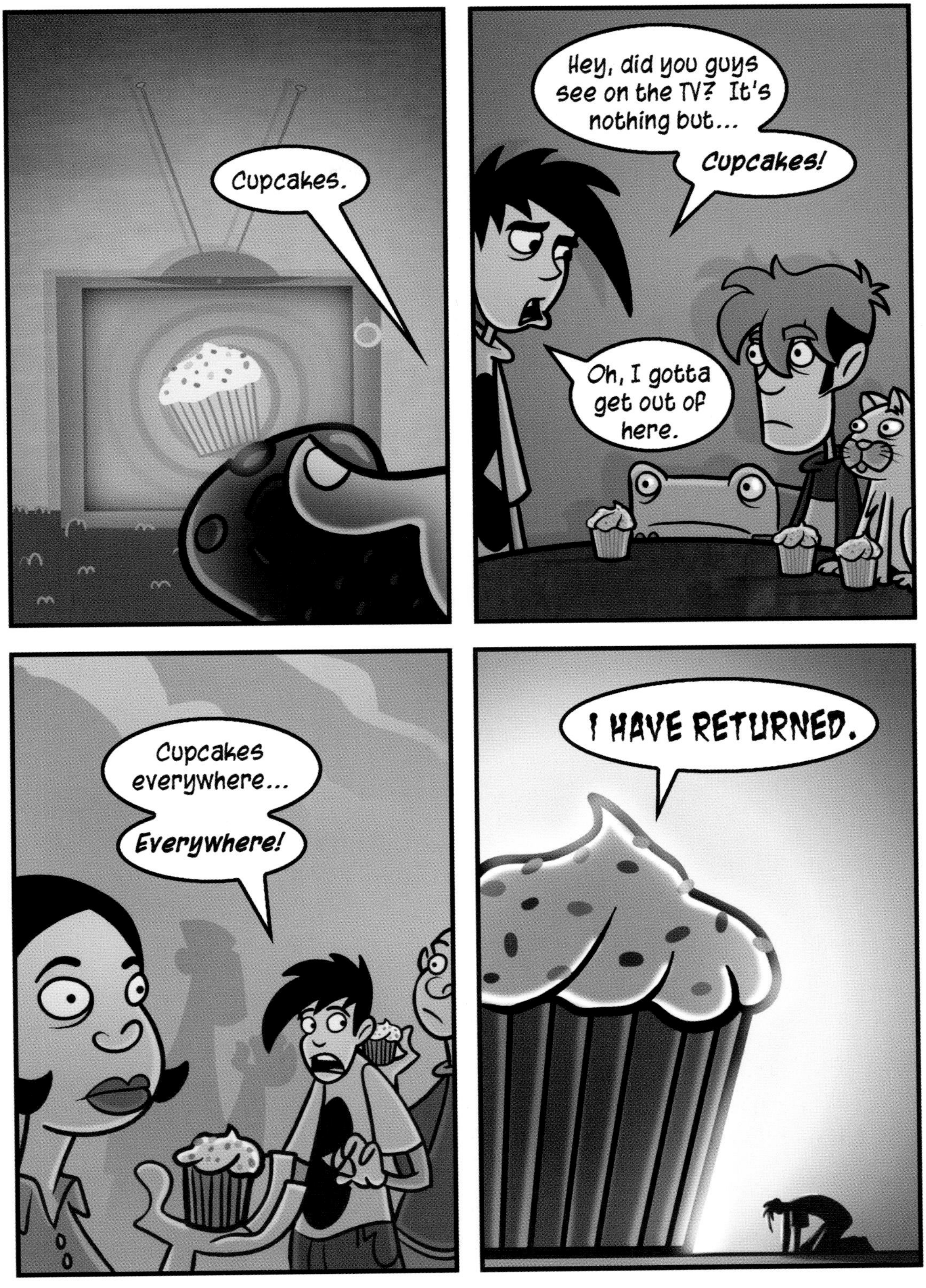
Cupcakes.
Hey, did you guys see on the TV? It's nothing but...
Cupcakes!
Oh, I gotta get out of here.
Cupcakes everywhere...
Everywhere!
I HAVE RETURNED.

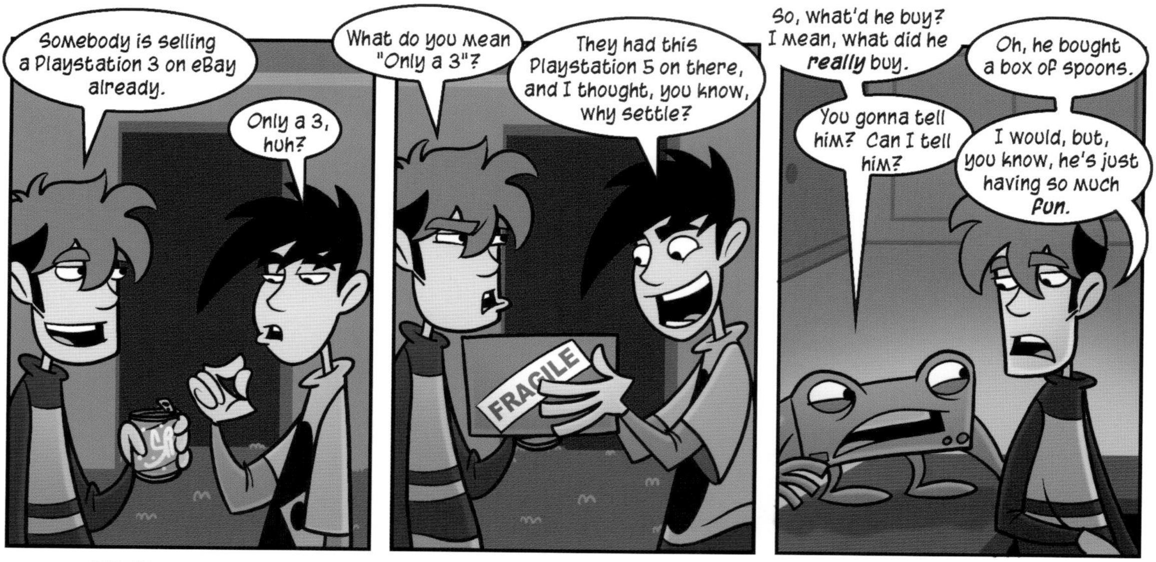
Somebody is selling a Playstation 3 on eBay already.
Only a 3, huh?
What do you mean "Only a 3"?
They had this Playstation 5 on there, and I thought, you know, why settle?
FRAGILE
So, what'd he buy? I mean, what did he *really* buy.
Oh, he bought a box of spoons.
You gonna tell him? Can I tell him?
I would, but, you know, he's just having so much *fun*.

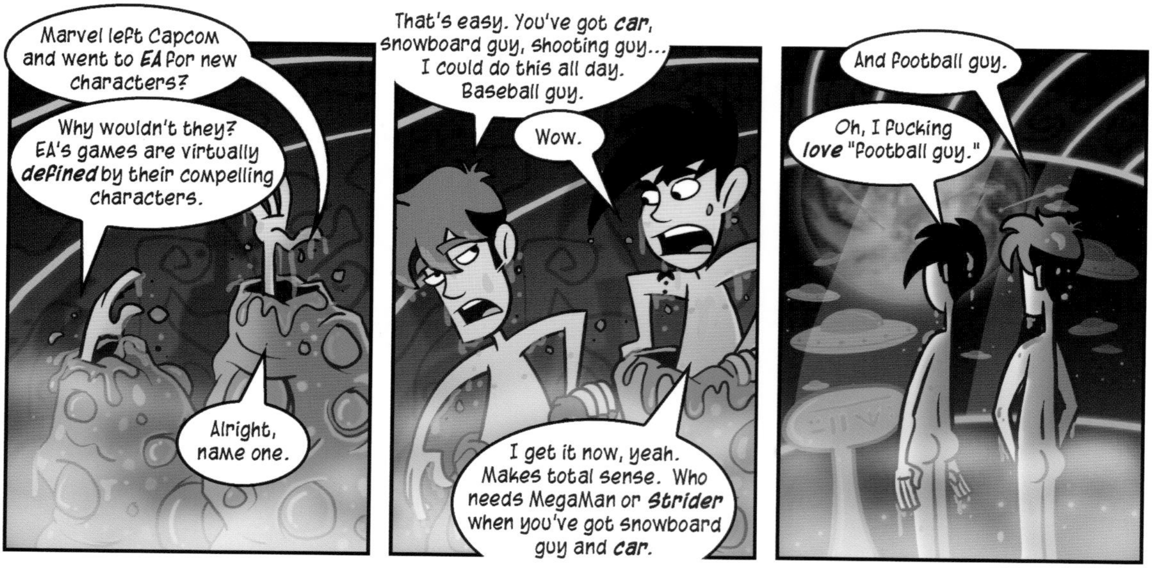
Marvel left Capcom and went to *EA* for new characters?
Why wouldn't they? EA's games are virtually *defined* by their compelling characters.
Alright, name one.
That's easy. You've got *car*, snowboard guy, shooting guy... I could do this all day. Baseball guy.
Wow.
I get it now, yeah. Makes total sense. Who needs MegaMan or *Strider* when you've got snowboard guy and *car*.
And football guy.
Oh, I fucking *love* "football guy."

A GOOD PLAN, IN THEORY

February 6, 2004 The obvious joke, the one I am doing my best to avoid, is the one where you suggest the amount of fun you can have with a spoon and a PS3 are roughly comparable. There was a long, dark, also *cold* period of time when you could make a joke like that and actually have it stick. Luckily, *most* luckily for those who were out six hundred smackers, that brutal season has since thawed.

EMERGING FROM HIDEOUS COCOONS

February 9, 2004 We had wanted to do a comic strip where we emerged from slime-encrusted cocoons for quite a while, but the opportunity never presented itself. You would think you could toss in some old cocoon just anywhere, but we really wanted to respect both the cocoons themselves and the larger notion of cocooning *itself* with the piece.

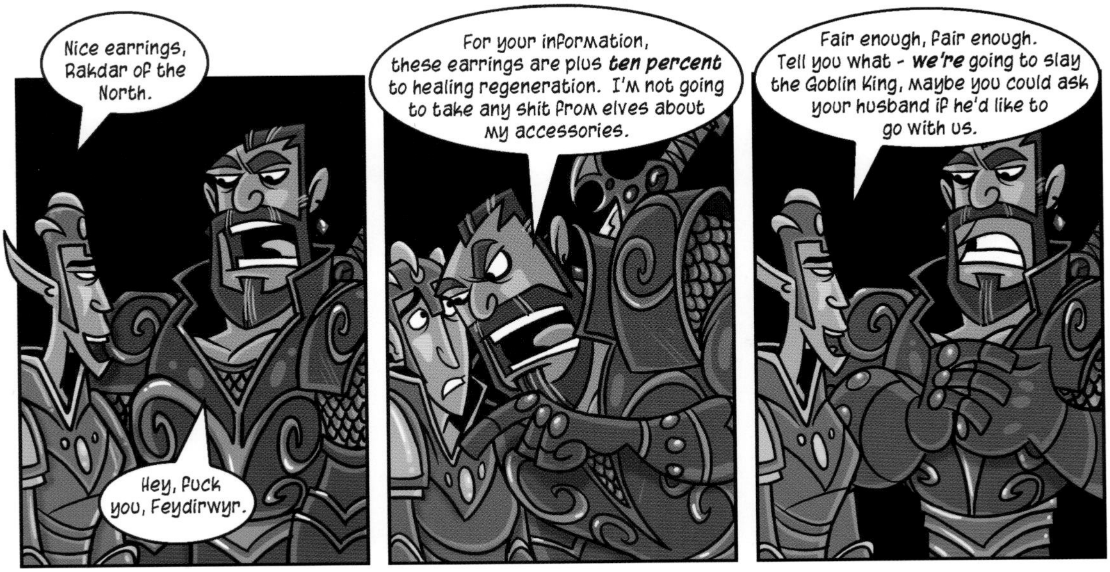
Nice earrings, Rakdar of the North.
Hey, fuck you, Feydirwyr.
For your information, these earrings are plus **ten percent** to healing regeneration. I'm not going to take any shit from elves about my accessories.
Fair enough, fair enough. Tell you what - **we're** going to slay the Goblin King, maybe you could ask your husband if he'd like to go with us.

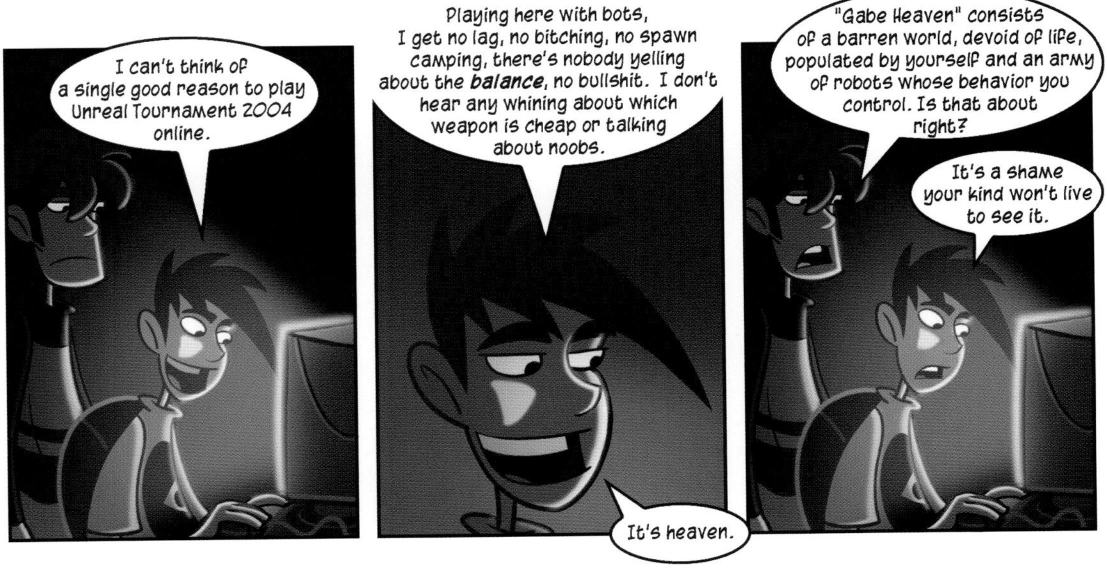
I can't think of a single good reason to play Unreal Tournament 2004 online.
Playing here with bots, I get no lag, no bitching, no spawn camping, there's nobody yelling about the **balance**, no bullshit. I don't hear any whining about which weapon is cheap or talking about noobs.
It's heaven.
"Gabe Heaven" consists of a barren world, devoid of life, populated by yourself and an army of robots whose behavior you control. Is that about right?
It's a shame your kind won't live to see it.

RUBIES: NOT JUST FOR SLIPPERS

February 13, 2004 This can happen in many games, but it's most pronounced in Massively Multiplayer titles where they can (and will!) make you comb the entire Goddamned universe for a unified ensemble. In World of Warcraft, I found a belt early on that did exactly what I wanted. It was like the calm eye of the storm around which my other clothes swirled. It was a *hideous* neon purple that probably damaged people's monitors, if not their retinas.

ONE MAN'S HEAVEN

February 16, 2004 We've never really broken out of the old PC paradigm of hosting your own voice server exclusively for friends, and as a result the wild realm of "party-line" style chatting with strangers always puts us ill at ease. We meet interesting people via the same mechanism, of course—people who have become good friends—which is why we don't mute the channel by default.

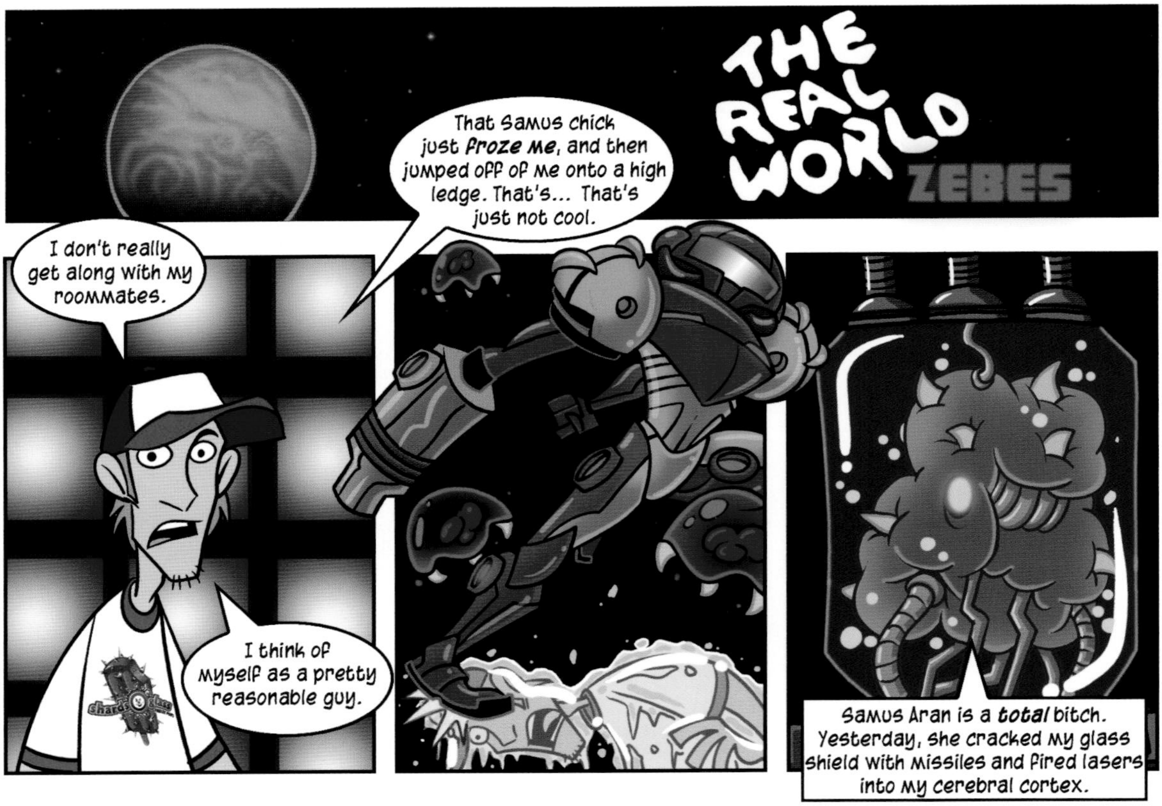
THE REAL WORLD
ZEBES
I don't really get along with my roommates.
I think of myself as a pretty reasonable guy.
That Samus chick just froze me, and then jumped off of me onto a high ledge. That's... That's just not cool.
Samus Aran is a total bitch. Yesterday, she cracked my glass shield with missiles and fired lasers into my cerebral cortex.

WHEN PEOPLE STOP BEING POLITE

February 11, 2004 From that day's post:

Did anybody else catch the first episode of Real World: Zebes? With fully seven distinct *species* and four different sexual orientations, it's the most diverse *Real World* yet. It makes the bridge of the Enterprise look like a KKK rally.

"Four different sexual orientations?" you exclaim. "Preposterous! There are only two thingies, and their interactions are well known." I don't deny that you are correct in your assertion. Every possible intersection of ding-dongs and hoo-has has been charted, mapped, and inverted, and each permutation of the above has been pontificated on for as long as the material components of physical love have been in circulation. But one of the wonders of science fiction is that not only can our minds be expanded by vivid scenarios of space travel, but also that truly remarkable new genitals can be conceived of by imaginative shut-ins, for whom even the activity of *human* genitalia has taken on the allure and mystery of fiction.

One of the other two sexual configurations is dreadfully mundane, I'm afraid—*asexual reproduction*. Nothing to write home about here. It's just like masturbating, except that when you get done there's somebody else in the room. The whole thing is pretty crazy. What would you talk about? It's not like you can deny what you do in your spare time.

The fourth one, however, might be enough to get your space-blood pumping—imagine if you will a *seven-dimensional penis* that can project *beyond* time, and even through solid matter. This meta-dong can be everywhere and nowhere at once; its exact physical state is constantly in flux. You might think of this scenario as somewhat emasculating, because if someone asks you (for example) if you have the *balls* to do something, you have to very earnestly reply that you might or you might not, it's kind of a quantum thing. On the other hand, ask that motherfucker if he can have sex with anyone who ever existed, *ever*, even if they were trapped inside a safe. See what I'm talking about? With an infinite wang, this and much more is possible. Well, I guess I should say probable. It's kind of a quantum thing.

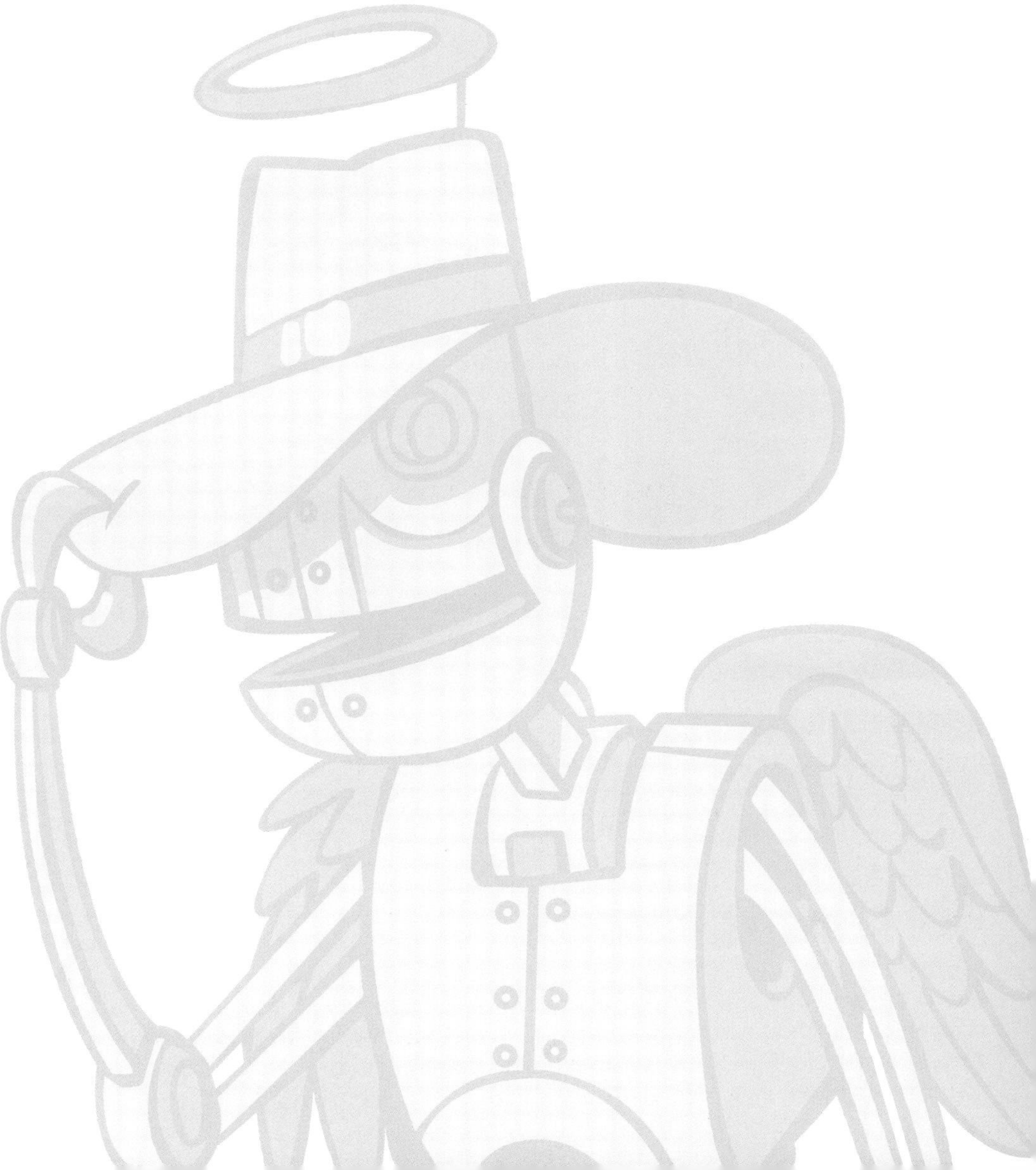

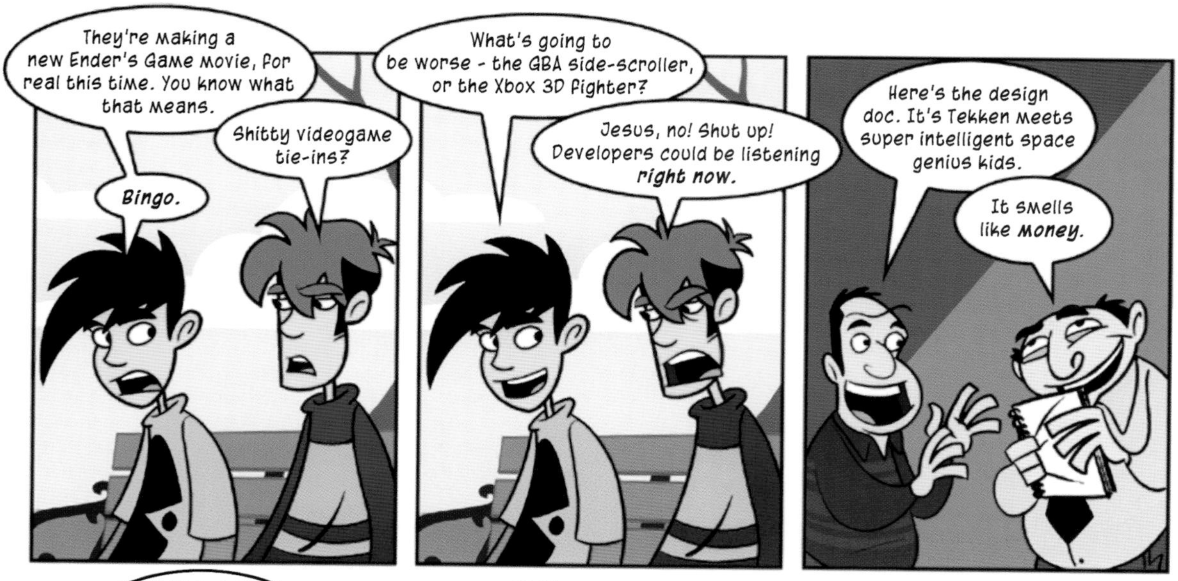
They're making a new Ender's Game movie, for real this time. You know what that means.
Shitty videogame tie-ins?
Bingo.
What's going to be worse - the GBA side-scroller, or the Xbox 3D fighter?
Jesus, no! Shut up! Developers could be listening right now.
Here's the design doc. It's Tekken meets super intelligent space genius kids.
It smells like money.

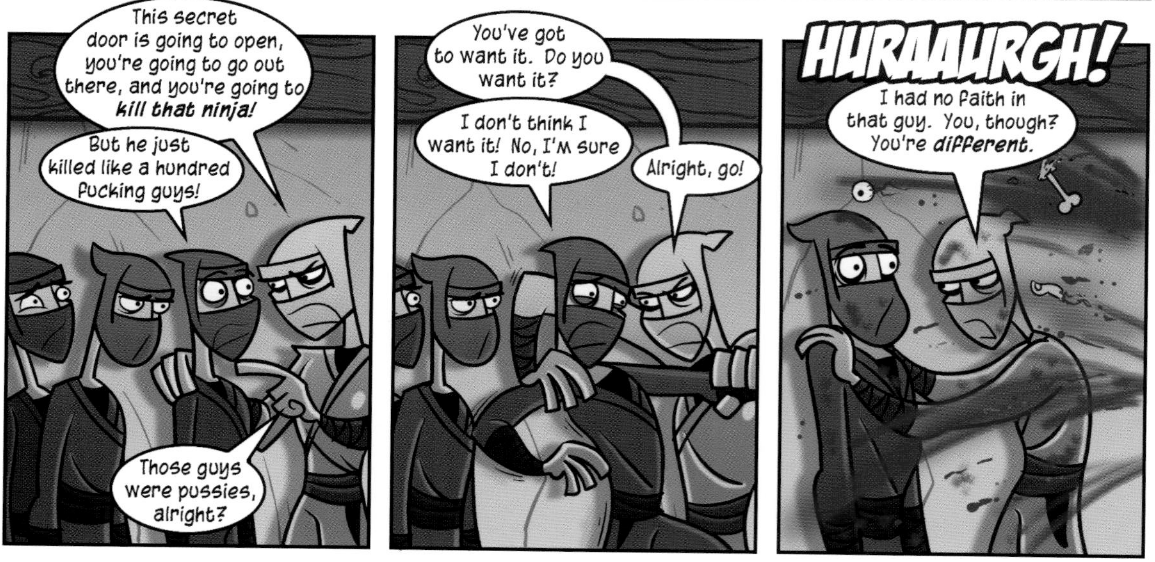
This secret door is going to open, you're going to go out there, and you're going to kill that ninja!
But he just killed like a hundred fucking guys!
Those guys were pussies, alright?
You've got to want it. Do you want it?
I don't think I want it! No, I'm sure I don't!
Alright, go!
HURAAAURGH!
I had no faith in that guy. You, though? You're different.

ENDER'S GAME(S)

February 18, 2004 Whatever happened to this thing? Not the vile tie-ins (and subsequent shoddy ports), but rather the Ender's Game movie? It's seriously like a sci-fi high school on a space station. It belongs on the WB. Or the CW, or whatever they are calling that shit now. You pretty much can't mess it up. So, what's the hold up? Is it all the genocide? Hard to say.

HIGH EMPLOYEE TURNOVER

February 20, 2004 Going back through the post for this strip, the demo of Ninja Gaiden (which this strip is based on) apparently didn't drive me wild with desire. It's strange to read something like that, because even now it's one of the few action games I'll ever pop back in and play. It's one of only two games for the original Xbox that I even kept, that and the third Splinter Cell, and it's interesting to see the entire platform boiled down in that way.

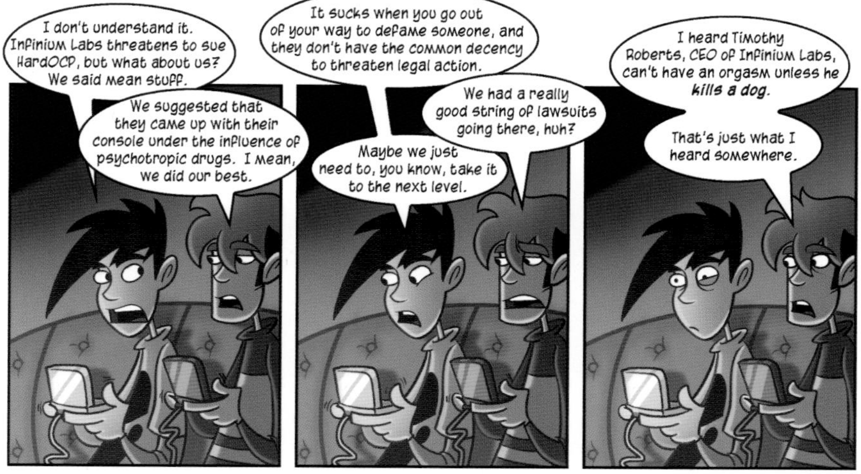
I don't understand it. Infinium Labs threatens to sue HardOCP, but what about us? We said mean stuff.
We suggested that they came up with their console under the influence of psychotropic drugs. I mean, we did our best.
It sucks when you go out of your way to defame someone, and they don't have the common decency to threaten legal action.
We had a really good string of lawsuits going there, huh?
Maybe we just need to, you know, take it to the next level.
I heard Timothy Roberts, CEO of Infinium Labs, can't have an orgasm unless he **kills a dog**.
That's just what I heard somewhere.

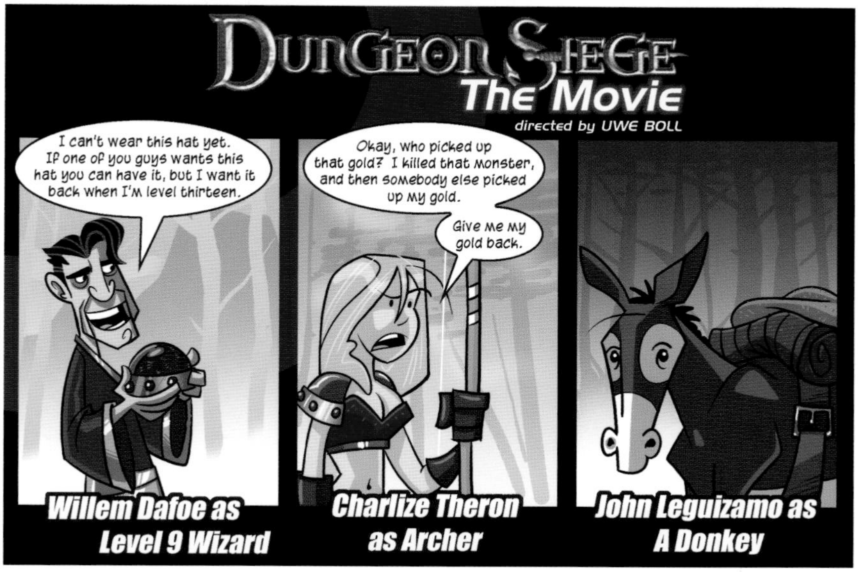
Dungeon Siege
The Movie
directed by UWE BOLL
I can't wear this hat yet. If one of you guys wants this hat you can have it, but I want it back when I'm level thirteen.
Willem Dafoe as Level 9 Wizard
Okay, who picked up that gold? I killed that monster, and then somebody else picked up my gold.
Give me my gold back.
Charlize Theron as Archer
John Leguizamo as A Donkey

STOP PRETENDING YOU'RE A REAL COMPANY

February 23, 2004 This is probably the weirdest, most foul "punch line" we've ever offered our readership. The idea that underpinned it was real, though. We'd done everything in our power to be noticed, only to lose their love to another, and it seemed like it was time to hike up the skirt. All HardOCP had done to draw their baleful eye was to take photographs of their office which proved that nobody was working there! We were mean for months and said vile, nasty things for no reason. We *earned* that lawsuit.

IF YOU SIEGE ONE DUNGEON THIS SUMMER

February 25, 2004 The *actual* movie is about wire-walking medieval ninjas, which is . . . I don't really know what that is. But a movie that was not only true to the source material but also how people actually play those games would be *completely excruciating*. The rush to put beloved franchises to work in the movie mines continues, and apparently this base urge applies even to franchises which are not especially beloved.

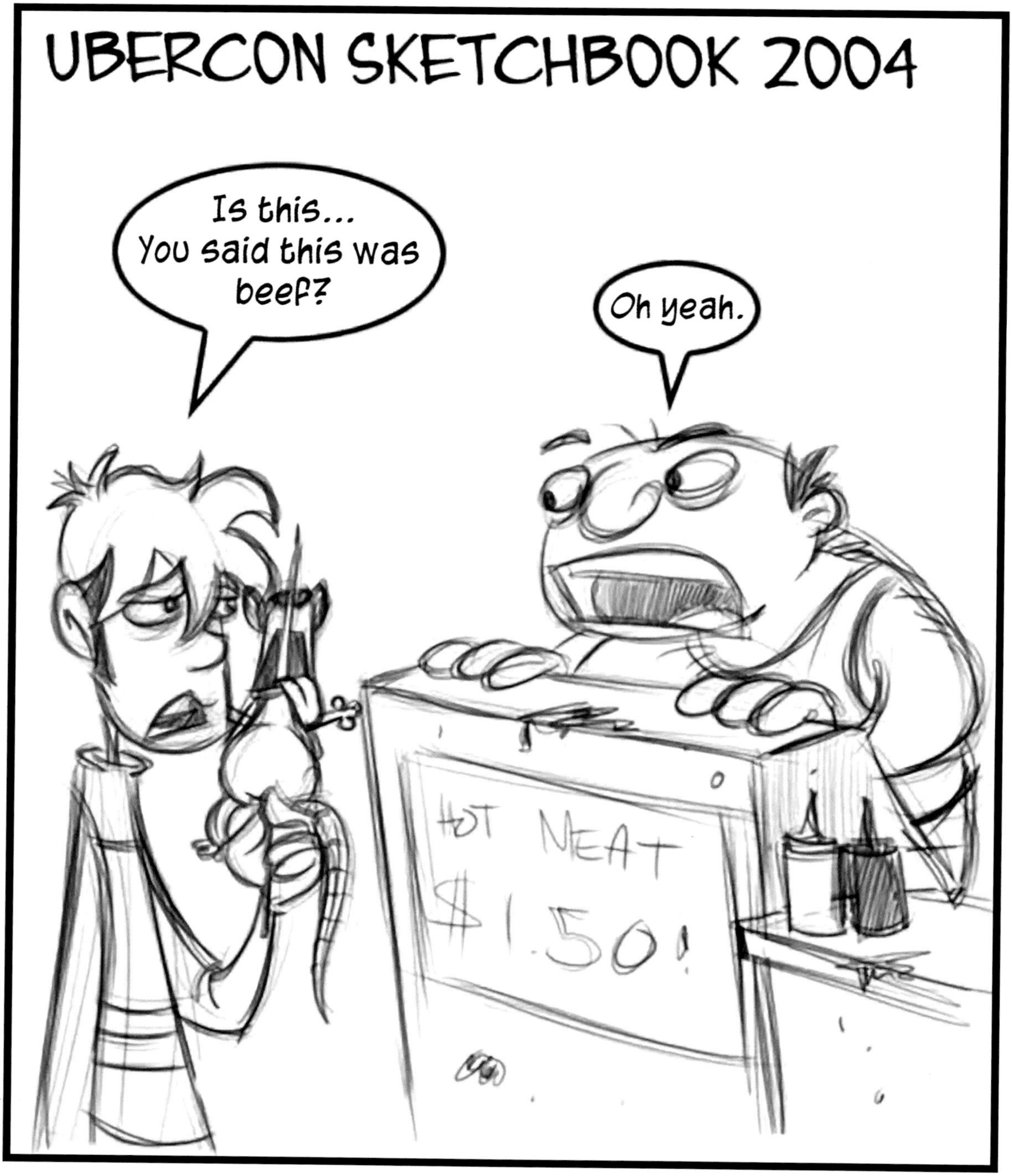

UBERCON SKETCHBOOK 2004
Is this... You said this was beef?
Oh yeah.
HOT MEAT $1.50!

UBERCON SKETCHBOOK: INADVISABLE CUISINE

February 27, 2004 Don't eat rats! I guess that's the message here.

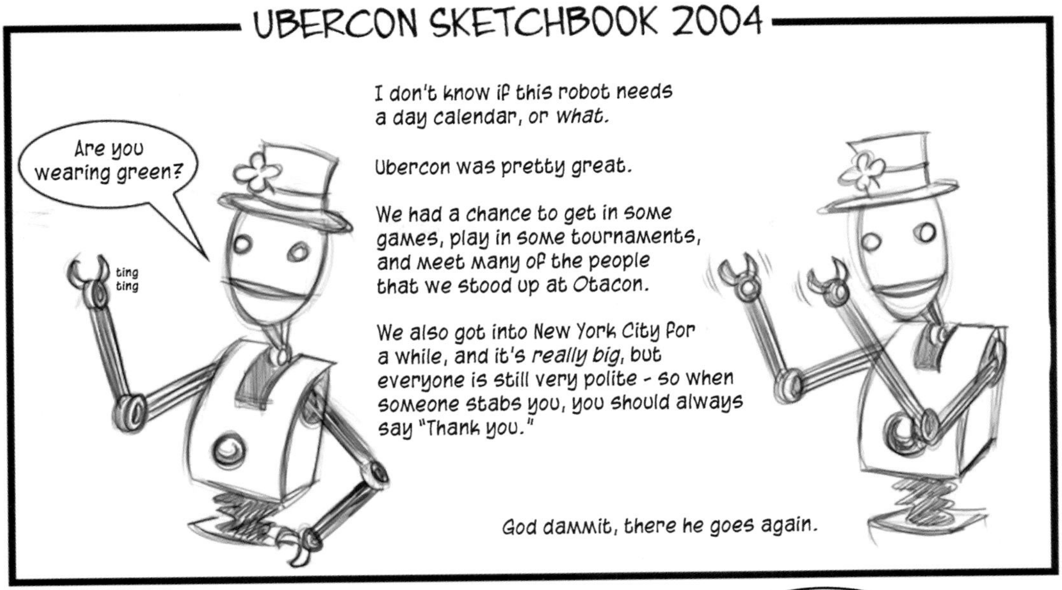
UBERCON SKETCHBOOK 2004
Are you wearing green?
ting ting
I don't know if this robot needs a day calendar, or *what.*
Ubercon was pretty great.
We had a chance to get in some games, play in some tournaments, and meet many of the people that we stood up at Otacon.
We also got into New York City for a while, and it's *really big*, but everyone is still very polite - so when someone stabs you, you should always say "Thank you."
God dammit, there he goes again.

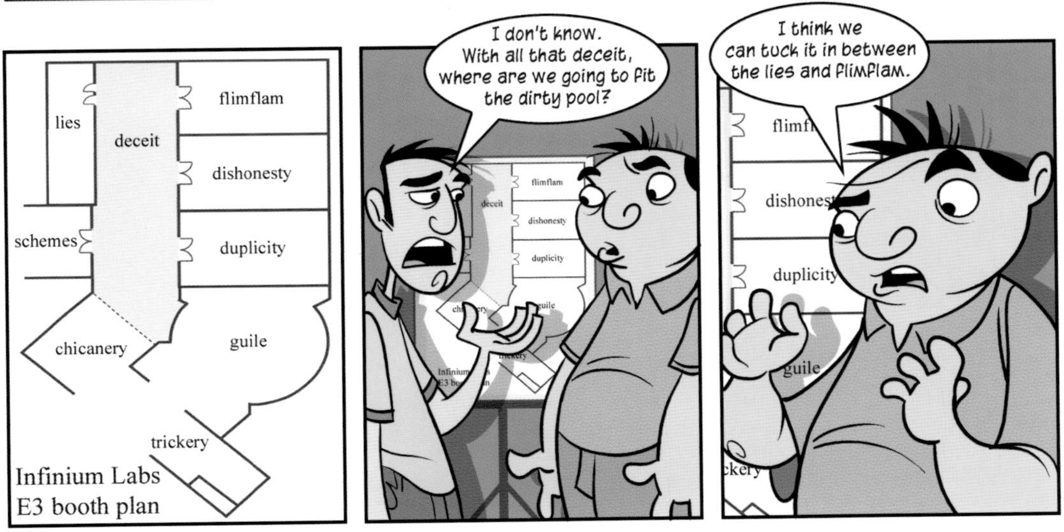
lies
deceit
flimflam
dishonesty
schemes
duplicity
chicanery
guile
trickery
Infinium Labs E3 booth plan
I don't know. With all that deceit, where are we going to fit the dirty pool?
I think we can tuck it in between the lies and flimflam.

UBERCON SKETCHBOOK: EPILOGUE

March 1, 2004 He's back! The dancing robot is *back*. Going to UberCon, more than anything else, created PAX. In fact, PAX was originally a joint venture with those guys, but when it became clear that they were just looking to host a west coast version of their existing show we decided to try and go it alone. We probably should have gone that way from the start, but we'd never done anything like this before, and anything we've never done before seems impossible.

THE PRECISE LOCATION OF VILLAINY

March 3, 2004 See? More *vile nastiness* from the rabid voles at Penny Arcade. This comic went up before that year's E3 ultrafest, and mostly as a joke we made an appointment with Infinium Labs to see their spectral Phantom personal console thing. We were shocked to find friendly people there who delivered an extremely sharp and professional presentation. They were still doomed, of course.

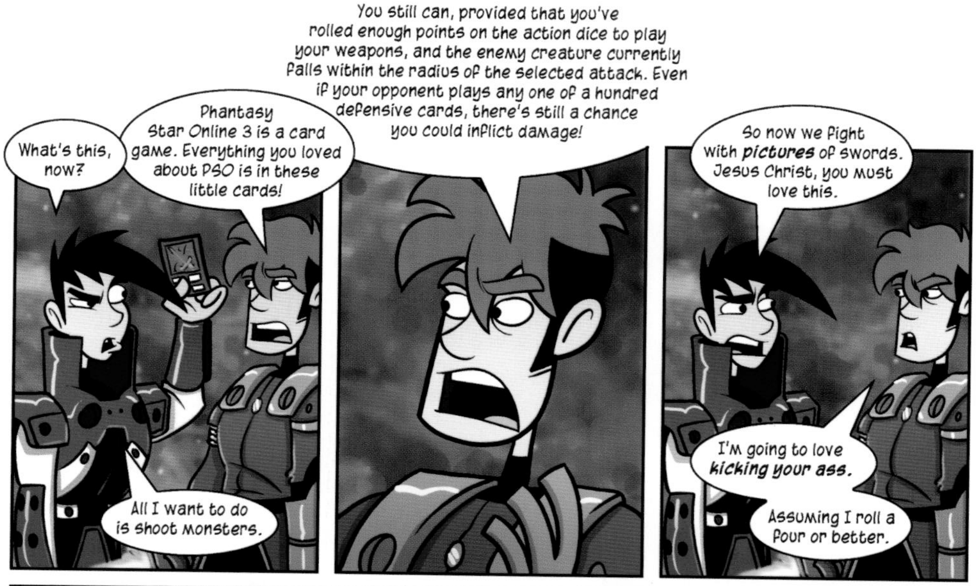
What's this, now?
Phantasy Star Online 3 is a card game. Everything you loved about PSO is in these little cards!
All I want to do is shoot monsters.
You still can, provided that you've rolled enough points on the action dice to play your weapons, and the enemy creature currently falls within the radius of the selected attack. Even if your opponent plays any one of a hundred defensive cards, there's still a chance you could inflict damage!
So now we fight with pictures of swords. Jesus Christ, you must love this.
I'm going to love kicking your ass.
Assuming I roll a four or better.

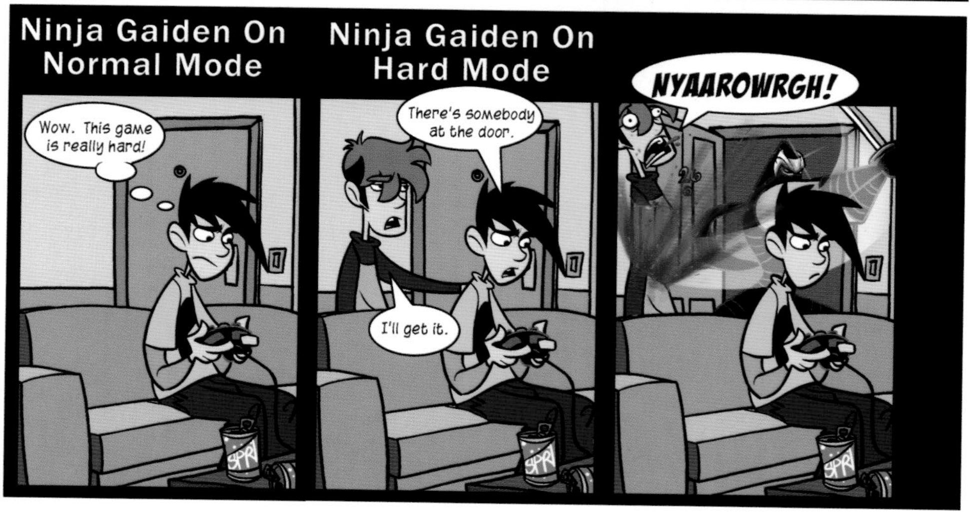
Ninja Gaiden On Normal Mode
Wow. This game is really hard!
Ninja Gaiden On Hard Mode
There's somebody at the door.
I'll get it.
NYAAROWRGH!

IF IT AIN'T BROKE

March 5, 2004 Phantasy Star Online 3 should have taken over my life, being a combination of card-based battlin' and Phantasy Star Online, which I revere. There is probably a person who could endure the early portions of the game to emerge in some eventual sunlit realm, but the realm in question might not even exist. I could never shake the feeling that the entire game was nothing more than an attempt to monetize old assets.

A BRIEF INDEX OF DIFFICULTY

March 8, 2004 A game so difficult that it kills people who are *walking by* seemed like a good way of putting it. I mentioned before that I still play Ninja Gaiden, which is true, but I've still never actually *beaten* it. Like mortar, the game often fills the cracks in the release schedule for new games. The game I play (which is a kind of subset of the game proper) is to traverse the first few levels while sustaining as little damage as possible.

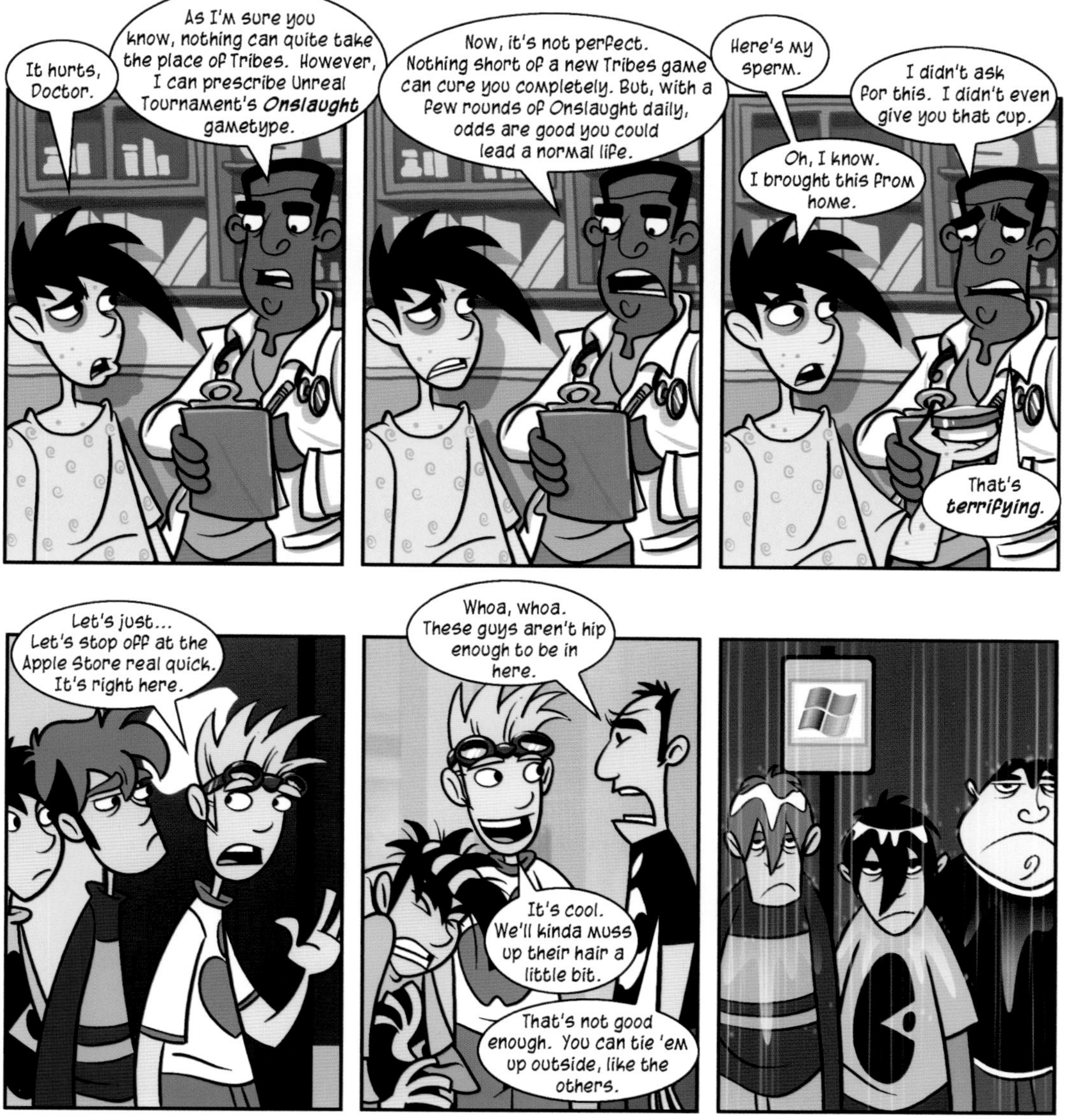
It hurts, Doctor.
As I'm sure you know, nothing can quite take the place of Tribes. However, I can prescribe Unreal Tournament's *Onslaught* gametype.
Now, it's not perfect. Nothing short of a new Tribes game can cure you completely. But, with a few rounds of Onslaught daily, odds are good you could lead a normal life.
Here's my sperm.
I didn't ask for this. I didn't even give you that cup.
Oh, I know. I brought this from home.
That's *terrifying*.
Let's just... Let's stop off at the Apple Store real quick. It's right here.
Whoa, whoa. These guys aren't hip enough to be in here.
It's cool. We'll kinda muss up their hair a little bit.
That's not good enough. You can tie 'em up outside, like the others.

A COMMON AILMENT

March 10, 2004 I wonder if they understood when they were making Tribes that they were establishing a worldwide cult. Fifteen percent of my best gaming memories are based on the thing—either the base game, its sequel, or the sophisticated mods that were made available. There are plenty of games that get team-based play right, but there's still nothing that empowers players to the extent that Tribes did.

THE HIPNESS THRESHOLD

March 12, 2004 As I was walking into the Apple Store to pick up my iPhone, the entire store erupted into applause. I wasn't even doing anything that difficult, but I felt ennobled by the act. I like the idea that you need to hitch Windows users up to some shameful post outside, but the reality is that I have experienced a tremendous amount of humanity at these places.

TORUN JAX, BLIND JEDI

March 15, 2004 Now we're picking on the *blind*? There is no hell hot enough. From that day's (weird) post:

I've had a couple weeks now with the Littermaid Plus, and I have to say that this is one of the worst-designed consumer devices ever made. I don't have any arguments with the concept—a machine that obviates the need to play with feline waste. I'm onboard. Men of science, *please* invent a machine that will collect and sequester the tiny pot roasts my cat leaves behind. It is, however, a deeply *ironic* device, and it has lessons to teach us about sloth and human folly. Indeed, this strange method of instruction is the only thing it accomplishes with any regularity. What we learn through using the device is that life is sometimes difficult, and to try and mediate that fact invites the scorn of the universe.

There is a sort of "comb" that trawls the litter, snaring the sweet surprises left within and theoretically depositing them into a sort of cat shit purgatory. While *mostly* successful, the waste must first travel up a steep ramp, like the ones in extreme sports videos. And sometimes it is flung out, as though by catapult, toward imaginary foes.

The thing is, the device really doesn't have a lot of room in it *for* cats, which strikes me as a design flaw. You would think they would try to put a cat in there, or find somebody who had a cat, shit, maybe just *imagine* a cat and try to design their litter box around that hypothetical, hairy customer. But they didn't. Cats must situate themselves diagonally in order to *make a deposit* as it were, so the container at the end where it's all supposed to go fills up at the sides first and then boils over into your house. This isn't even the worst problem.

Cat pee and litter is like wet cement; it's like a new state of matter. In an ordinary, non-robot litter box it has time to "set" so that you can remove it and then go do something that is important to you. If, on the other hand, a mechanical arm reaches out and spreads it the length and breadth of the device, now you have a completely disgusting *new* task you could never have imagined in trade for the one you thought you were giving up forever.

It is the sort of thing you would design if you had only a vague description of a cat and you didn't really give a fuck if it worked or not.

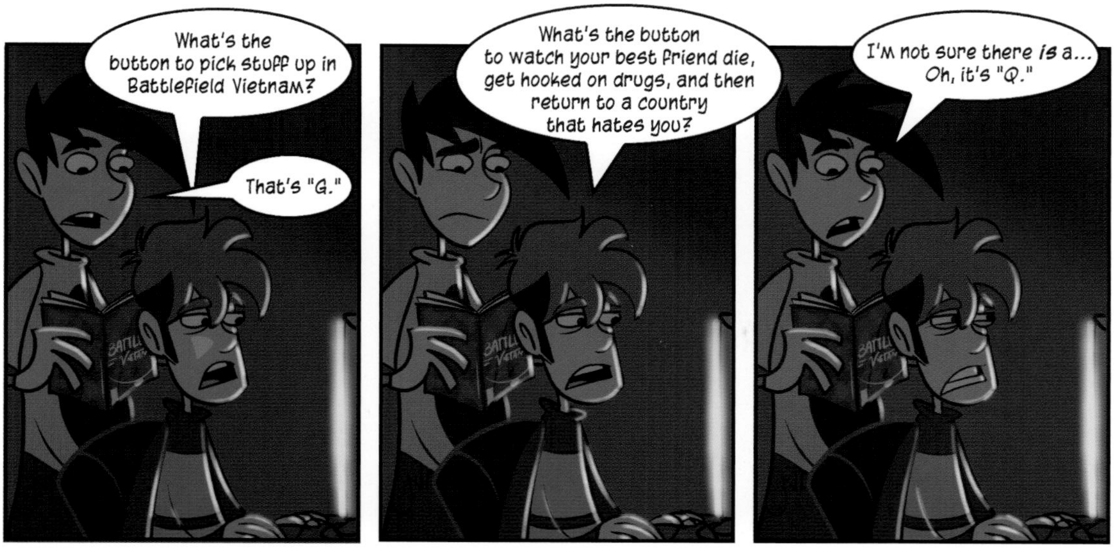
What's the button to pick stuff up in Battlefield Vietnam?
That's "G."
What's the button to watch your best friend die, get hooked on drugs, and then return to a country that hates you?
I'm not sure there *is* a... Oh, it's "Q."

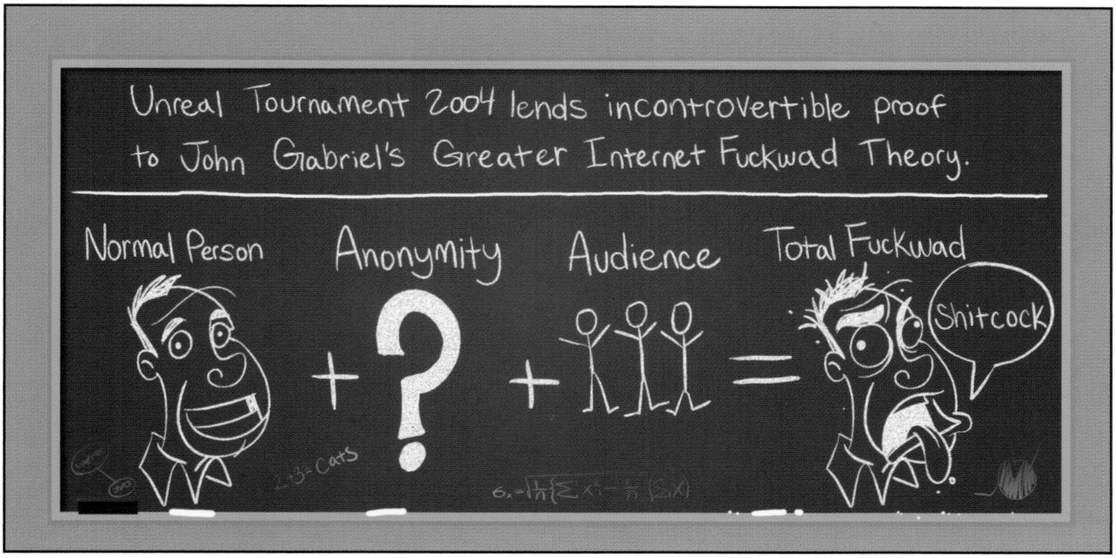
Unreal Tournament 2004 lends incontrovertible proof to John Gabriel's Greater Internet Fuckwad Theory.
Normal Person
Anonymity
Audience
Total Fuckwad
Shitcock
2+3=Cats

VIETNAM IS ACTUALLY KIND OF COMPLEX

March 17, 2004 My favorite part of Battlefield Vietnam, and probably one of the most expensive on EA's part, was the list of licensed period music you could queue up when you were driving a vehicle. The method for doing so was pretty rudimentary, a little text-based thing with their other quick keys, but for some reason blaring out a piece of authentic music added a tremendous amount to the experience. Passengers of mine could expect to hear either "Fortunate Son" or "Ride of the Valkyries."

GREEN BLACKBOARDS (AND OTHER ANOMALIES)

March 19, 2004 It's a very elegant way of presenting the concept, and the chalkboard delivery lends the idea a great deal of authenticity. We had the opportunity to speak at MIT, for people who are a great deal smarter than we are, and the opportunity to scrawl this formula on one of its hallowed boards was an honor.

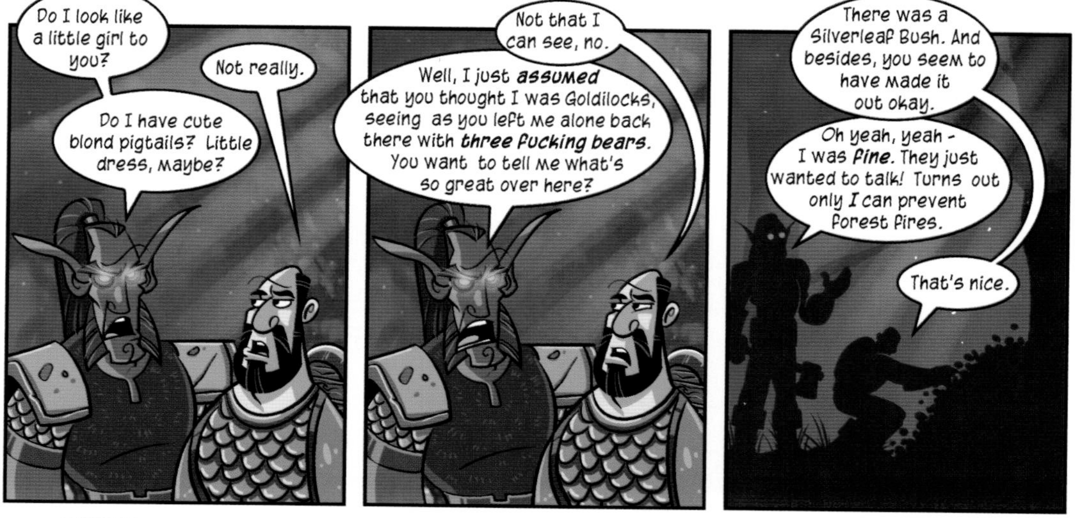

Do I look like a little girl to you?
Do I have cute blond pigtails? Little dress, maybe?
Not really.
Not that I can see, no.
Well, I just **assumed** that you thought I was Goldilocks, seeing as you left me alone back there with **three fucking bears**. You want to tell me what's so great over here?
There was a Silverleaf Bush. And besides, you seem to have made it out okay.
Oh yeah, yeah - I was **fine**. They just wanted to talk! Turns out only *I* can prevent forest fires.
That's nice.

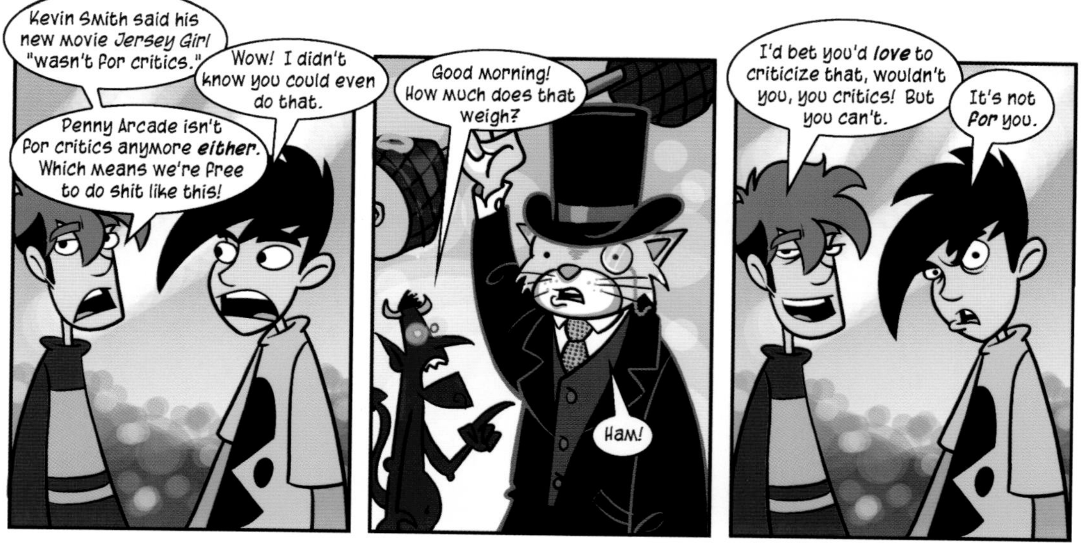

Kevin Smith said his new movie *Jersey Girl* "wasn't for critics."
Wow! I didn't know you could even do that.
Penny Arcade isn't for critics anymore **either**. Which means we're free to do shit like this!
Good morning! How much does that weigh?
Ham!
I'd bet you'd **love** to criticize that, wouldn't you, you critics! But you can't.
It's not **for** you.

HERBS AND SPICES

March 22, 2004 Because it was our constant obsession, it was hard to keep WoW out of the comic. Eventually we instituted hard rules about how often we could do comics based on that game. These rules were "hard" not only because they were unyielding, but also because they were difficult to actually follow. When you're pouring this much of yourself into a game of this kind, it can put down pretty deep roots.

THE ADVENTURES OF TWISP AND CATSBY

March 24, 2004 Twisp and Catsby were born here, in this weird comic about Kevin Smith, or *Jersey Girl*, or *whatever*. They were an incredible non sequitur that really made this thing work, but in creating them we had accidentally made something that we liked. Many readers seemed to respond to them as well, and I couldn't help but name them. And then, once I'd named them, they were *real*. Then, once they were real, I wanted to know what they were up to . . .

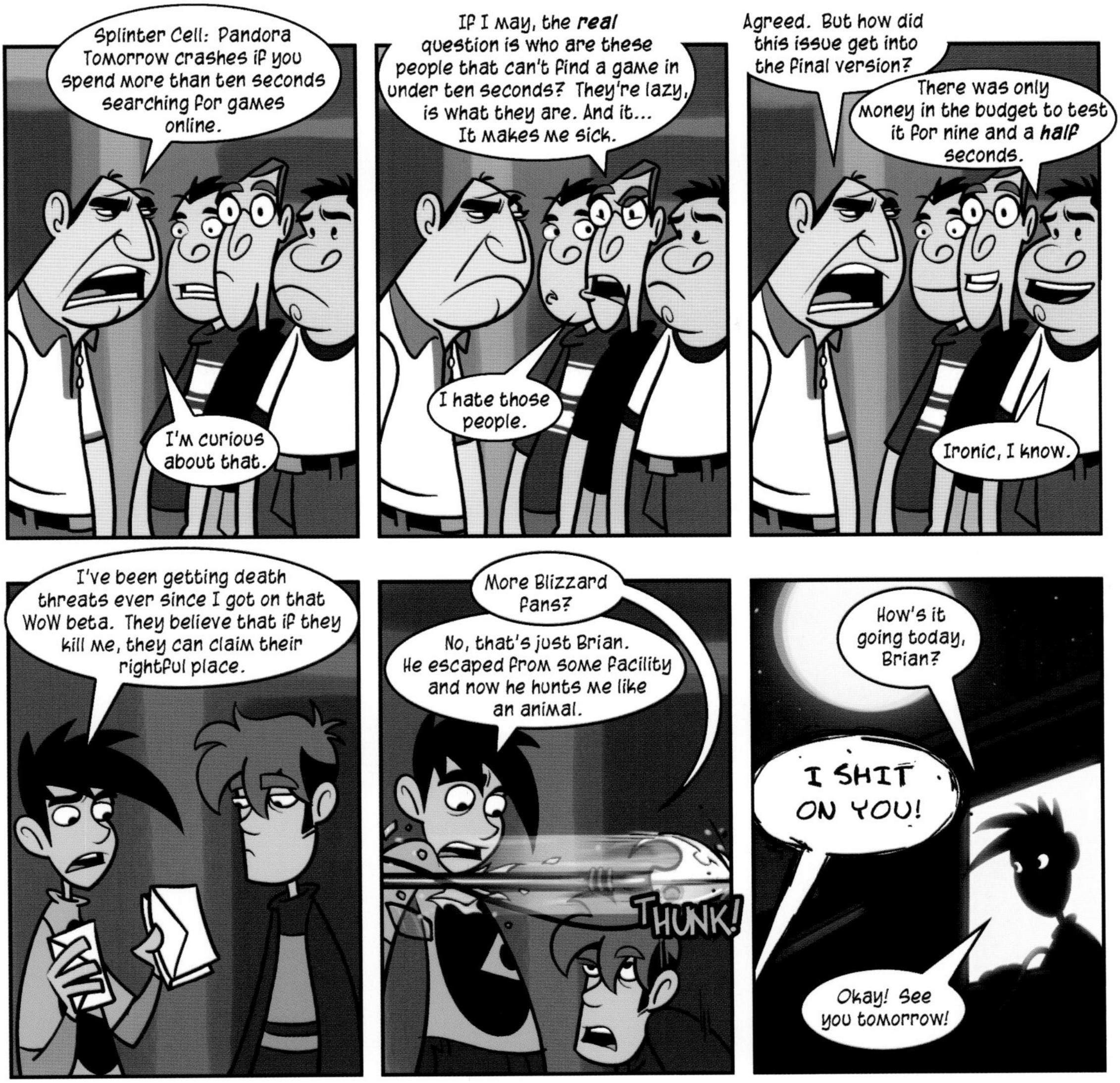
Splinter Cell: Pandora Tomorrow crashes if you spend more than ten seconds searching for games online.
I'm curious about that.
If I may, the **real** question is who are these people that can't find a game in under ten seconds? They're lazy, is what they are. And it... It makes me sick.
I hate those people.
Agreed. But how did this issue get into the final version?
There was only money in the budget to test it for nine and a **half** seconds.
Ironic, I know.
I've been getting death threats ever since I got on that WoW beta. They believe that if they kill me, they can claim their rightful place.
More Blizzard fans?
No, that's just Brian. He escaped from some facility and now he hunts me like an animal.
THUNK!
How's it going today, Brian?
I SHIT ON YOU!
Okay! See you tomorrow!

THE PROXIMITY OF DEVILS AND DETAILS

March 26, 2004 This same bug showed up in a couple different products, right out the gate; the Rainbow Six that came out around then suffered from exactly the same crash, for presumably the same reason. Once the server browser was populated with more than a set number of servers, the games crashed straight up. In a testing environment, where the number of available servers was always constrained, it never showed up.

WOW LOG, SUPPLEMENTAL

March 29, 2004 Some people were super angry that we had been allowed into the World of Warcraft Beta, which isn't a great idea, because when a person gets really angry our first instinct is to stoke the furnace of their rage with a bellows of . . . like, *hate* or something. I understand why they would be mad, though. I burned in a similar way during the Alpha—when I knew that mysterious, undeserving *others* were questing epically, blades drawn to farm elite mobs.

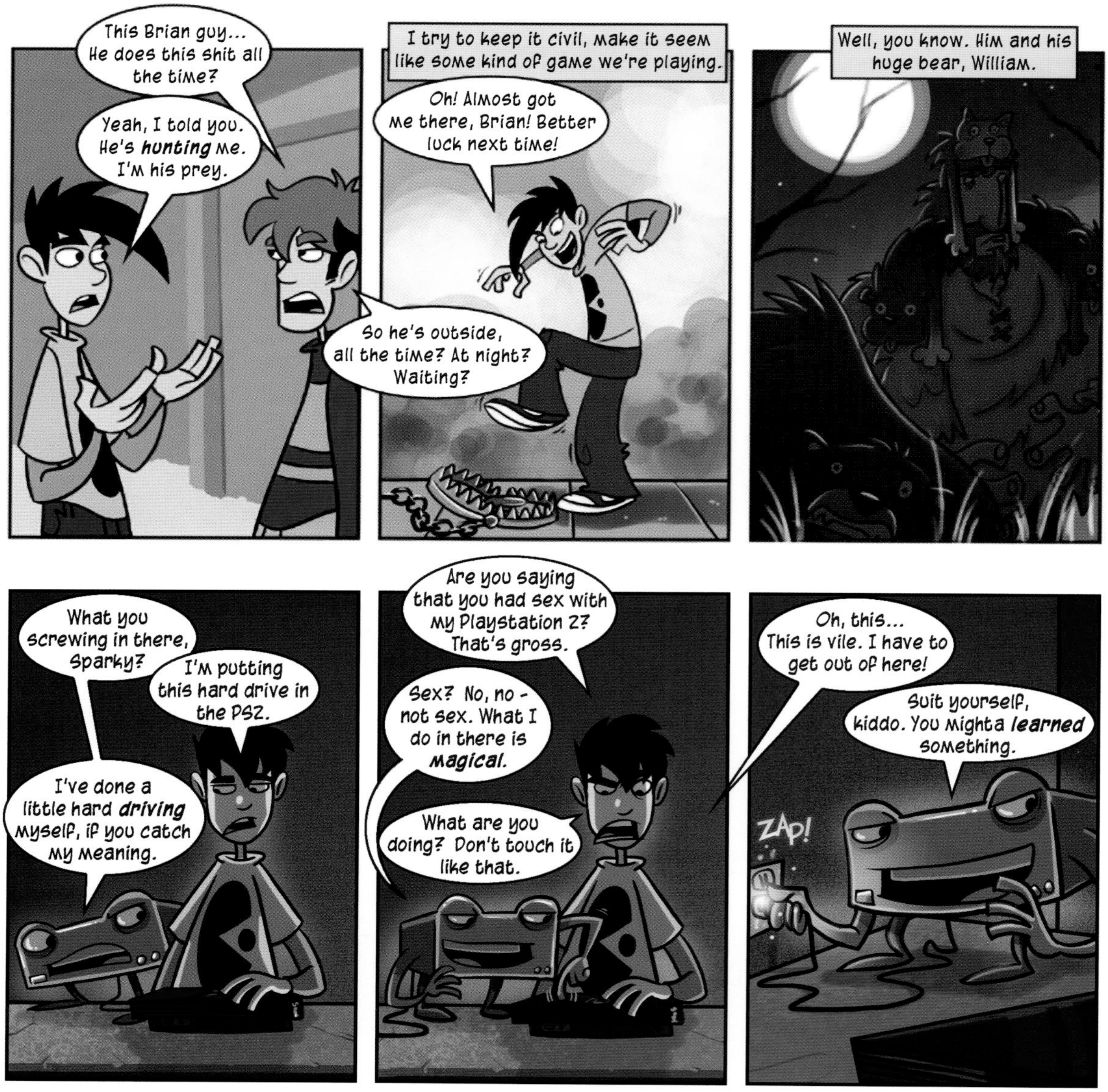
This Brian guy... He does this shit all the time?
Yeah, I told you. He's **hunting** me. I'm his prey.
So he's outside, all the time? At night? Waiting?
I try to keep it civil, make it seem like some kind of game we're playing.
Oh! Almost got me there, Brian! Better luck next time!
Well, you know. Him and his huge bear, William.
What you screwing in there, Sparky?
I'm putting this hard drive in the PS2.
I've done a little hard **driving** myself, if you catch my meaning.
Are you saying that you had sex with my Playstation 2? That's gross.
Sex? No, no - not sex. What I do in there is **magical.**
What are you doing? Don't touch it like that.
Oh, this... This is vile. I have to get out of here!
Suit yourself, kiddo. You mighta **learned** something.
ZAP!

WOW LOG, CONTINUED

March 31, 2004 We have tried on more than one occasion to bring back the mad trapper Brian and his ursine accomplice, but I think it's conceivable that they will just lie here in the archive for all eternity. Suburban trapping doesn't really have a lot of meat on it.

COMPATIBILITY

April 5, 2004 I don't even remember what we were even using the hard drive *for* . . . Oh, that's right. It wasn't ours. We were putting in Robert's at the time, because he's essentially a slut for Final Fantasy, and he wanted to tap into the online iteration that has so gripped many of its players. He played all day, all the way up until he died and lost a level, which must have resulted in some mental calculation. After that, he never played again.

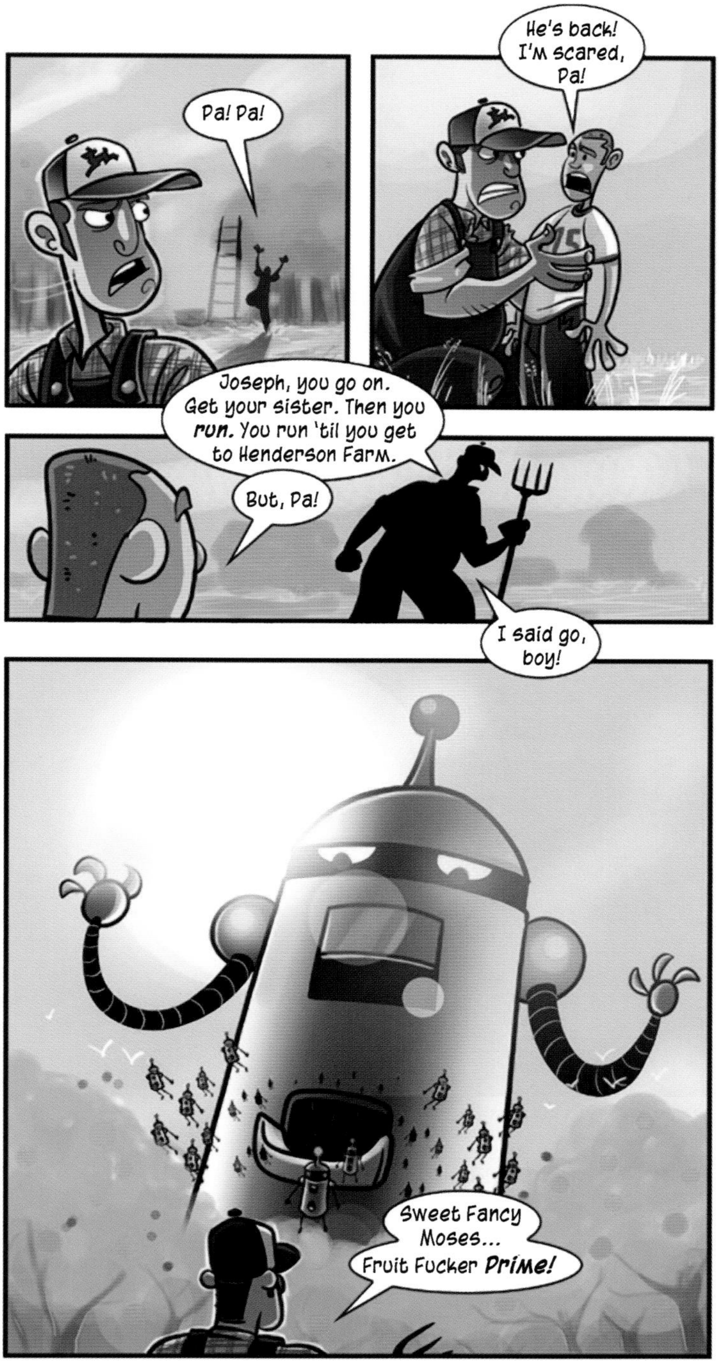
Pa! Pa!
He's back! I'm scared, Pa!
Joseph, you go on. Get your sister. Then you *run.* You run 'til you get to Henderson Farm.
But, Pa!
I said go, boy!
Sweet Fancy Moses... Fruit Fucker *Prime!*

NO PRODUCE IS SAFE

April 2, 2004 As is now perfectly clear to all, Fruit Fucker Prime extends far beyond this particular comic and into the bizarre cosmic horror setting in Precipice. Or, more completely, On The Rain-Slick Precipice Of Darkness: Episode One. We originally considered *additional* subtitles after that, but soon thought better of it.

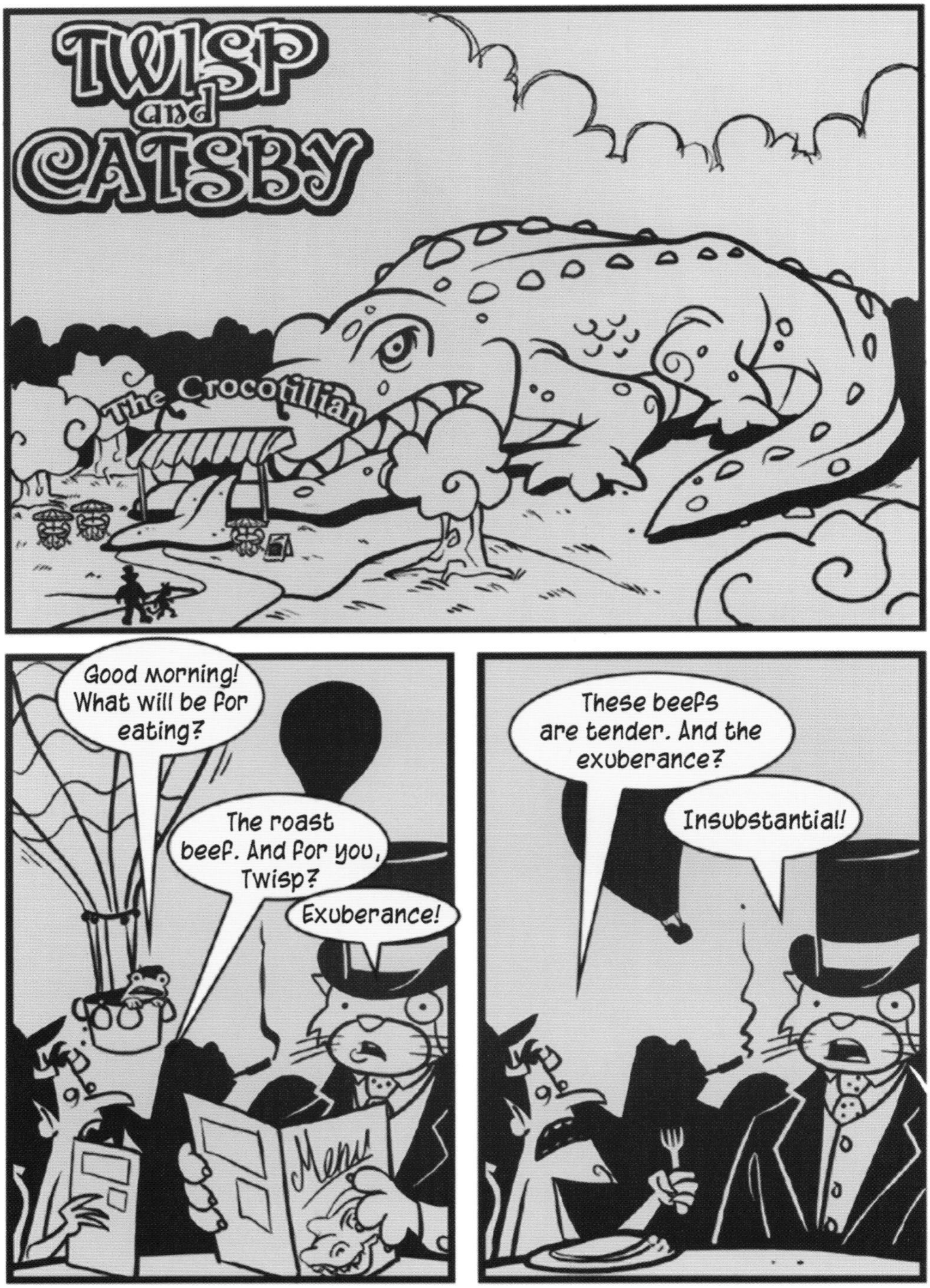
TWISP and CATSBY
The Crocotillian
Good morning! What will be for eating?
The roast beef. And for you, Twisp?
Exuberance!
Menu
These beefs are tender. And the exuberance?
Insubstantial!

TWISP & CATSBY IN: THE CROCOTILLIAN

April 7, 2004 As you can see, we couldn't resist the pull for long.

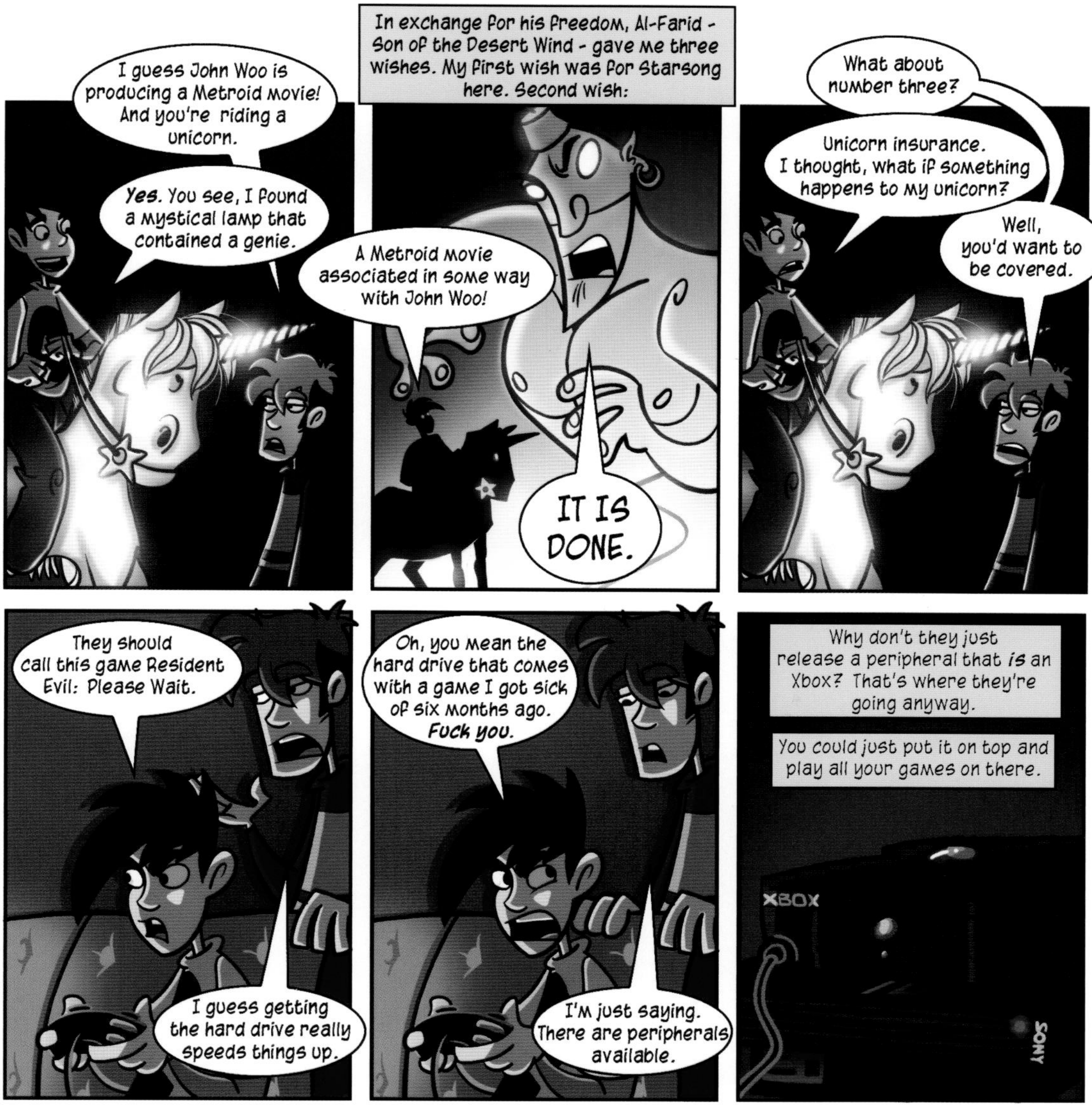
I guess John Woo is producing a Metroid movie! And you're riding a unicorn.
Yes. You see, I found a mystical lamp that contained a genie.
In exchange for his freedom, Al-Farid - Son of the Desert Wind - gave me three wishes. My first wish was for Starsong here. Second wish:
A Metroid movie associated in some way with John Woo!
IT IS DONE.
What about number three?
Unicorn insurance. I thought, what if something happens to my unicorn?
Well, you'd want to be covered.
They should call this game Resident Evil: Please Wait.
I guess getting the hard drive really speeds things up.
Oh, you mean the hard drive that comes with a game I got sick of six months ago. Fuck you.
I'm just saying. There are peripherals available.
Why don't they just release a peripheral that is an Xbox? That's where they're going anyway.
You could just put it on top and play all your games on there.
XBOX
SONY

DJINN AND JUICE

April 9, 2004 Where did this movie even *go*? The Goddamned thing was ordained by a genie, and still nothing. We were robbed. *Metroid* done right would make for a pretty high-concept film. It would take people who believed in the actual franchise from top to bottom, though. Essentially, it would require a universe that is radically different from the one we inhabit.

A CROWN OF THORNS

April 12, 2004 What a complete mess. Microsoft entered the console market with what was essentially a locked-down computer, against deeply entrenched opponents. In the space of one generation, Microsoft axed the hard drive to create a more mainstream product, while Sony delivered a highly specialized computer. And then, while they're each trying to decide what business they're actually in, Nintendo swept in and took all the marbles.

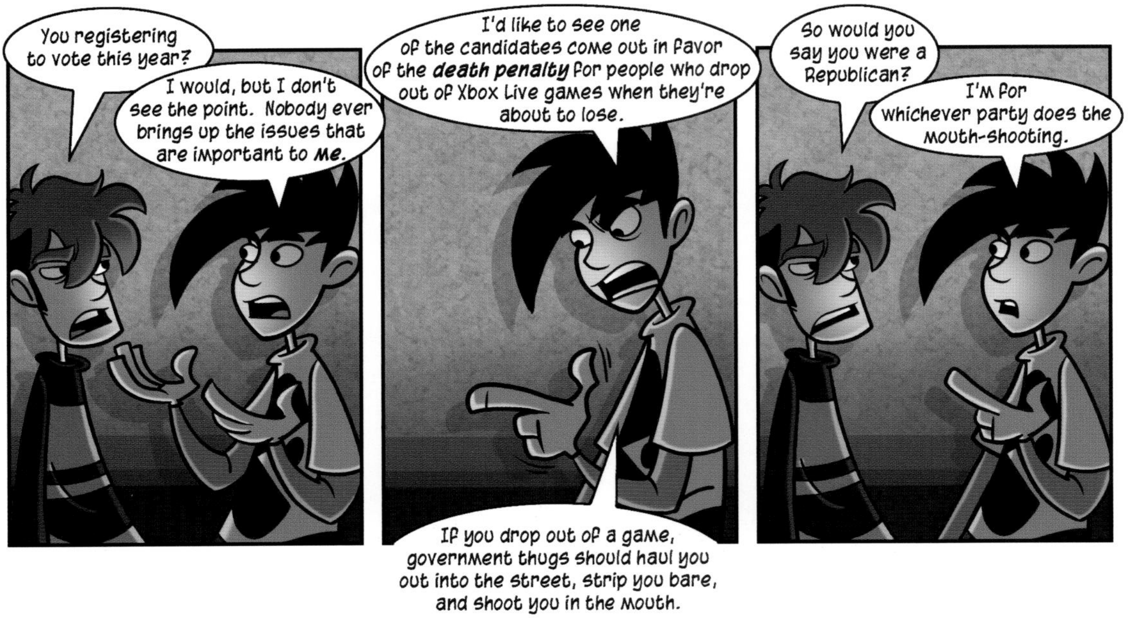
You registering to vote this year?
I would, but I don't see the point. Nobody ever brings up the issues that are important to *me*.
I'd like to see one of the candidates come out in favor of the ***death penalty*** for people who drop out of Xbox Live games when they're about to lose.
If you drop out of a game, government thugs should haul you out into the street, strip you bare, and shoot you in the mouth.
So would you say you were a Republican?
I'm for whichever party does the mouth-shooting.

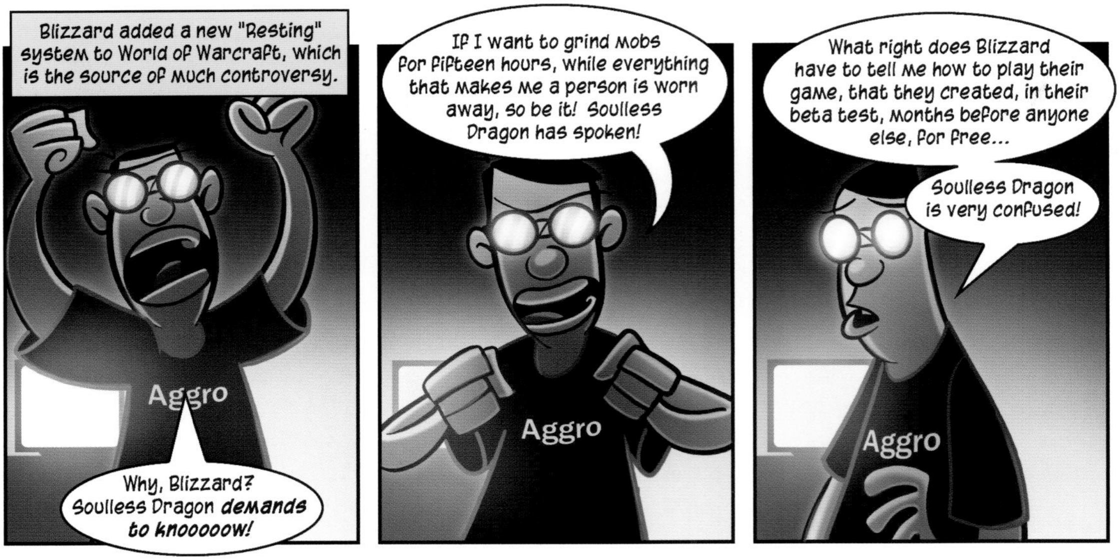
Blizzard added a new "Resting" system to World of Warcraft, which is the source of much controversy.
Aggro
Why, Blizzard? Soulless Dragon ***demands*** *to knooooow!*
If I want to grind mobs for fifteen hours, while everything that makes me a person is worn away, so be it! Soulless Dragon has spoken!
Aggro
What right does Blizzard have to tell me how to play their game, that they created, in their beta test, months before anyone else, for free...
Soulless Dragon is very confused!
Aggro

GABRIEL'S PRIMARY CONCERN

April 14, 2004 There's still no movement on this critical policy initiative. Maybe we can get this thing on the local ballot? Obviously, though it was a concern at the time (most likely in Splinter Cell: Pandora Tomorrow), this isn't really a platform issue. Jackasses drop constantly from all games, on all systems. More people are probably dropping than playing right now. People drop from online rounds of *Pokémon*, which is especially sad.

AND LO

April 16, 2004 I guess this was a really big deal at the time. With something like ten million subscribers globally, it doesn't appear to have affected its success.

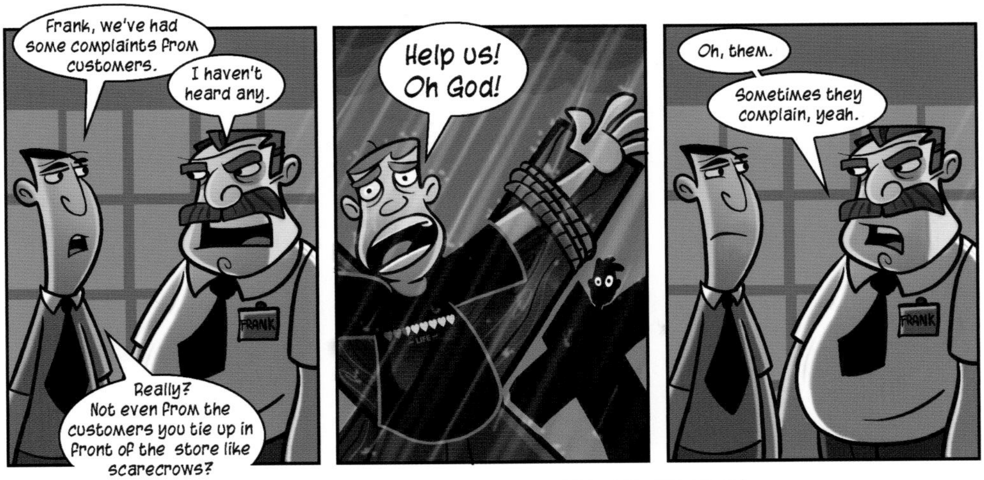
Frank, we've had some complaints from customers.
I haven't heard any.
Really? Not even from the customers you tie up in front of the store like scarecrows?
Help us! Oh God!
Oh, them.
Sometimes they complain, yeah.
FRANK

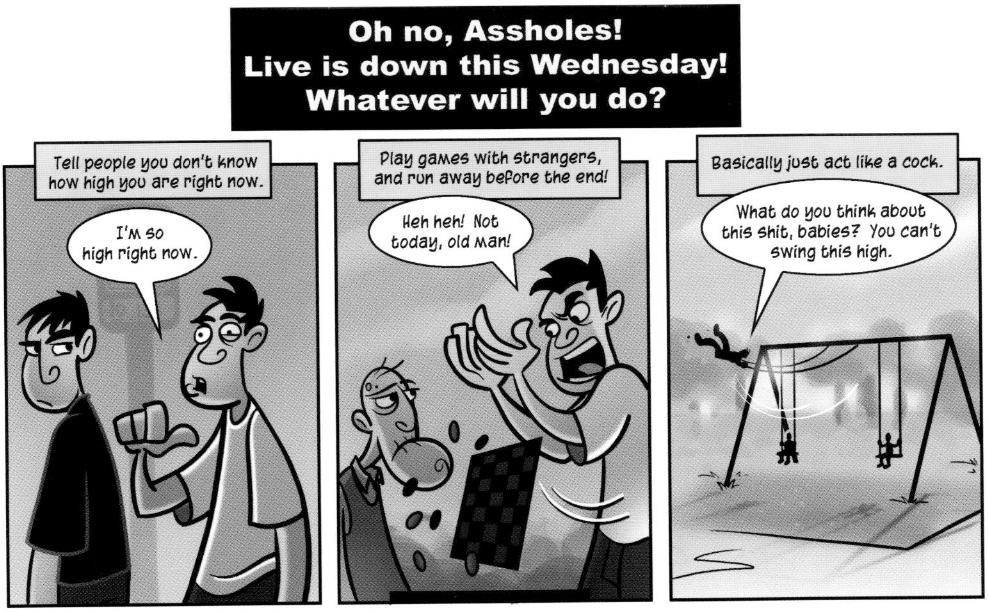
Oh no, Assholes!
Live is down this Wednesday!
Whatever will you do?
Tell people you don't know how high you are right now.
I'm so high right now.
Play games with strangers, and run away before the end!
Heh heh! Not today, old man!
Basically just act like a cock.
What do you think about this shit, babies? You can't swing this high.

THE DISTRICT MANAGER

April 19, 2004 I think I just wrote "I Love Frank" in all capital letters in the last book, and I would do so again here if I thought I could get away with it. I suppose this *is* a new book, though, so maybe it's alright. This comic is so *weird* that I can't help but like it. It's got Frank at his best, and the guys on the crosses really do their part to sell their terrifying ordeal. Especially the one in the back, whose panicked eyes search wildly for help.

HE COULD HAVE BEEN NICER TO THOSE BABIES

April 21, 2004 Xbox Live has a tawdry reputation, and rightly so, because it is filled with *people*. Last night, an opponent claimed to be having sex with my mother at that *very instant*—only he didn't say "sex," and I've left out several other choice bits. I can't really speak to the veracity of his claims, but Microsoft should probably get federal money for keeping these slavering mongooses off the streets.

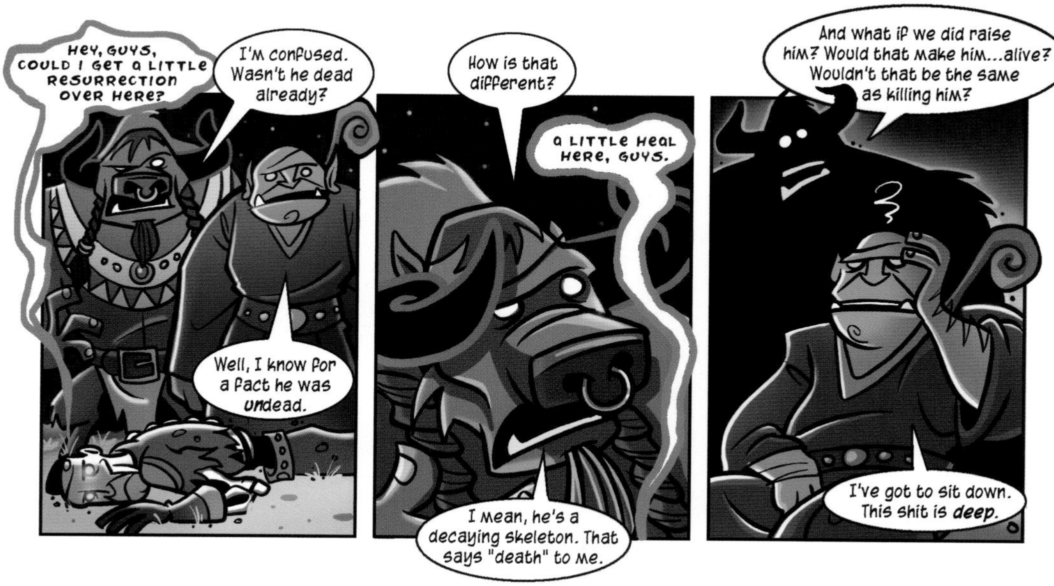

Hey, guys, could I get a little resurrection over here?
I'm confused. Wasn't he dead already?
Well, I know for a fact he was undead.
How is that different?
a little heal here, guys.
I mean, he's a decaying skeleton. That says "death" to me.
And what if we did raise him? Would that make him...alive? Wouldn't that be the same as killing him?
I've got to sit down. This shit is deep.

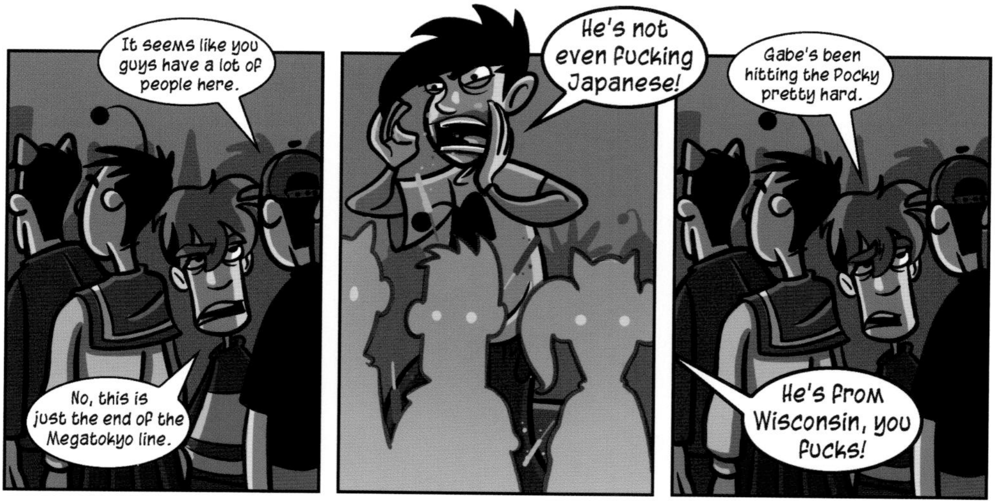

It seems like you guys have a lot of people here.
No, this is just the end of the Megatokyo line.
He's not even fucking Japanese!
Gabe's been hitting the Pocky pretty hard.
He's from Wisconsin, you fucks!

A MATTER OF LIFE AND DEATH

April 23, 2004 They had just made the Horde races available for the first time, and so on our unbelievable treks through those wild lands we stumbled on quandaries like this one. Horde never stuck with me, though I know that many swear by their bison guy or whatnot. Of course, my class of choice was Paladin, and when I was still playing there was no such thing as a Horde Paladin. That has since changed.

HERE HE GOES AGAIN ON HIS OWN

April 26, 2004 This was in 2004, which is to say that it was long after the webcomic feuds that characterized our initial forays into the medium. Fred Gallagher (the man discussed in this comic) is both "not fucking Japanese," and "from Wisconsin, you fucks," but he's an amazing talent who is revered globally for his American manga, *Megatokyo*. Actually, I don't know if he *is* from Wisconsin. But the parts about talent and being revered globally are both true.

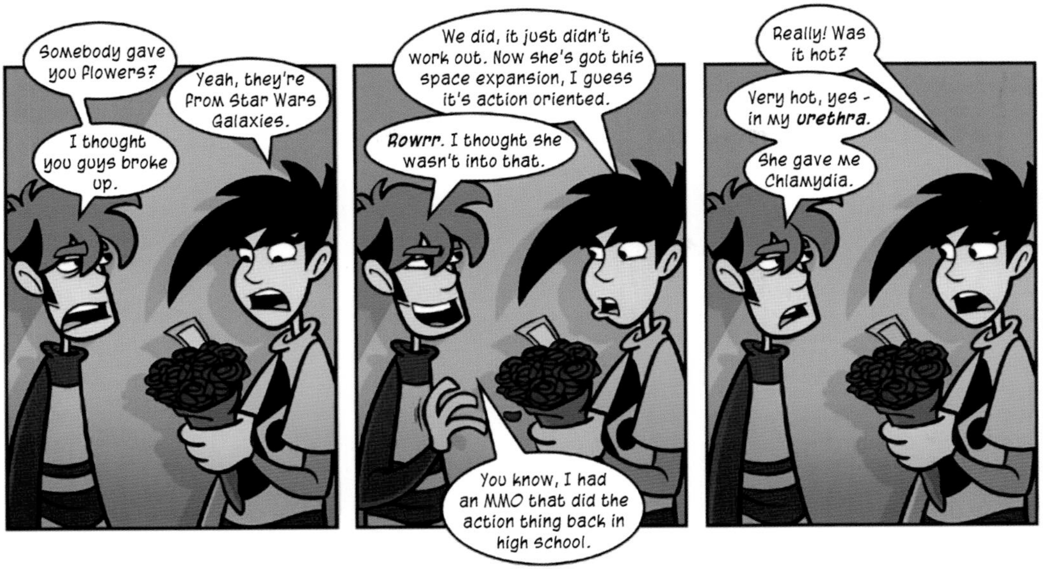

Somebody gave you flowers?
Yeah, they're from Star Wars Galaxies.
I thought you guys broke up.
We did, it just didn't work out. Now she's got this space expansion, I guess it's action oriented.
Rowrr. I thought she wasn't into that.
You know, I had an MMO that did the action thing back in high school.
Really! Was it hot?
Very hot, yes - in my urethra.
She gave me Chlamydia.

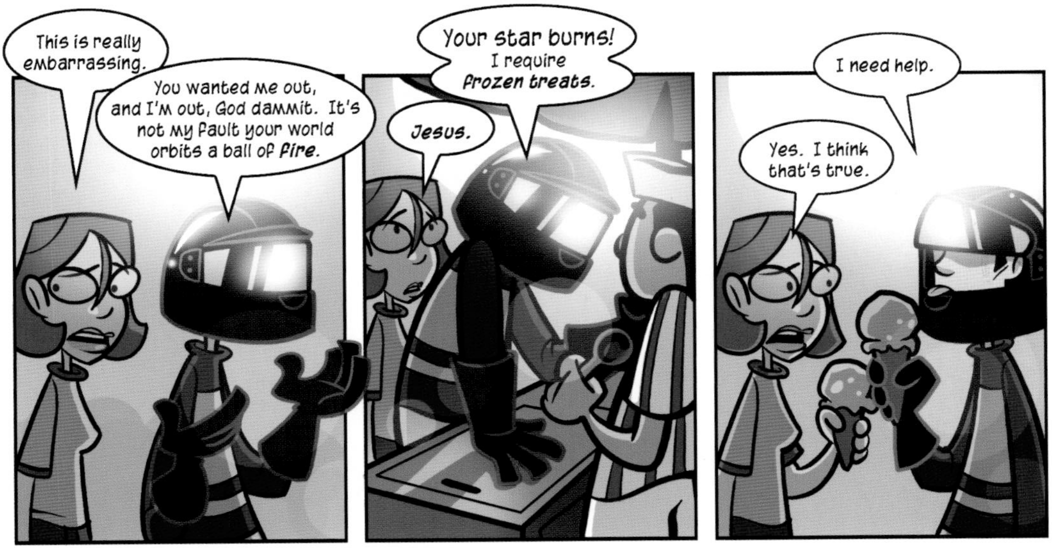

This is really embarrassing.
You wanted me out, and I'm out, God dammit. It's not my fault your world orbits a ball of fire.
Your star burns! I require frozen treats.
Jesus.
I need help.
Yes. I think that's true.

JUMP TO LIGHT-THPEED

April 28, 2004 I have told you before that it is Gabriel's primary goal to insert Div or Randy Pinkwood into every comic strip we produce, and I have a similar affliction. As I related in this day's newspost, it is of the utmost importance that I drop the word "urethra" into each and every script. I once wrote (and submitted) a comic about a urethra that goes to the urethra store. One strip was comprised entirely of the word urethra, over and over, save for the odd bit of punctuation.

WELCOME TO MATRIMONY THEATRE

April 30, 2004 We've been able to use "Motorcycle Helmet Tycho" (who might also be "Helljumper Tycho," I suppose) on a few occasions, most notably on the "Beach" poster we made. It seems like if we ever get around to making toys, the Tycho figurine should come with the helmet *and* the protective black gauntlets. In any case, that is how it occurs in my fantasy.

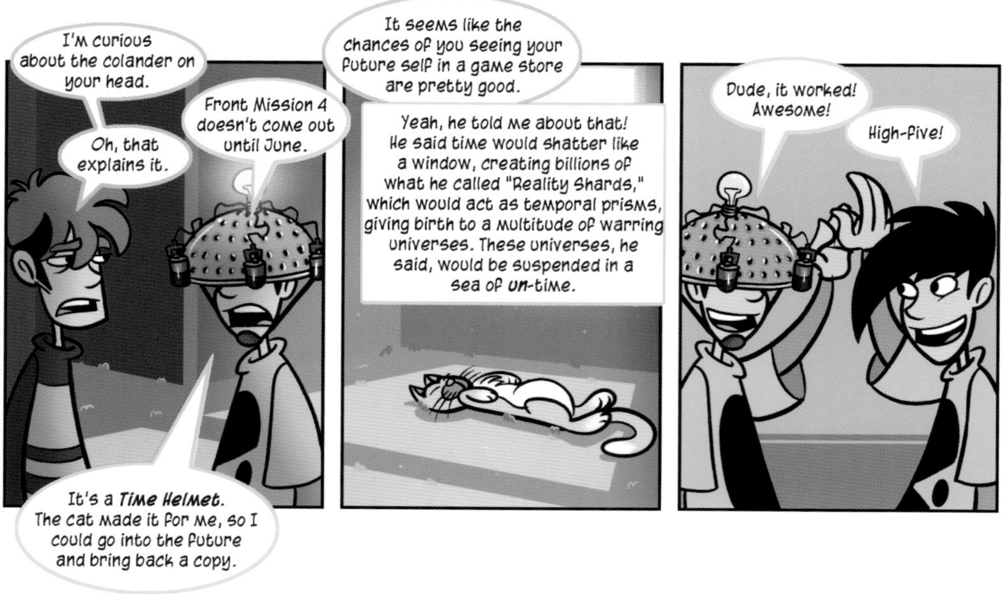
I'm curious about the colander on your head.
Oh, that explains it.
Front Mission 4 doesn't come out until June.
It's a *Time Helmet.* The cat made it for me, so I could go into the future and bring back a copy.
It seems like the chances of you seeing your future self in a game store are pretty good.
Yeah, he told me about that! He said time would shatter like a window, creating billions of what he called "Reality Shards," which would act as temporal prisms, giving birth to a multitude of warring universes. These universes, he said, would be suspended in a sea of *un*-time.
Dude, it worked! Awesome!
High-five!

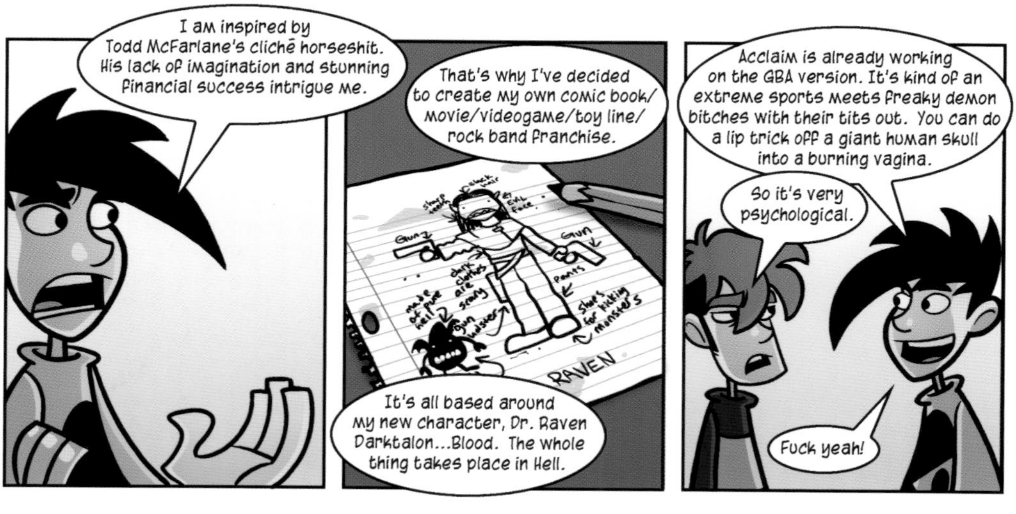
I am inspired by Todd McFarlane's cliché horseshit. His lack of imagination and stunning financial success intrigue me.
That's why I've decided to create my own comic book/movie/videogame/toy line/rock band franchise.
RAVEN
It's all based around my new character, Dr. Raven Darktalon...Blood. The whole thing takes place in Hell.
Acclaim is already working on the GBA version. It's kind of an extreme sports meets freaky demon bitches with their tits out. You can do a lip trick off a giant human skull into a burning vagina.
So it's very psychological.
Fuck yeah!

PARSLEY, SAGE, ROSEMARY, AND TIME

May 3, 2004 To say that I like the Front Mission series is not sufficient. To say that I crave it is closer. I don't know that I worship it, though I do maintain a quiet shrine. A number of imported figurines guard my desk from mercenary incursions, and I have customized their loadouts to deliver *maximum* firepower. I often test people with the series. I will ask them if they are familiar with it, and if they say no, *I stab them.* It's always a big surprise.

THE NEW NAME OF FEAR

May 5, 2004 We came up with Dr. Raven Darktalon Blood this year, too? That's another character we like a lot, but there's rarely an opportunity for a pistol-packing gothic shit-kicker to boil up into ordinary continuity. Not that we really *have* a very substantial continuity, but there's enough there that if a cloaked sorcerer keeps popping in, you're going to notice.

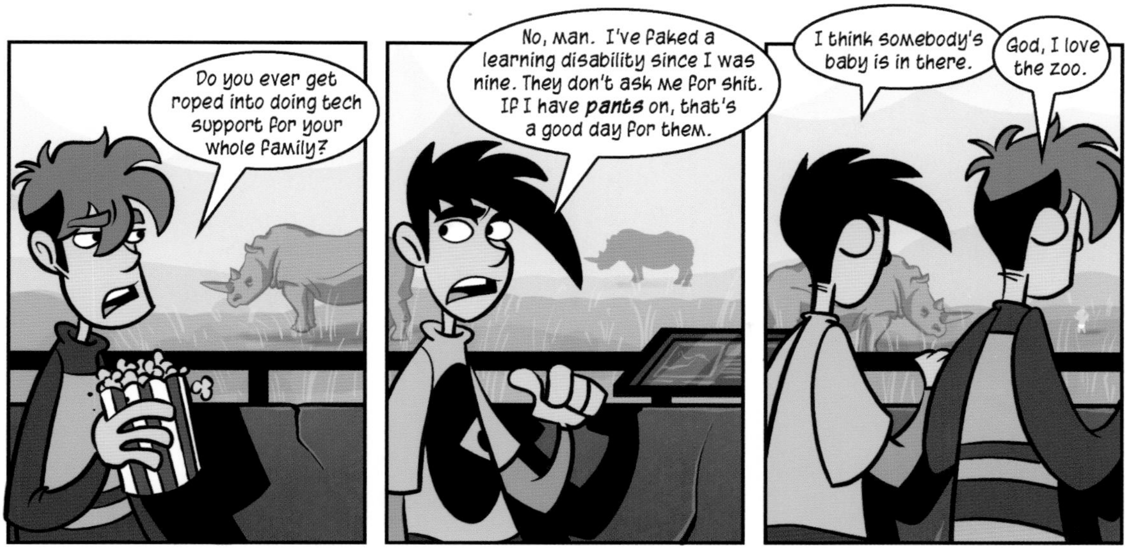
Do you ever get roped into doing tech support for your whole family?
No, man. I've faked a learning disability since I was nine. They don't ask me for shit. If I have pants on, that's a good day for them.
I think somebody's baby is in there.
God, I love the zoo.

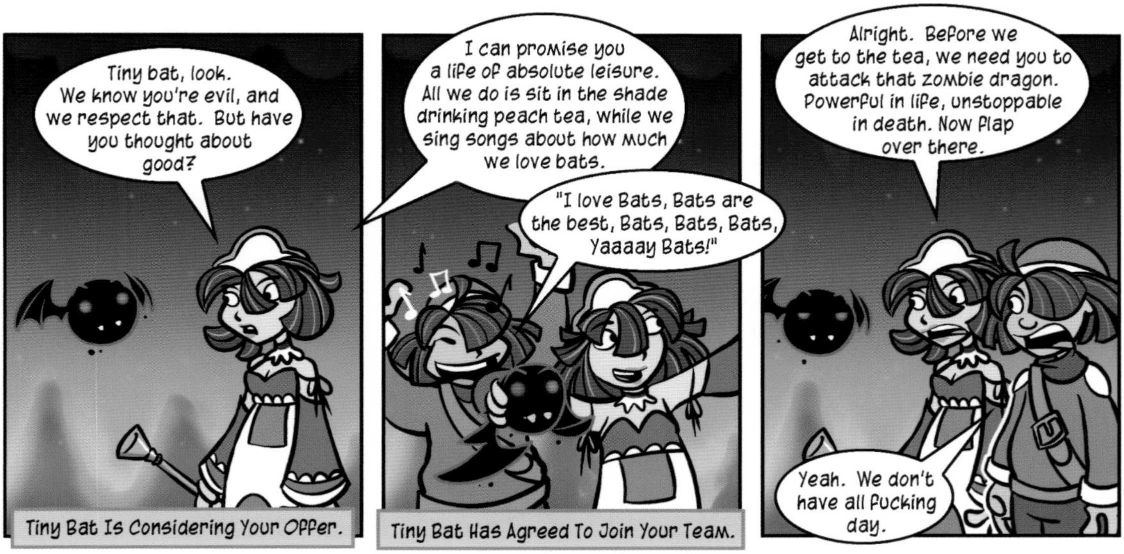
Tiny bat, look. We know you're evil, and we respect that. But have you thought about good?
Tiny Bat Is Considering Your Offer.
I can promise you a life of absolute leisure. All we do is sit in the shade drinking peach tea, while we sing songs about how much we love bats.
"I love Bats, Bats are the best, Bats, Bats, Bats, Yaaaay Bats!"
Tiny Bat Has Agreed To Join Your Team.
Alright. Before we get to the tea, we need you to attack that zombie dragon. Powerful in life, unstoppable in death. Now flap over there.
Yeah. We don't have all fucking day.

BABY VERSUS RHINO

May 7, 2004 The concept behind the strip struck us as pretty universal. Not the baby/rhino junction, which is hopefully quite rare, but the fact that if you know anything about computers at all you invariably get roped into trying to resuscitate grandma's wheezing old XT. And when you get married, wow. People catch on fast. Even at the wedding itself, I was helping these people fashion Excel macros on a copy of my vows.

HOW TO MAKE FRIENDS AND INFLUENCE BATS

May 10, 2004 We're nuts about NIS strategy games, which often look very similar in screenshots but bear strategic subtleties. Part of the reason they look similar is because their art is breathtaking, with a style that carries through their catalog. I've been waiting for their leap to the next generation, hungry to see their luscious 2D elements honored by today's (comparatively crazy) resolutions.

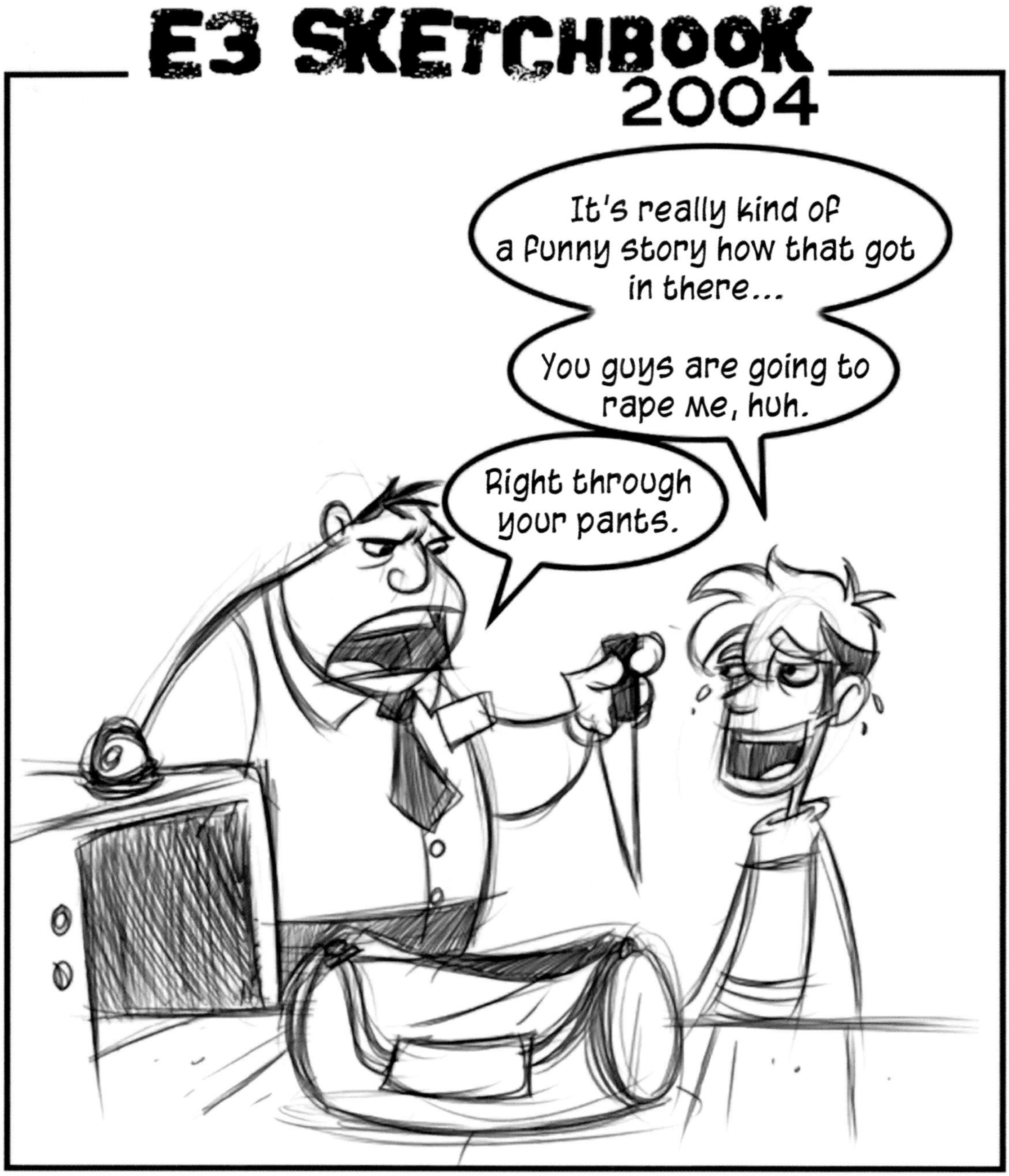
E3 SKETCHBOOK 2004
It's really kind of a funny story how that got in there...
You guys are going to rape me, huh.
Right through your pants.

E32K4 SKETCHBOOK: BAD TOUCHES

May 11, 2004 From that day's post:

There are hiking trails near Mount Rainier, and if you want to brave such things that's fine, but the forest service does ask that you bring a few emergency supplies. This is probably to delay the onset of cannibal acts for a few hours while rangers attempt to track down the next batch of city folk.

It was these terrifically useful items I removed by the handful from the pack Brenna had been using up there, and I was relatively certain that I had gotten them all by the time I began replacing that stuff with the things I'd want to die in a forest with, like ironic game shirts and a phone charger that fits any outlet.

I never get stopped at those airport baggage things. No stranger ever diddles me with a latex glove because I am absolutely ordinary in every way. So when I was made to wait without my shoes—which is oddly dehumanizing—while a man I was not familiar with began to stir the contents of my bag like a large kettle, I began to sass back in various ways regarding the dangerous Game Boy hinge or lethal mouse cord. I don't know what made me do that. Certainly the man did not enjoy it, and continued to insist that there was something really dangerous in there. "Probably not," I said, though I did bring a potentially hazardous box of mints to his attention.

The security man proceeded to draw a long knife out of my bag. The thing was practically a sword, and as he held that shape over the bag I could feel a frigid, unseen hand grip my scrotum. The knife had a black wooden handle and a serrated edge. It was not, in fact, a mint. Or, if it was, this was the sort of mint you should eat only as a last resort.

His supervisor came over, holding the knife and looking at me as though I were an animal in need of a reprimand, a creature somewhat outside the reach of language. "This is a knife." I knew that much. "You can't bring it on the plane." I knew that too, actually. They don't give that kind of shit back, by the way—the weapons you try to sneak on board? Nope. Turns out they keep that stuff.

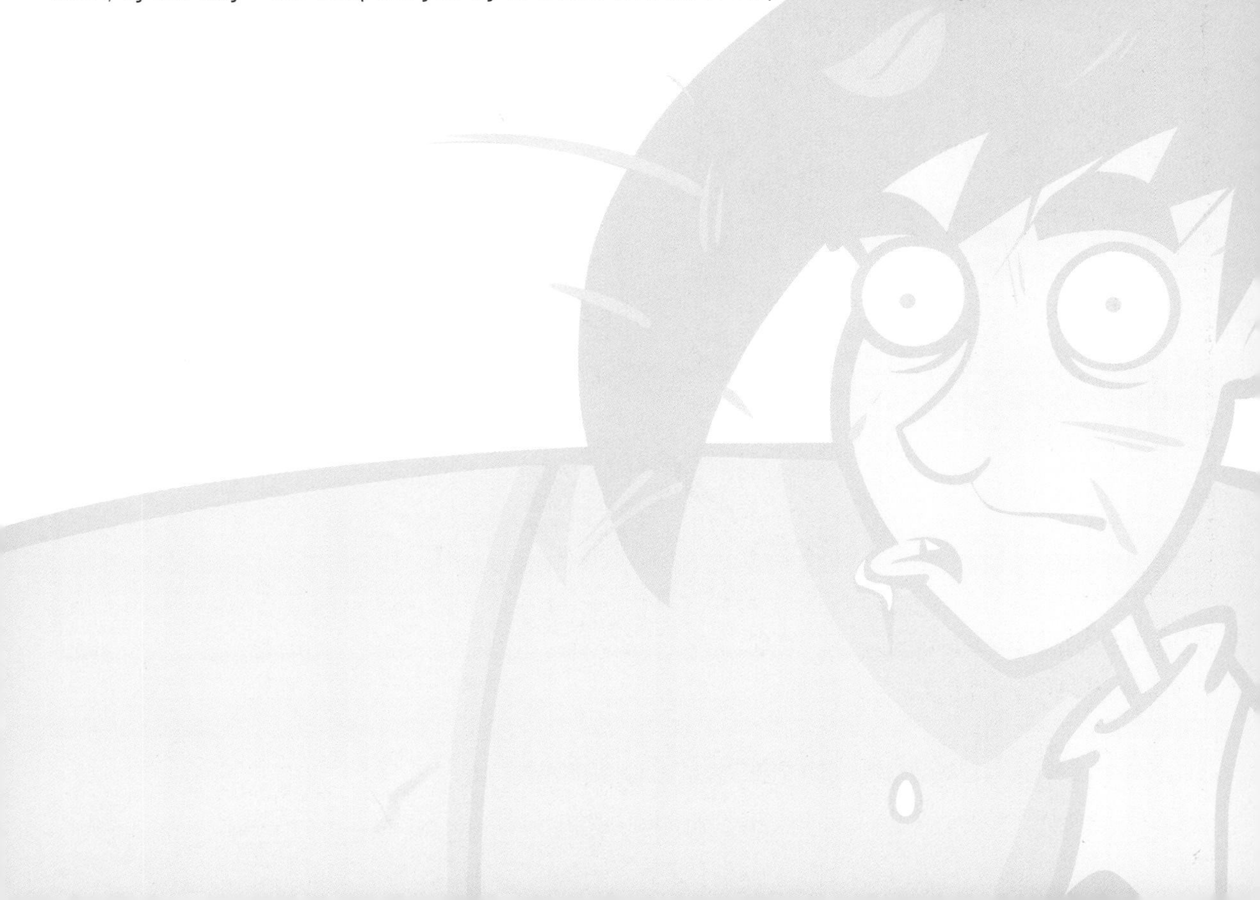

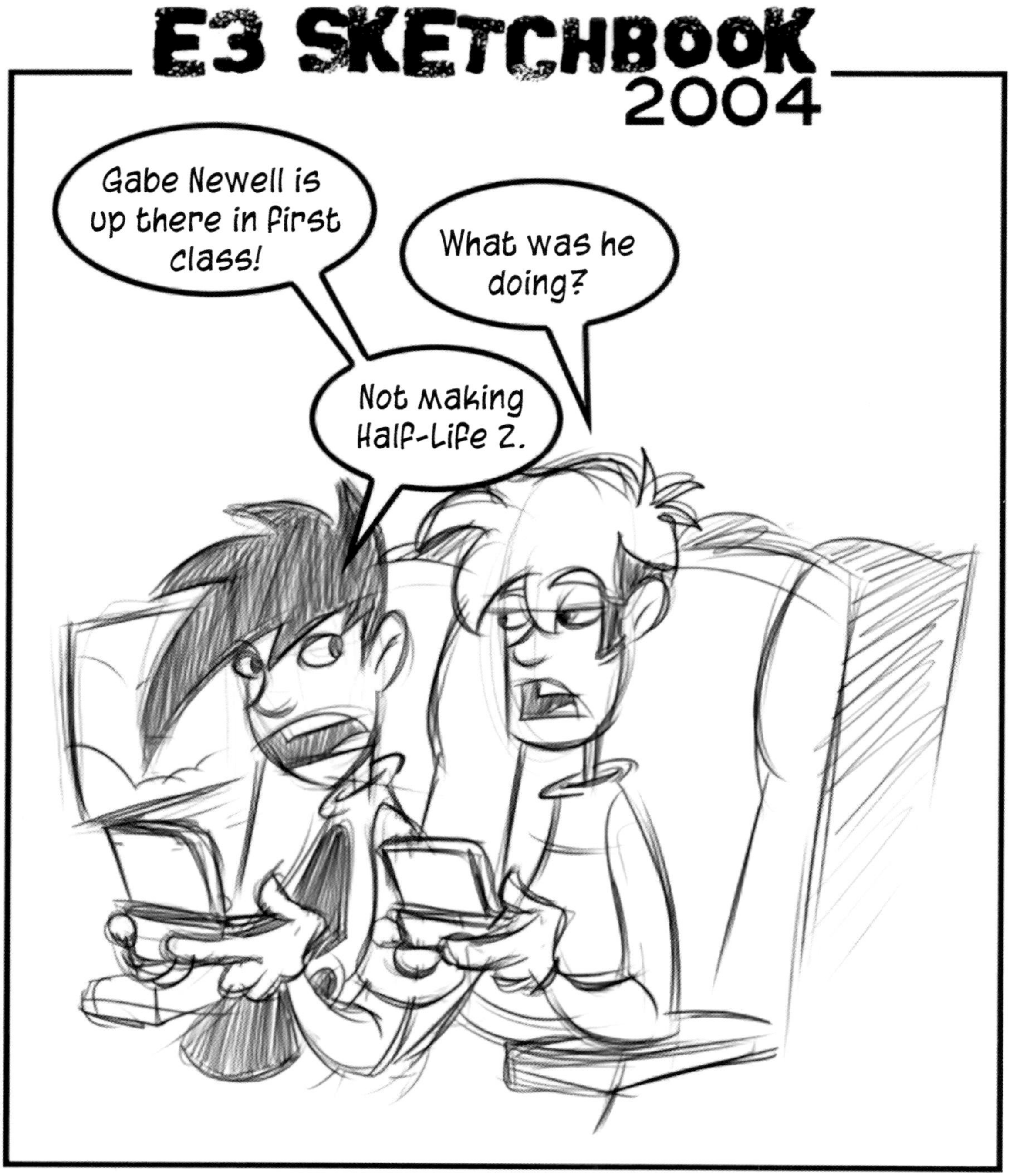
E3 SKETCHBOOK 2004
Gabe Newell is up there in first class!
What was he doing?
Not making Half-Life 2.

E32K4 SKETCHBOOK: EXTREME COMFORT

May 12, 2004 | I think we were still stinging from the most recent delay.

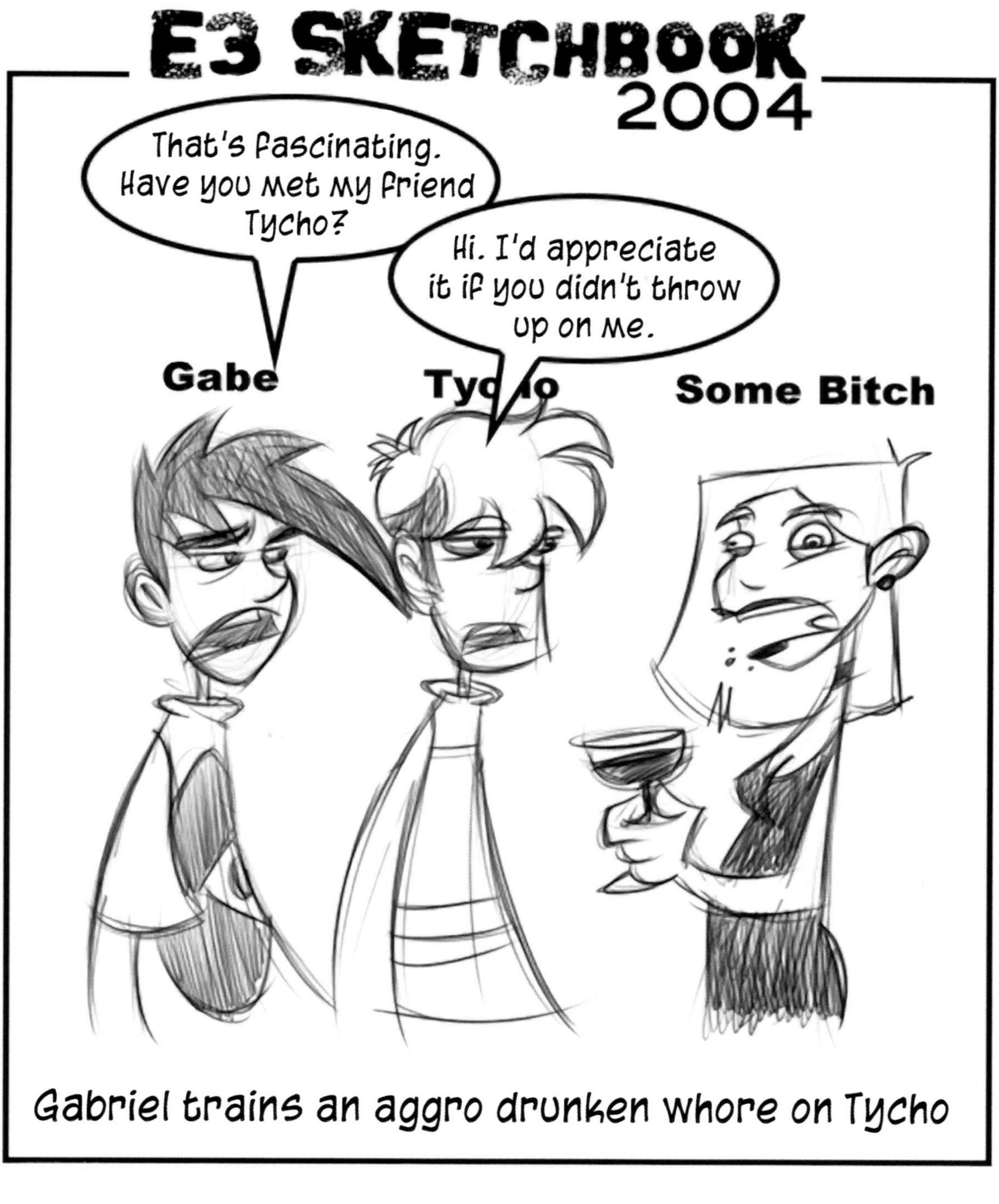
E3 SKETCHBOOK
2004
That's fascinating. Have you met my friend Tycho?
Hi. I'd appreciate it if you didn't throw up on me.
Gabe
Tycho
Some Bitch
Gabriel trains an aggro drunken whore on Tycho

E32K4 SKETCHBOOK: LEVEL 25 DRUNK BITCH

May 14, 2004 I explained this fascinating process in a recent post, describing my role as a kind of "social tank."

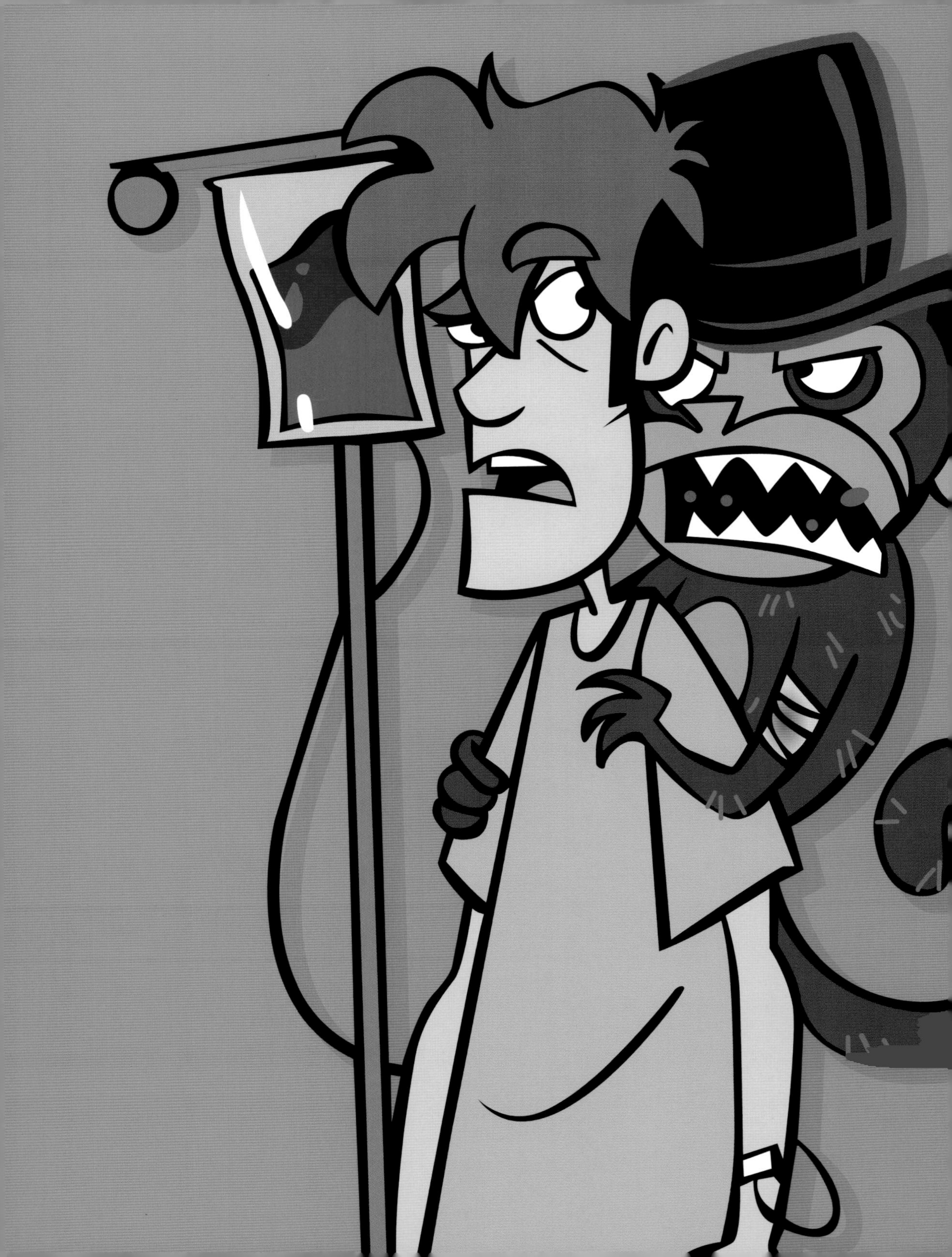

E3: The Disappointments

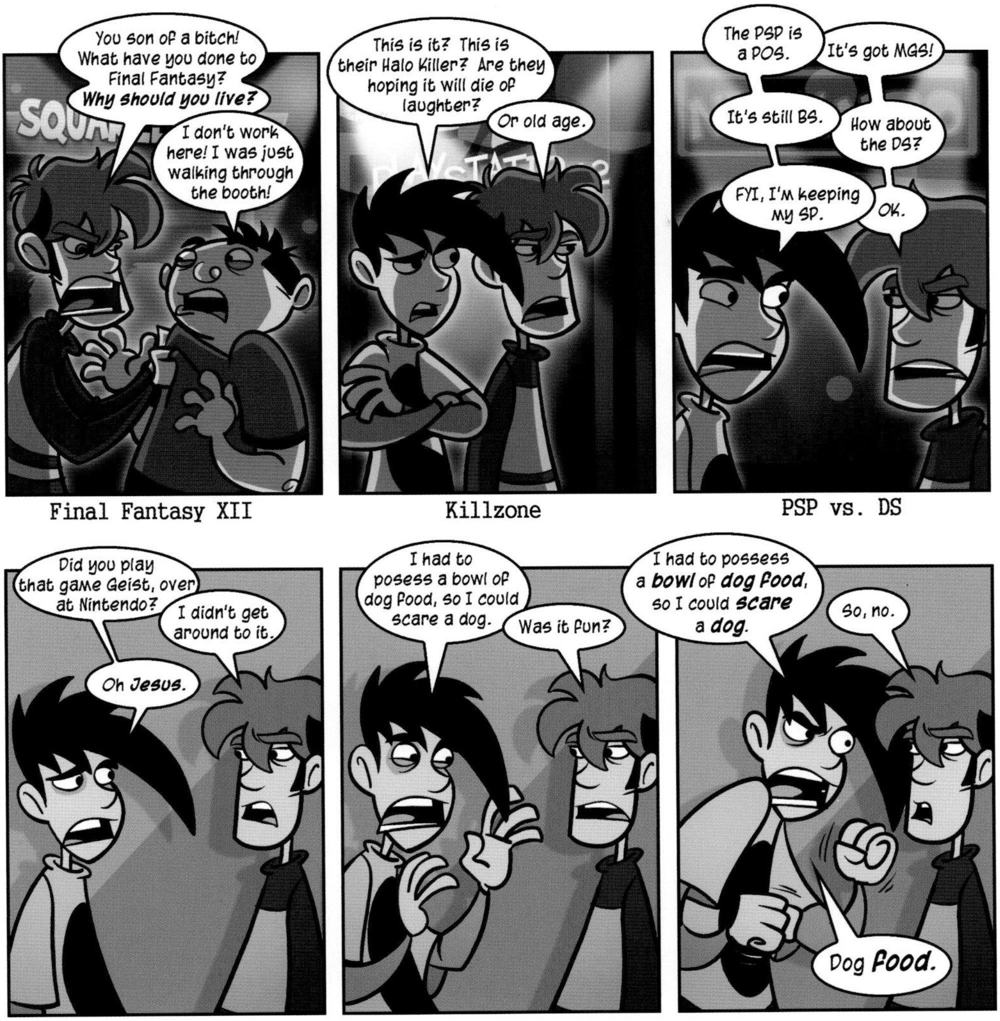
You son of a bitch! What have you done to Final Fantasy? *Why should you live?*
I don't work here! I was just walking through the booth!
This is it? This is their Halo killer? Are they hoping it will die of laughter?
Or old age.
The PSP is a POS.
It's got MGS!
It's still BS.
How about the DS?
FYI, I'm keeping my SP.
OK.
Did you play that game Geist, over at Nintendo?
I didn't get around to it.
Oh Jesus.
I had to posess a bowl of dog food, so I could scare a dog.
Was it fun?
I had to possess a **bowl** of **dog food**, so I could **scare** a **dog**.
So, no.
Dog **food.**

Final Fantasy XII

Killzone

PSP vs. DS

LES DISAPPOINTMENTS

May 17, 2004 As regards the first panel, I would maintain my orthodoxy on the subject. It's since become Gabriel's favorite Final Fantasy of all time. The *heretic*. It worked out for me, though, because the writing, story, and presentation were executed flawlessly. I loved the game, provided I wasn't playing it.

GERMAN WORDS ARE SCARY

May 19, 2007 The dog food thing is . . . I mean, come on. But there is definitely a reason that Nintendo had n-Space keep plugging away at this thing, and that is because there are some really cool ideas there. You could see the game shifting over the years at E3 as their tuning and tweaking took hold. There were a couple "boss battles" that had a flow radically different than anything we'd ever experienced: a man and his elite guards entered the room, and we leapt to each of his closest confidants as we killed him. It was actually very disturbing.

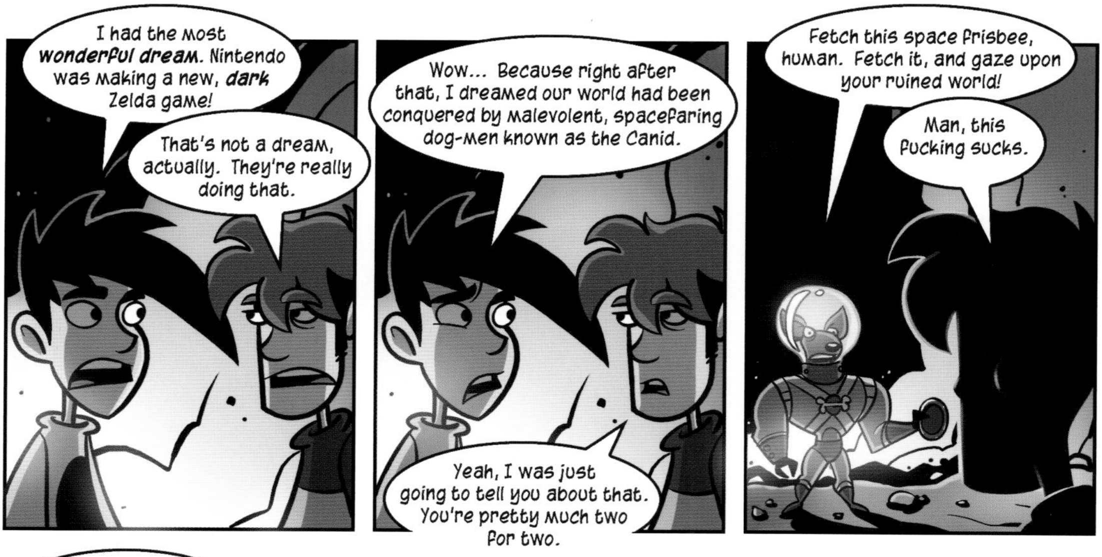
I had the most **wonderful dream**. Nintendo was making a new, ***dark*** Zelda game!
That's not a dream, actually. They're really doing that.
Wow... Because right after that, I dreamed our world had been conquered by malevolent, spacefaring dog-men known as the Canid.
Yeah, I was just going to tell you about that. You're pretty much two for two.
Fetch this space frisbee, human. Fetch it, and gaze upon your ruined world!
Man, this fucking sucks.

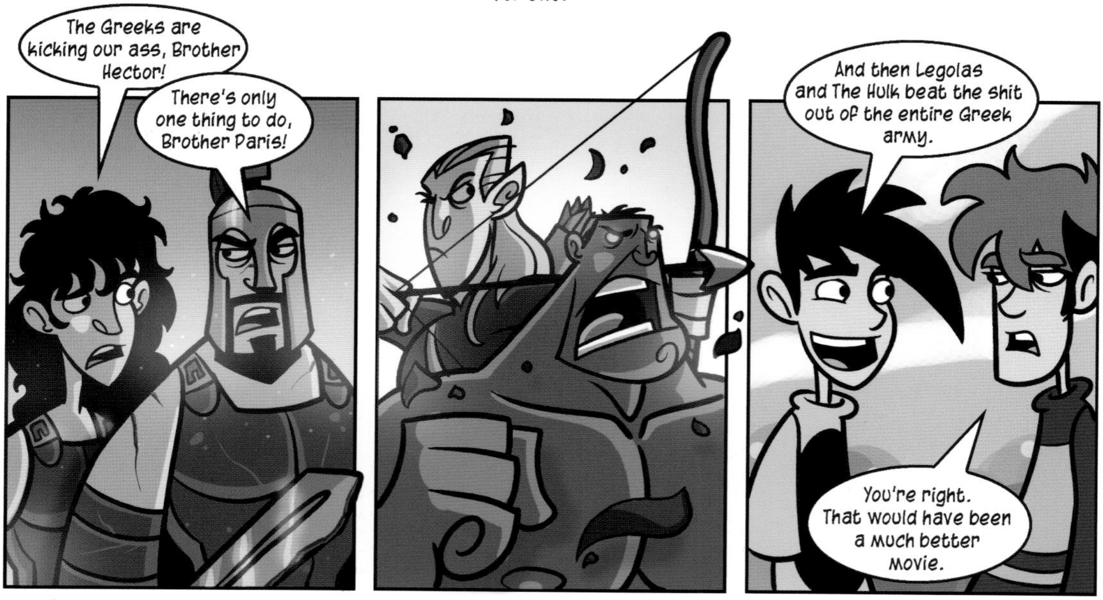
The Greeks are kicking our ass, Brother Hector!
There's only one thing to do, Brother Paris!
And then Legolas and The Hulk beat the shit out of the entire Greek army.
You're right. That would have been a much better movie.

THEY HAIL FROM CANIDON

May 21, 2004 What's not to like? The palette is appropriately apocalyptic, and also there's some kind of Chihuahua operating a cybernetic harness. There's an online CCG called Star Chamber—it's operated by Sony, these days—but back when it was a one-man indie gaming operation he asked us to make a couple cards for the game. We were glad to, or at any rate I was glad to make Gabriel do it, offering up the Canid Impounder and Canid Smuggler.

TROY, THE GABRIEL CUT

May 24, 2004 I never saw *Troy*, so I had to take his word for it. I certainly bought the premise, which is that history would have been more interesting had it been strewn about with elfin marksmen and indestructible giants.

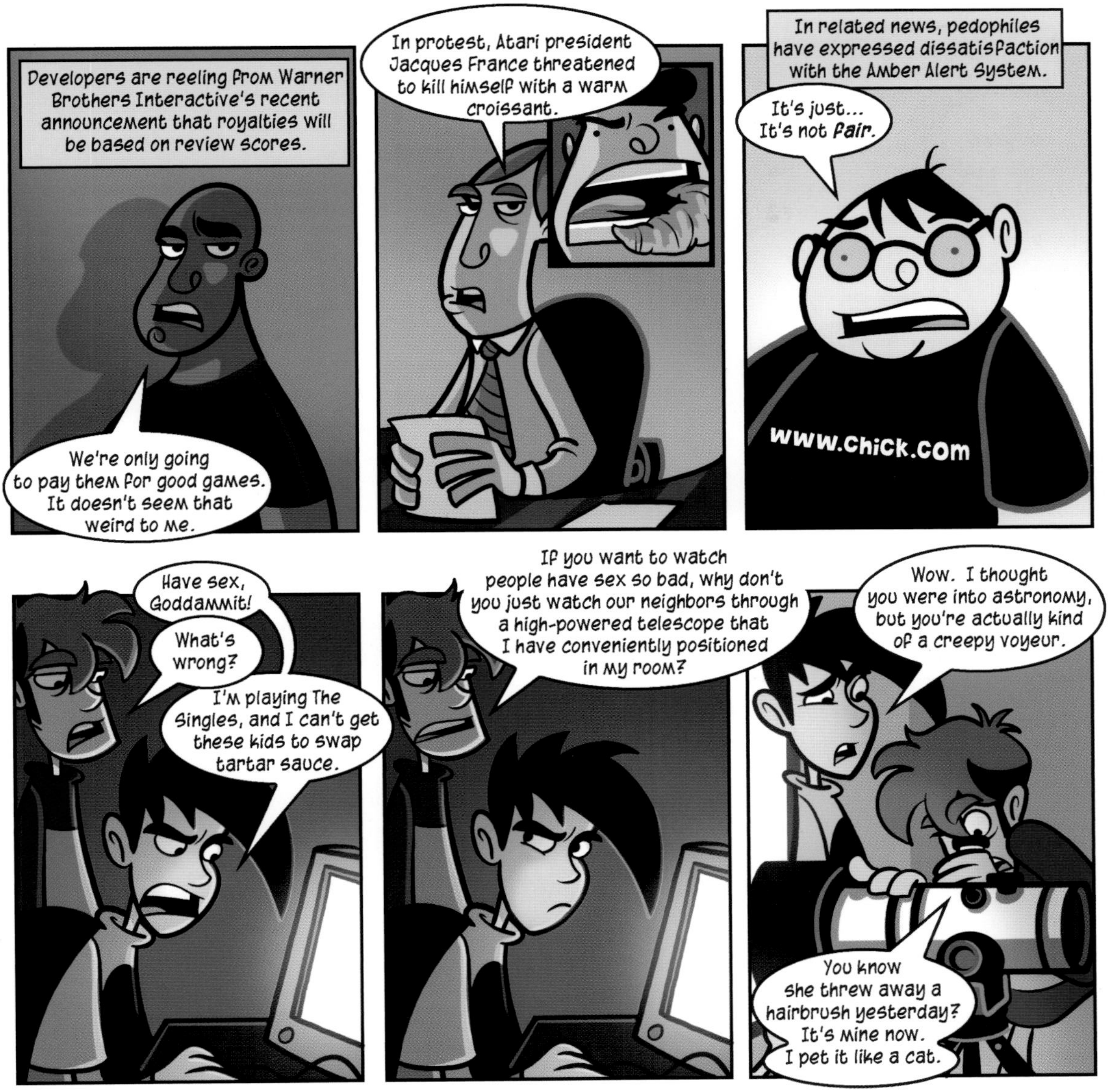
Developers are reeling from Warner Brothers Interactive's recent announcement that royalties will be based on review scores.
We're only going to pay them for good games. It doesn't seem that weird to me.
In protest, Atari president Jacques France threatened to kill himself with a warm croissant.
In related news, pedophiles have expressed dissatisfaction with the Amber Alert System.
It's just... It's not fair.
www.chick.com
Have sex, Goddammit!
What's wrong?
I'm playing The Singles, and I can't get these kids to swap tartar sauce.
If you want to watch people have sex so bad, why don't you just watch our neighbors through a high-powered telescope that I have conveniently positioned in my room?
Wow. I thought you were into astronomy, but you're actually kind of a creepy voyeur.
You know she threw away a hairbrush yesterday? It's mine now. I pet it like a cat.

THE DOUBLE-YOU BEE

May 26, 2004 Warner Brothers Interactive eventually backed off from the policy publicly, but I understand that this isn't terribly uncommon. Aggregate review scores (on a Metacritic or Gamerankings type site) are pretty serious business, and many things are indexed to them—it's one of the things that makes escaping those all-important numbers in reviews so difficult.

THE TYCHO YOU DIDN'T KNOW

May 28, 2004 Singles, which is also known as "Not The Sims," was like *Big Brother* in some ways. And I don't mean the version of *Big Brother* in the US, I mean the non-stop orgies of the European versions. Essentially, it was The Sims for perverts, which I'm sure they would have put *right on the box* if they could.

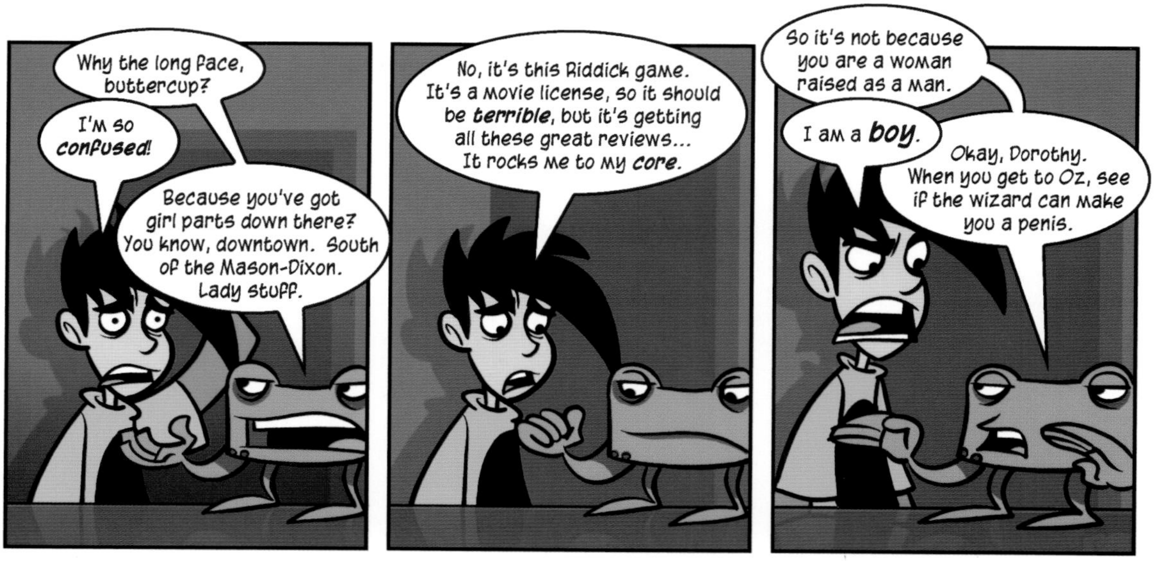
Why the long face, buttercup?
I'm so confused!
Because you've got girl parts down there? You know, downtown. South of the Mason-Dixon. Lady stuff.
No, it's this Riddick game. It's a movie license, so it should be terrible, but it's getting all these great reviews... It rocks me to my core.
So it's not because you are a woman raised as a man.
I am a boy.
Okay, Dorothy. When you get to Oz, see if the wizard can make you a penis.

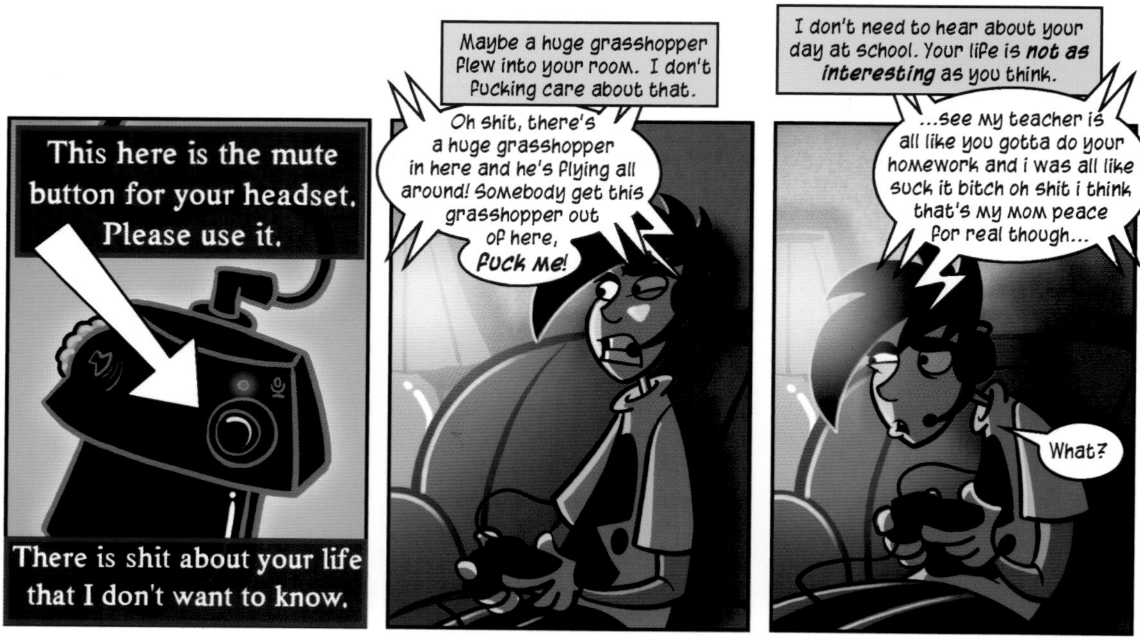
This here is the mute button for your headset. Please use it.
There is shit about your life that I don't want to know.
Maybe a huge grasshopper flew into your room. I don't fucking care about that.
Oh shit, there's a huge grasshopper in here and he's flying all around! Somebody get this grasshopper out of here, fuck me!
I don't need to hear about your day at school. Your life is not as interesting as you think.
...see my teacher is all like you gotta do your homework and i was all like suck it bitch oh shit i think that's my mom peace for real though...
What?

AVOIDING THE OBVIOUS PUN

May 31, 2004 We received a mail at this time saying that they thought we were implying that Gabriel was a hermaphrodite, which was . . . not our intention. It was our intention to prove that Div is an asshole, a thesis that is easy to support.

ILL COMMUNICATION

June 2, 2004 Oh, but there are interesting conversations too. We met a guy who works for Purdue, "processing" chickens, and he tells us that they just steal and eat chicken all day. Also, they have a machine that freezes and cooks chicken simultaneously, which is *horrifying*.

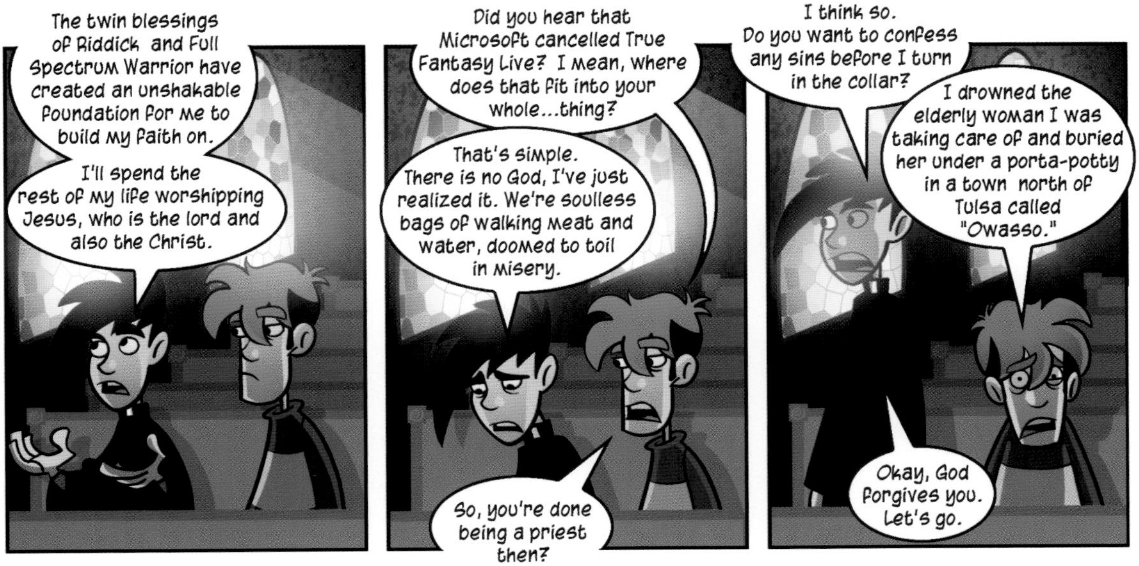
The twin blessings of Riddick and Full Spectrum Warrior have created an unshakable foundation for me to build my faith on.
I'll spend the rest of my life worshipping Jesus, who is the lord and also the Christ.
Did you hear that Microsoft cancelled True Fantasy Live? I mean, where does that fit into your whole...thing?
That's simple. There is no God, I've just realized it. We're soulless bags of walking meat and water, doomed to toil in misery.
So, you're done being a priest then?
I think so. Do you want to confess any sins before I turn in the collar?
I drowned the elderly woman I was taking care of and buried her under a porta-potty in a town north of Tulsa called "Owasso."
Okay, God forgives you. Let's go.

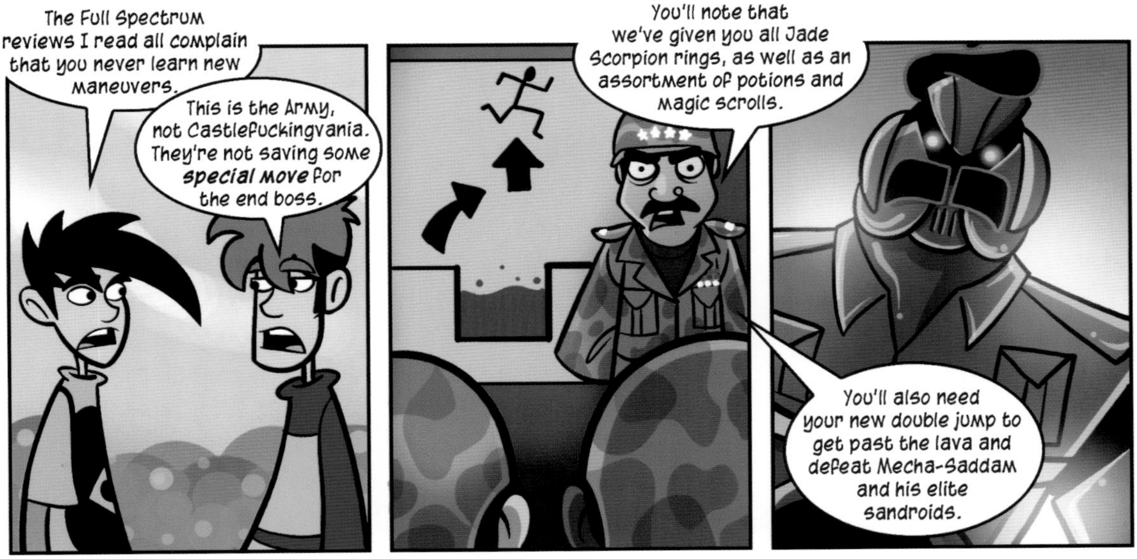
The Full Spectrum reviews I read all complain that you never learn new maneuvers.
This is the Army, not Castlefuckingvania. They're not saving some **special move** for the end boss.
You'll note that we've given you all Jade Scorpion rings, as well as an assortment of potions and magic scrolls.
You'll also need your new double jump to get past the lava and defeat Mecha-Saddam and his elite sandroids.

ADDITIONAL REVELATIONS

June 4, 2004 It really is a shame, and not just for Microsoft, who could really have used a game like True Fantasy Live to break that ground on their first box. No, it's because Level 5—whose oeuvre is legendary by now—were putting together an MMO, and it fell through. They're focusing on a lot of single-player RPG content at the moment, which is great, because they excel at it. I just would have loved to see their take on the genre.

POWERFUL NEW TECHNIQUES

June 7, 2004 God damn I loved that game, I mean, God *damn*. Seriously, I thought I knew all about warriors by that point. Fact is, their spectrums were incomplete. They were only partial spectrums. The sequel did poorly, which is a shame, because that's probably it for the franchise. It had a clever way of modeling your commands that really deserved to be fleshed out.

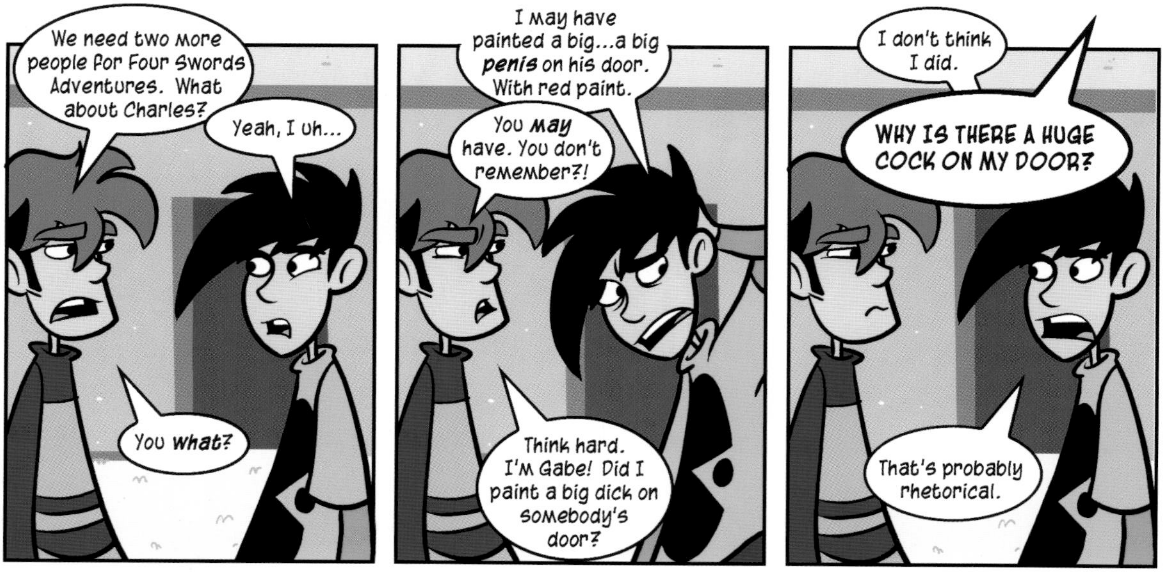
We need two more people for Four Swords Adventures. What about Charles?
Yeah, I uh...
You **what**?
I may have painted a big...a big **penis** on his door. With red paint.
You **may** have. You don't remember?!
Think hard. I'm Gabe! Did I paint a big dick on somebody's door?
I don't think I did.
WHY IS THERE A HUGE COCK ON MY DOOR?
That's probably rhetorical.

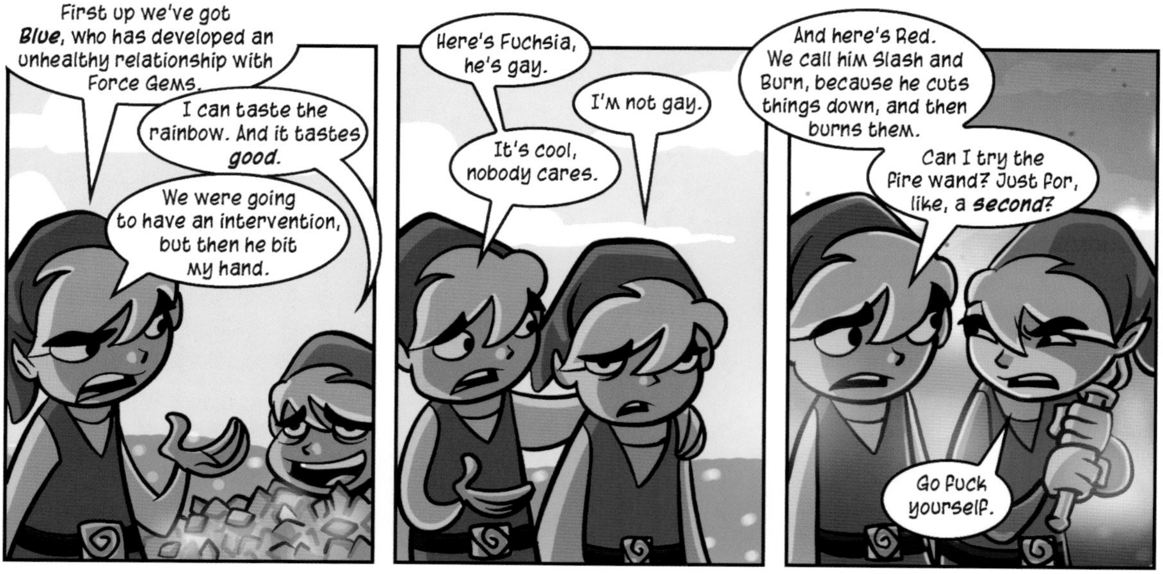
First up we've got **Blue**, who has developed an unhealthy relationship with Force Gems.
I can taste the rainbow. And it tastes **good**.
We were going to have an intervention, but then he bit my hand.
Here's Fuchsia, he's gay.
I'm not gay.
It's cool, nobody cares.
And here's Red. We call him Slash and Burn, because he cuts things down, and then burns them.
Can I try the fire wand? Just for, like, a **second**?
Go fuck yourself.

REMINISCENT OF EGYPT / THE GANG

June 9, 2004 / June 11, 2004 There are now a few takes on Zelda in multiplayer, but the largely cooperative affair of Four Swords was unique. Then again, we took any opportunity to haul out those little cables and plug our GBAs into the Gamecube. We got a lot more enjoyment out of that system than most, because we had a handful of friends who all gamed together regularly in the same physical location. Final Fantasy: Crystal Chronicles is one of our favorites, precisely for that reason, and that's a game that is almost universally reviled. Remote multiplayer is a virtuous endeavor, and I support it wholeheartedly. At the same time, Nintendo seems to understand instinctively the value of actual proximity.

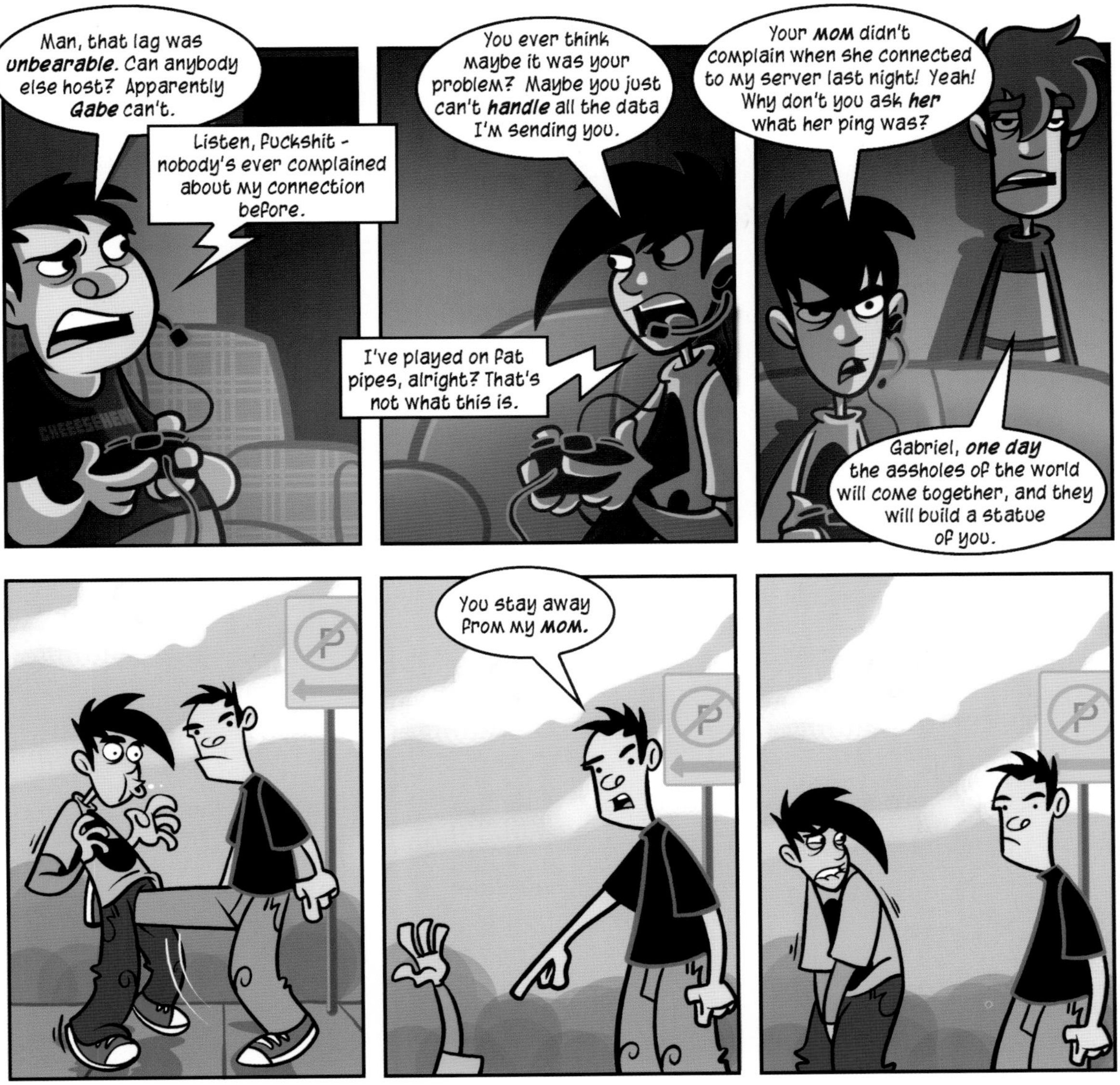
Man, that lag was *unbearable*. Can anybody else host? Apparently *Gabe* can't.
Listen, fuckshit - nobody's ever complained about my connection before.
You ever think maybe it was your problem? Maybe you just can't *handle* all the data I'm sending you.
I've played on fat pipes, alright? That's not what this is.
Your *MOM* didn't complain when she connected to my server last night! Yeah! Why don't you ask *her* what her ping was?
Gabriel, *one day* the assholes of the world will come together, and they will build a statue of you.
You stay away from my *MOM*.

MANWIDTH

June 14, 2004 This is a perfect example of what I was just talking about. At an actual LAN party, there's no lag of any kind. What percentage of your time online is spent experiencing lag, discussing lag, or being told at length about somebody else's Goddamned lag? It has to be over a hundred percent, which should be impossible, but the value is so vast that it distends the scale.

INITIATIVE

June 16, 2004 This was originally a completely different comic. I believe it was about the N-Gage being "bad." It was just so much sillier with less text and this weird-ass kid that we liked it better.

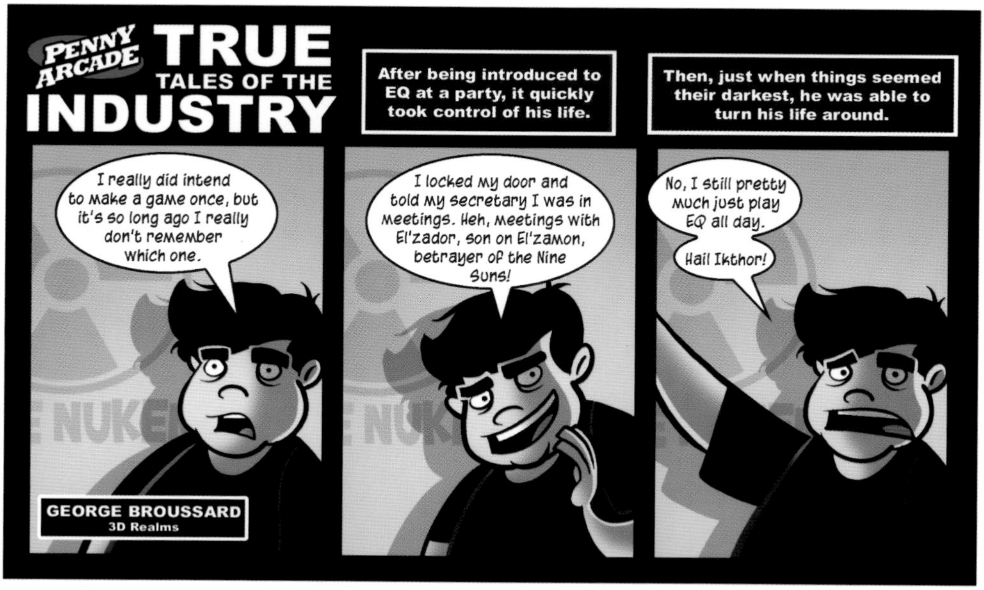
PENNY ARCADE TRUE TALES OF THE INDUSTRY
After being introduced to EQ at a party, it quickly took control of his life.
Then, just when things seemed their darkest, he was able to turn his life around.
I really did intend to make a game once, but it's so long ago I really don't remember which one.
GEORGE BROUSSARD
3D Realms
I locked my door and told my secretary I was in meetings. Heh, meetings with El'zador, son on El'zamon, betrayer of the Nine Suns!
No, I still pretty much just play EQ all day.
Hail Ikthor!

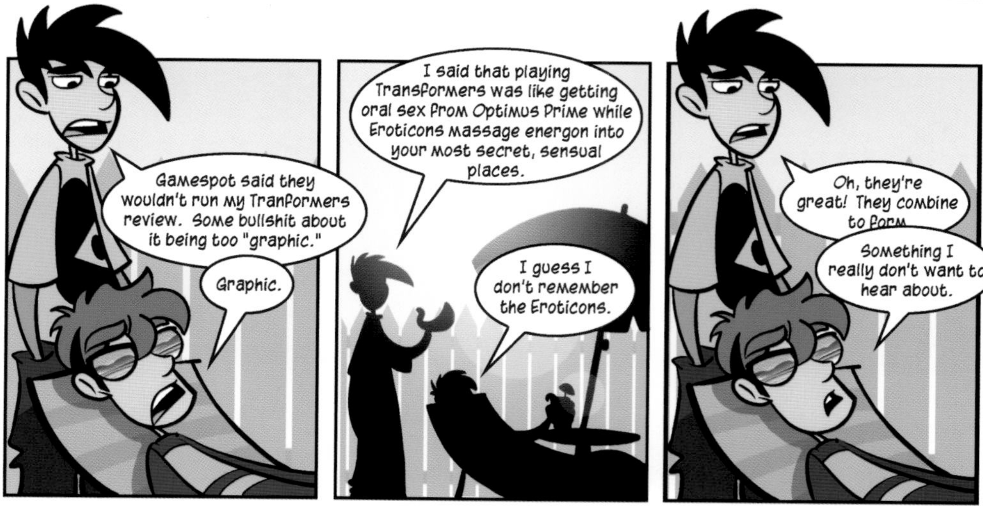
Gamespot said they wouldn't run my Tranformers review. Some bullshit about it being too "graphic."
Graphic.
I said that playing Transformers was like getting oral sex from Optimus Prime while Eroticons massage energon into your most secret, sensual places.
I guess I don't remember the Eroticons.
Oh, they're great! They combine to form
Something I really don't want to hear about.

NEXT TIME, ON TRUE TALES

June 18, 2004 We presented this as a joke slash rumor, but the person who told us the story claimed it was absolutely true. We weren't in a position to verify it, but the story he told us was essentially a comic already: that the development team of Duke Nukem Forever had become so addicted to Everquest that it had derailed the entire development process.

I DON'T BLAME THEM

June 21, 2004 The Transformers game that came out back then really clicked with us, for some reason. We weren't able to appreciate the cartoon it was based on, possibly because we are *grown men,* but the game provided enough exciting ramps and mid-air transformations to please the young men we once were. Using collectible Mini-cons—also known as Pokémon—you could tune how the game played significantly.

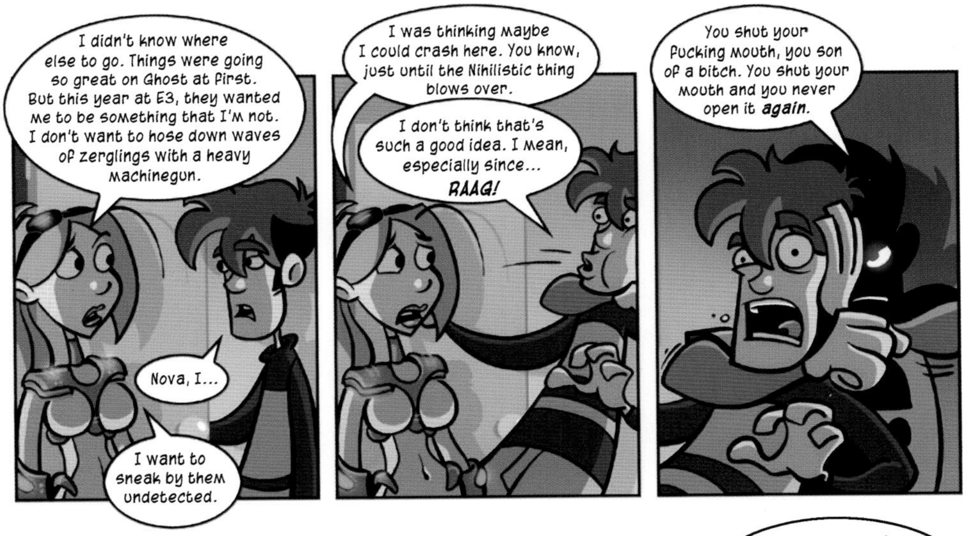
I didn't know where else to go. Things were going so great on Ghost at first. But this year at E3, they wanted me to be something that I'm not. I don't want to hose down waves of zerglings with a heavy machinegun.
Nova, I...
I want to sneak by them undetected.
I was thinking maybe I could crash here. You know, just until the Nihilistic thing blows over.
I don't think that's such a good idea. I mean, especially since... RAAG!
You shut your fucking mouth, you son of a bitch. You shut your mouth and you never open it again.

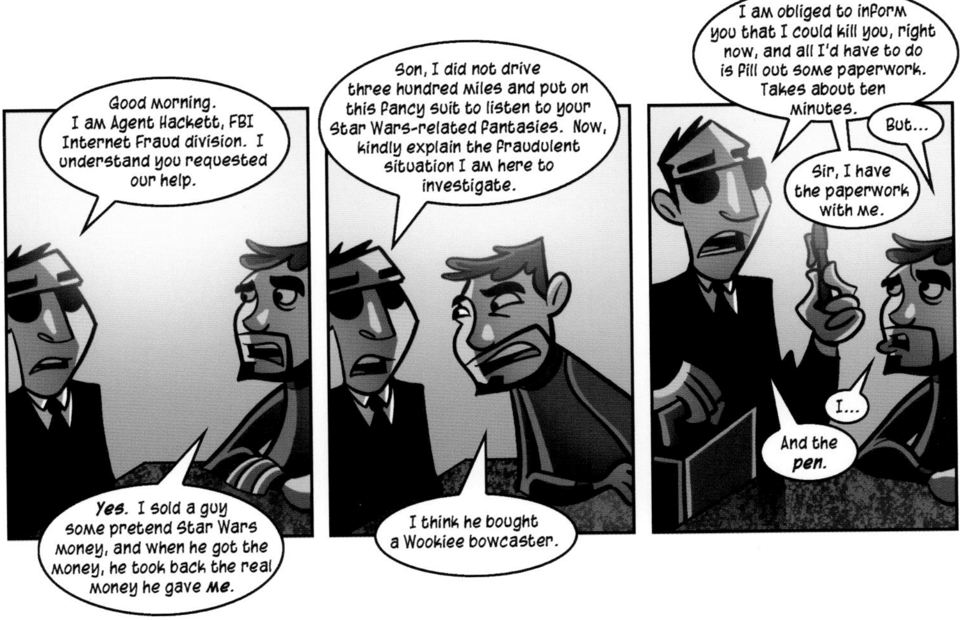
Good morning. I am Agent Hackett, FBI Internet Fraud division. I understand you requested our help.
Yes. I sold a guy some pretend Star Wars money, and when he got the money, he took back the real money he gave me.
Son, I did not drive three hundred miles and put on this fancy suit to listen to your Star Wars-related fantasies. Now, kindly explain the fraudulent situation I am here to investigate.
I think he bought a Wookiee bowcaster.
I am obliged to inform you that I could kill you, right now, and all I'd have to do is fill out some paperwork. Takes about ten minutes.
But...
Sir, I have the paperwork with me.
I...
And the pen.

HOT FUTURE GIRL CAN STAY

June 23, 2004 The first time they showed Ghost, it was an incredible-looking stealth/action game set in the legendary Starcraft universe. After going underground and then losing a developer, Blizzard bought another developer and set them to work. We saw two more radically different versions since then, including one at Blizzcon that was so far along that people were playing multiplayer matches on the show floor. Then, *poof*—it was gone again.

GOOD LUCK

June 25, 2004 I really do wonder how long the value that gamers create in virtual worlds will go unregulated. Not because it's reasonable to do so, but with the GDP of Azeroth being what it is you've got to imagine that it works like an aphrodisiac on a senator's physiology.

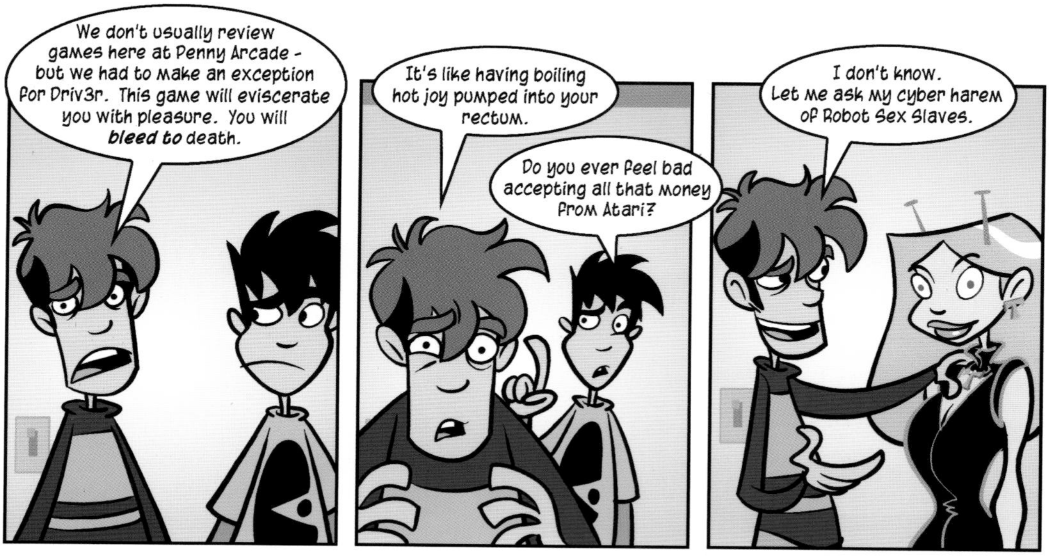
We don't usually review games here at Penny Arcade - but we had to make an exception for Driv3r. This game will eviscerate you with pleasure. You will **bleed to** death.
It's like having boiling hot joy pumped into your rectum.
Do you ever feel bad accepting all that money from Atari?
I don't know. Let me ask my cyber harem of Robot Sex Slaves.

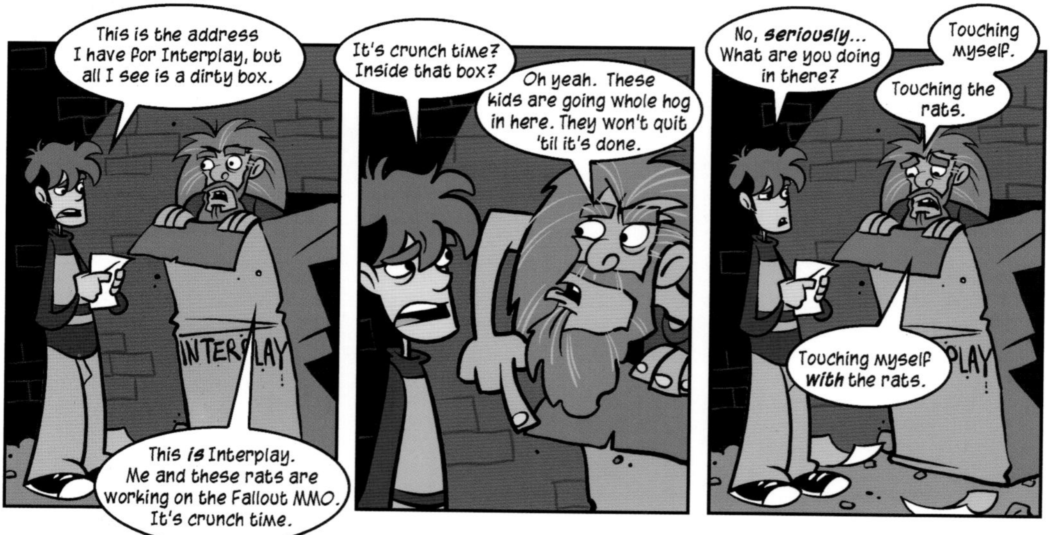
This is the address I have for Interplay, but all I see is a dirty box.
INTERPLAY
This *is* Interplay. Me and these rats are working on the Fallout MMO. It's crunch time.
It's crunch time? Inside that box?
Oh yeah. These kids are going whole hog in here. They won't quit 'til it's done.
No, *seriously*... What are you doing in there?
Touching myself.
Touching the rats.
Touching myself *with* the rats.
PLAY

THEY POSSESS A STARTLING ARRAY OF FEATURES

June 30, 2004 An explosive story ran on Spong in the summer of 2004, claiming that Atari had enacted a number of shady policies to try and crank up the review score. Attempts to guarantee high scores by dishing out early code made up the bulk of the charges, though occasionally anonymous sources would plead darker cases. I can't see what ever came of it, and it's never mentioned these days. Consumer consciousness is a fluid thing.

THE TRUTH COMES OUT

July 2, 2004 As a young man only just coming into my gamer identity, Interplay virtually defined the medium. The Bard's Tale and Wasteland together are synonymous with summers whiled away in epic conquest. Their contributions to the medium through Interplay Prime and through their Black Isle division really can't be overstated. Well, maybe they could. But it would be difficult.

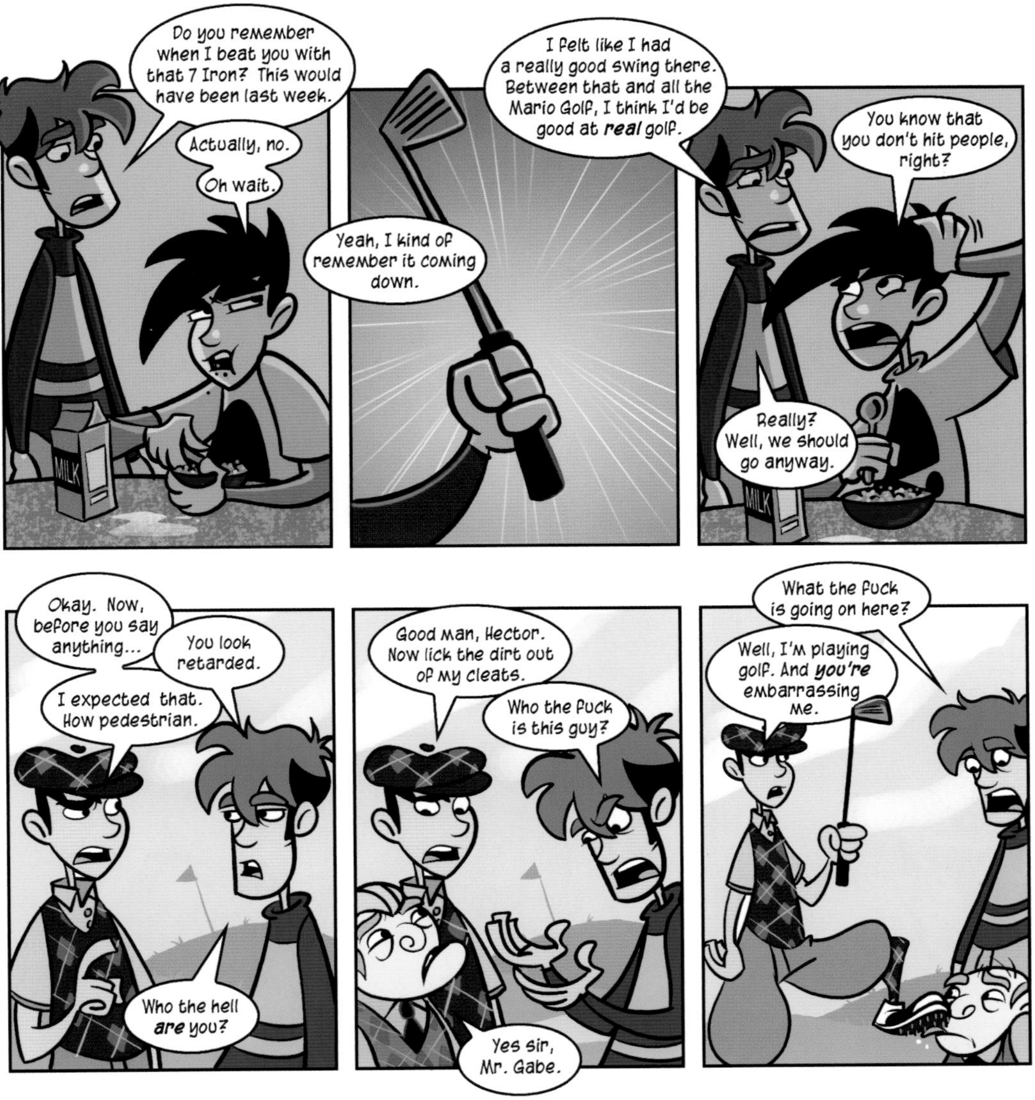
Do you remember when I beat you with that 7 Iron? This would have been last week.
Actually, no.
Oh wait.
Yeah, I kind of remember it coming down.
I felt like I had a really good swing there. Between that and all the Mario Golf, I think I'd be good at *real* golf.
You know that you don't hit people, right?
Really? Well, we should go anyway.
MILK
MILK
Okay. Now, before you say anything...
You look retarded.
I expected that. How pedestrian.
Who the hell *are* you?
Good man, Hector. Now lick the dirt out of my cleats.
Who the fuck is this guy?
Yes sir, Mr. Gabe.
What the fuck is going on here?
Well, I'm playing golf. And *you're* embarrassing me.

AN ALTERNATIVE LIFESTYLE, PART ONE

June 28, 2004 I'm glad I was able to sell him on panel two, a solid shot of a seven iron raised in anger. Electronical golfings have long been a fascination for us, and he eventually suggested we hit the links proper—and I agreed, without even knowing which part of the course contained the links. We have since golfed a number of times, in a variety of exotic locales. We once golfed on the astral corpse of a forgotten god!

AN ALTERNATIVE LIFESTYLE, PART TWO

July 5, 2004 How it happened that we would make a series about golfing is really quite beyond me, but every interest, every desire, and every paranoid fantasy of ours eventually finds its way into the body of the work. In a bizarre twist, it turns out that Gabriel actually played Varsity golf in high school. I don't actually know what Varsity means, because I never intersected with any coordinate in that continuum.

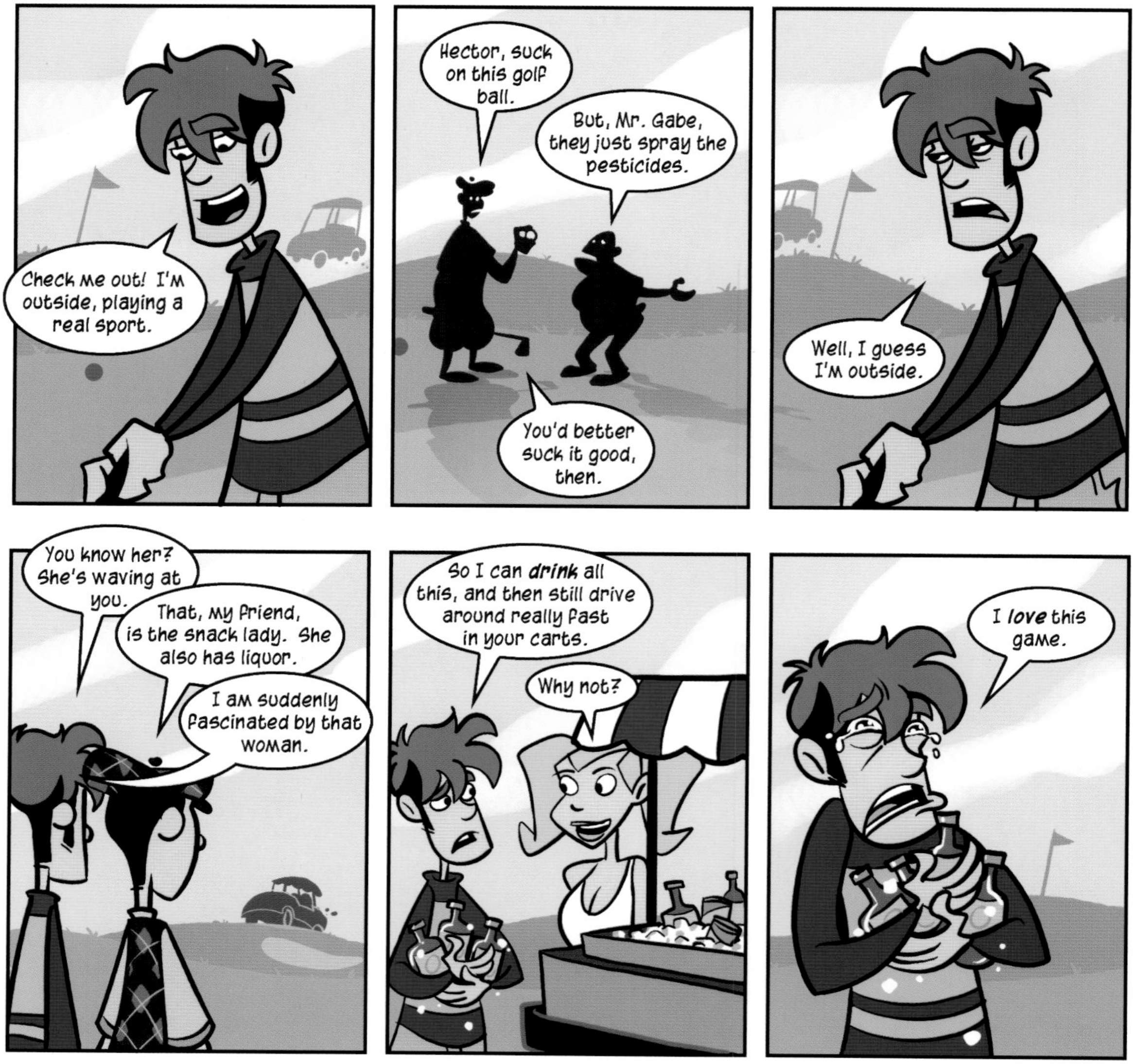
Check me out! I'm outside, playing a real sport.
Hector, suck on this golf ball.
But, Mr. Gabe, they just spray the pesticides.
You'd better suck it good, then.
Well, I guess I'm outside.
You know her? She's waving at you.
That, my friend, is the snack lady. She also has liquor.
I am suddenly fascinated by that woman.
So I can *drink* all this, and then still drive around really fast in your carts.
Why not?
I *love* this game.

AN ALTERNATIVE LIFESTYLE, PART THREE

July 7, 2004 It needs to be established that I—Tycho, or Jerry Holkins if you prefer—*I* am Hector. I enjoy going to golf courses, and being with people who are currently golfing, but the actual *game* of golf is so incredibly frustrating that I can't imagine why any rational person would do it. I'm essentially his slave at these things, as though non-golfers constitute some lesser form of life.

AN ALTERNATIVE LIFESTYLE, PART FOUR

July 9, 2004 Oh, yeah. This is the other reason that I go.

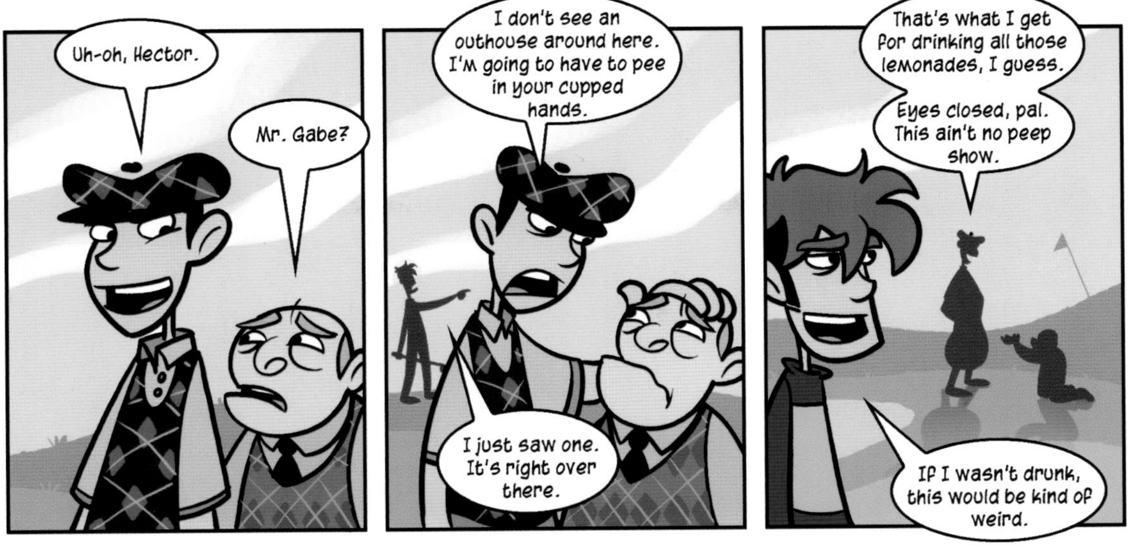
Uh-oh, Hector.
Mr. Gabe?
I don't see an outhouse around here. I'm going to have to pee in your cupped hands.
I just saw one. It's right over there.
That's what I get for drinking all those lemonades, I guess.
Eyes closed, pal. This ain't no peep show.
If I wasn't drunk, this would be kind of weird.

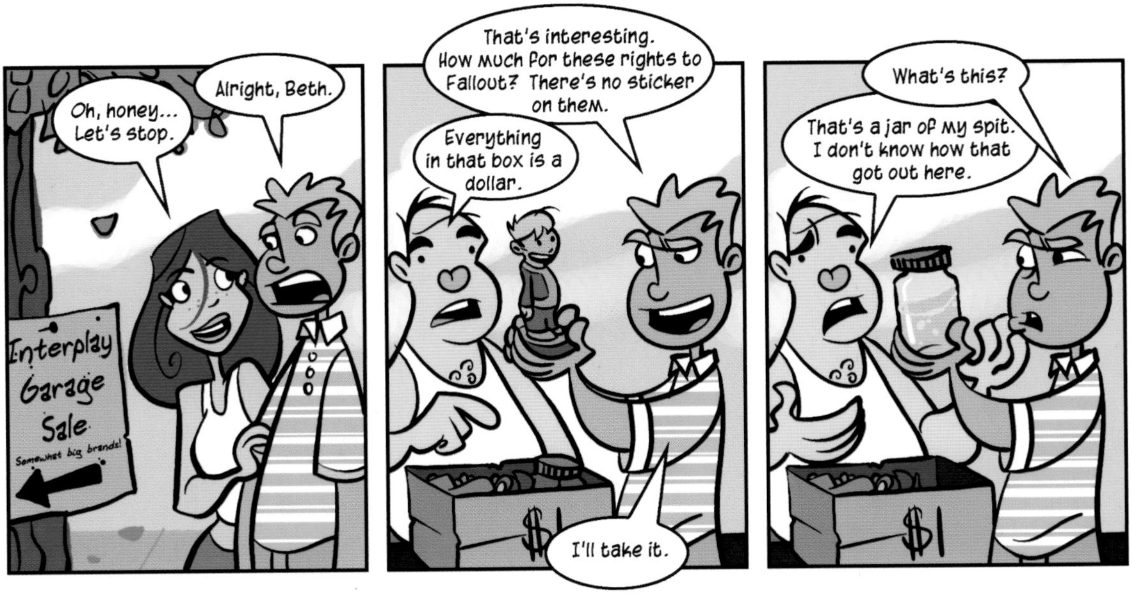
Oh, honey... Let's stop.
Alright, Beth.
Interplay Garage Sale
Somewhat big brands!
Everything in that box is a dollar.
That's interesting. How much for these rights to Fallout? There's no sticker on them.
I'll take it.
$1
What's this?
That's a jar of my spit. I don't know how that got out here.
$1

AN ALTERNATIVE LIFESTYLE, PART FIVE

July 12, 2004 Five strips is just about all we ever allow ourselves for a storyline—less than two full weeks. This is partially a politeness, and partially because events in the gaming world move so fast that we're quick to regain our agility. Armadeaddon is the only time we've ever indulged ourselves completely, because built into the thing was a shining core of rich fanservice.

BETH AND GARY SOFT

July 14, 2004 In the Interplay Fire Sale, you could snatch up legendary gaming treasures for pennies on the dollar—if *that*. Fallout would be an incredible buy at any price, but they were able to pick it up for just under six million dollars—half of what Microsoft spent merely promoting Halo. Bethesda's take on the series is set to be released only a couple months after this book hits shelves.

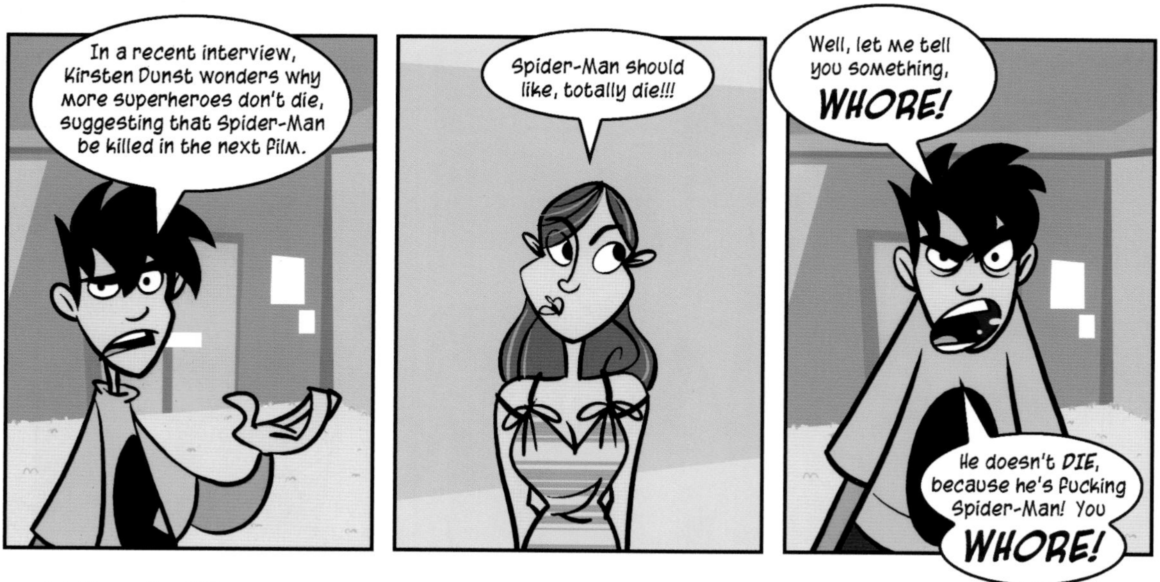
In a recent interview, Kirsten Dunst wonders why more superheroes don't die, suggesting that Spider-Man be killed in the next film.
Spider-Man should like, totally die!!!
Well, let me tell you something, WHORE!
He doesn't DIE, because he's fucking Spider-Man! You WHORE!

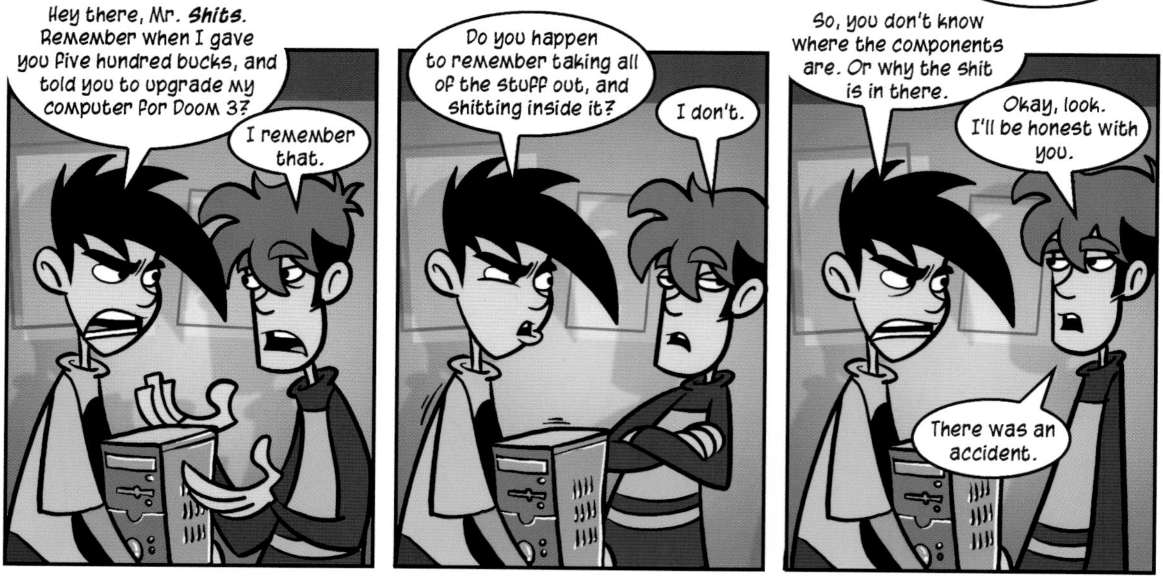
Hey there, Mr. Shits. Remember when I gave you five hundred bucks, and told you to upgrade my computer for Doom 3?
I remember that.
Do you happen to remember taking all of the stuff out, and shitting inside it?
I don't.
So, you don't know where the components are. Or why the shit is in there.
Okay, look. I'll be honest with you.
There was an accident.

SHE MIGHT HAVE STRUCK A NERVE

July 16, 2004 I don't have a strong opinion on spiders, let alone men, so if an opinion is expressed about someone at the *intersection* of Spider and Man I will probably nod and then return to my novel. Should you desire a grave manifesto on the topic, please let me direct you to my esteemed colleague. Here are your earplugs and complimentary taser.

THE NEWEST TECHNOLOGY

July 19, 2004 "Mr. Shits" was a mysterious pooper who fouled the lavatory on our level of the office building daily. We would return from that place of evil utterly haunted by it, mauled by the experience like shattered veterans. Science has no name for the dark processes of this man's tainted body, no laws that could contain this shitwizard and his cursed bung.

COMIC-CON SKETCHBOOK 2004

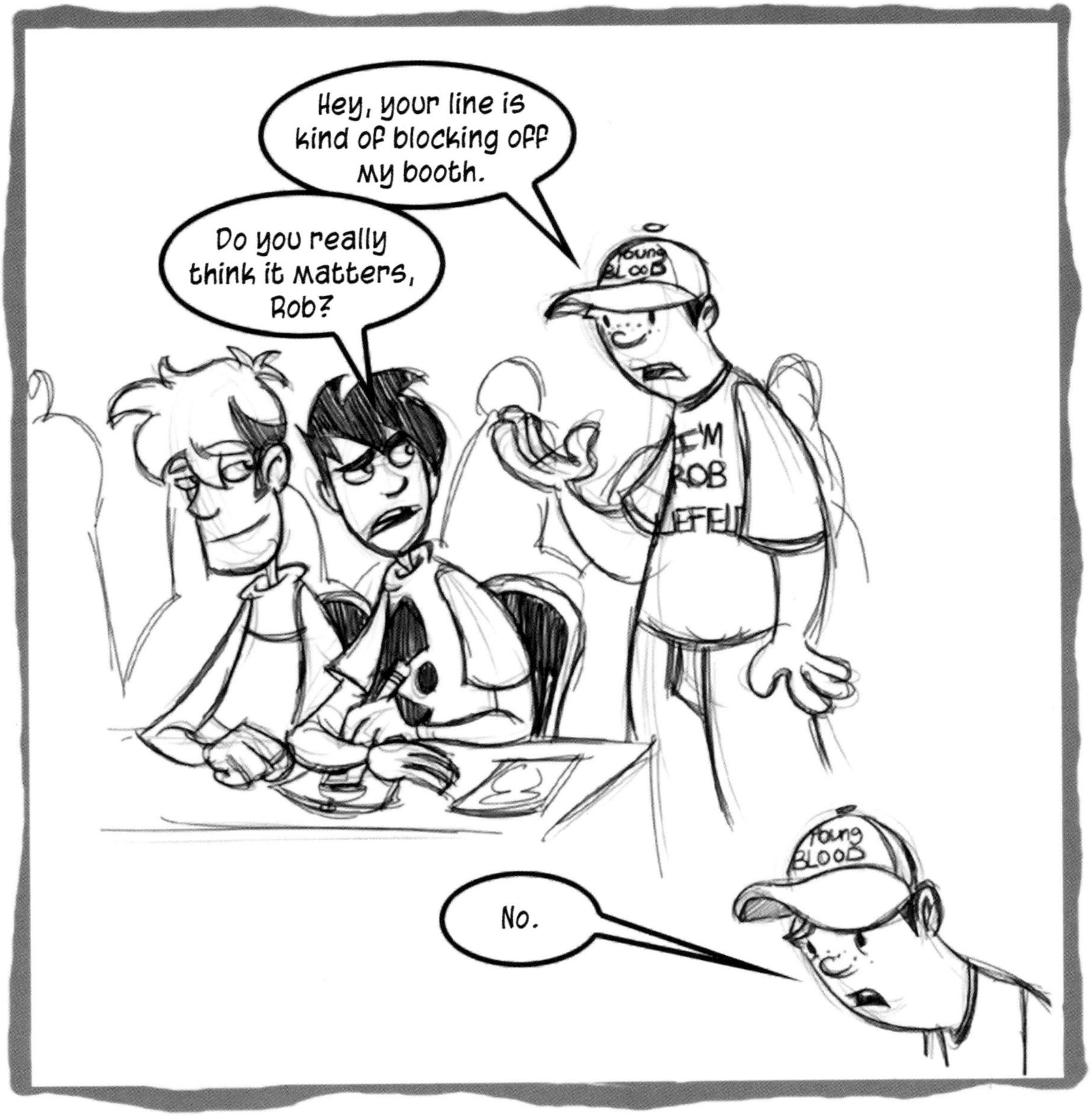
Hey, your line is kind of blocking off my booth.
Do you really think it matters, Rob?
Young BLOOD
No.

SAN DIEGO SKETCHBOOK: THE PAIN OF ROB LIEFELD

July 22, 2004 Sometimes you must wait quite a while to be put firmly back in your place, as the justice machinery of the universe operates on its own strange schedule. It wouldn't be long for us, though: as we relate in a later strip, we found ourselves opposite Rob at another convention, our booth not merely inconvenienced by but *entirely eclipsed* by his line. The lesson was so precise in its meaning and execution that it seemed to argue a strong case for a wry God.

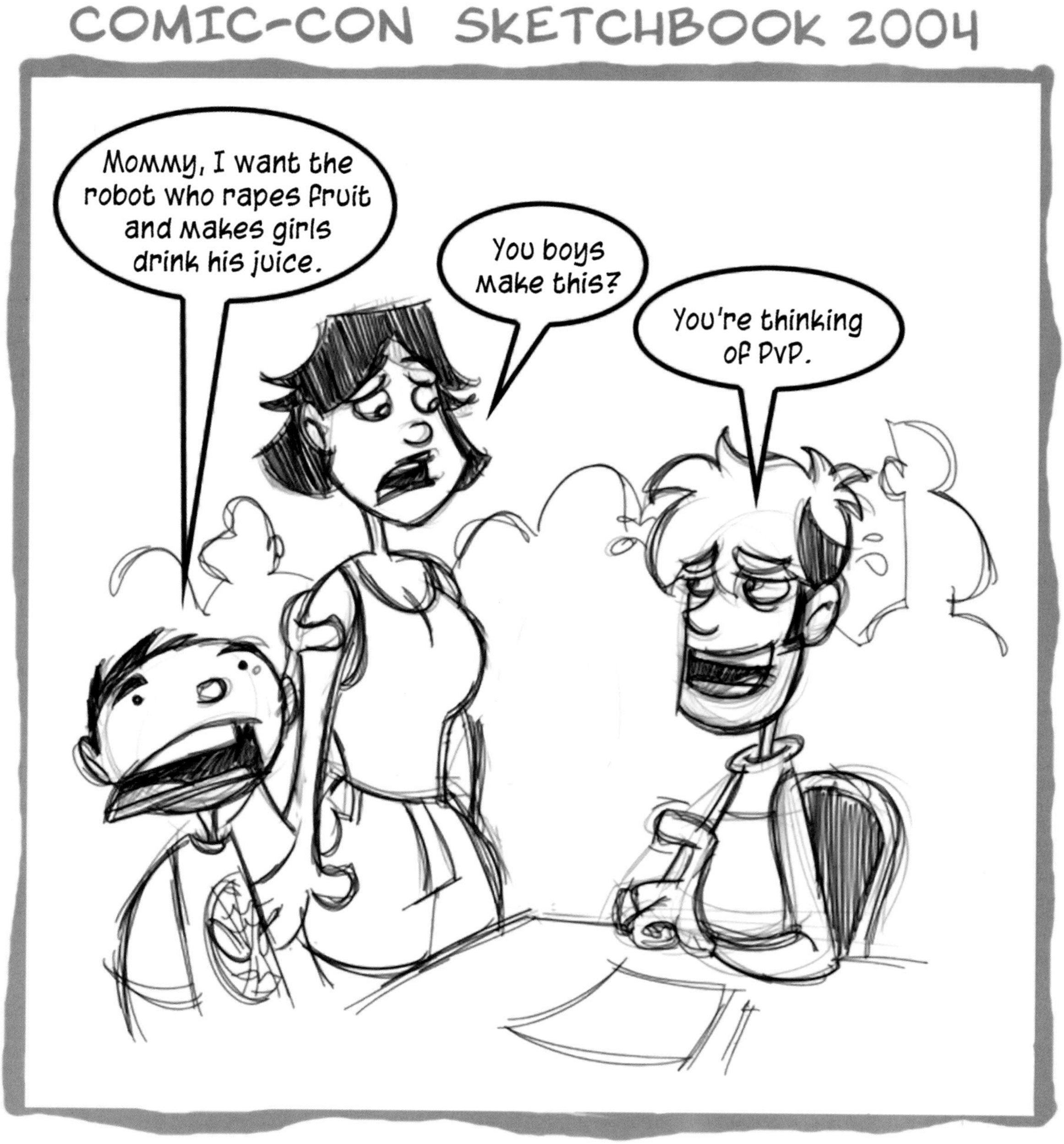
COMIC-CON SKETCHBOOK 2004
Mommy, I want the robot who rapes fruit and makes girls drink his juice.
You boys make this?
You're thinking of PvP.

SAN DIEGO SKETCHBOOK: ADULT CONTENT

July 23, 2004 We just wanted to make sure that people knew about Scott's booth and the incredible bargains he had in store. That is how I choose to contextualize this damning, incontrovertible evidence.

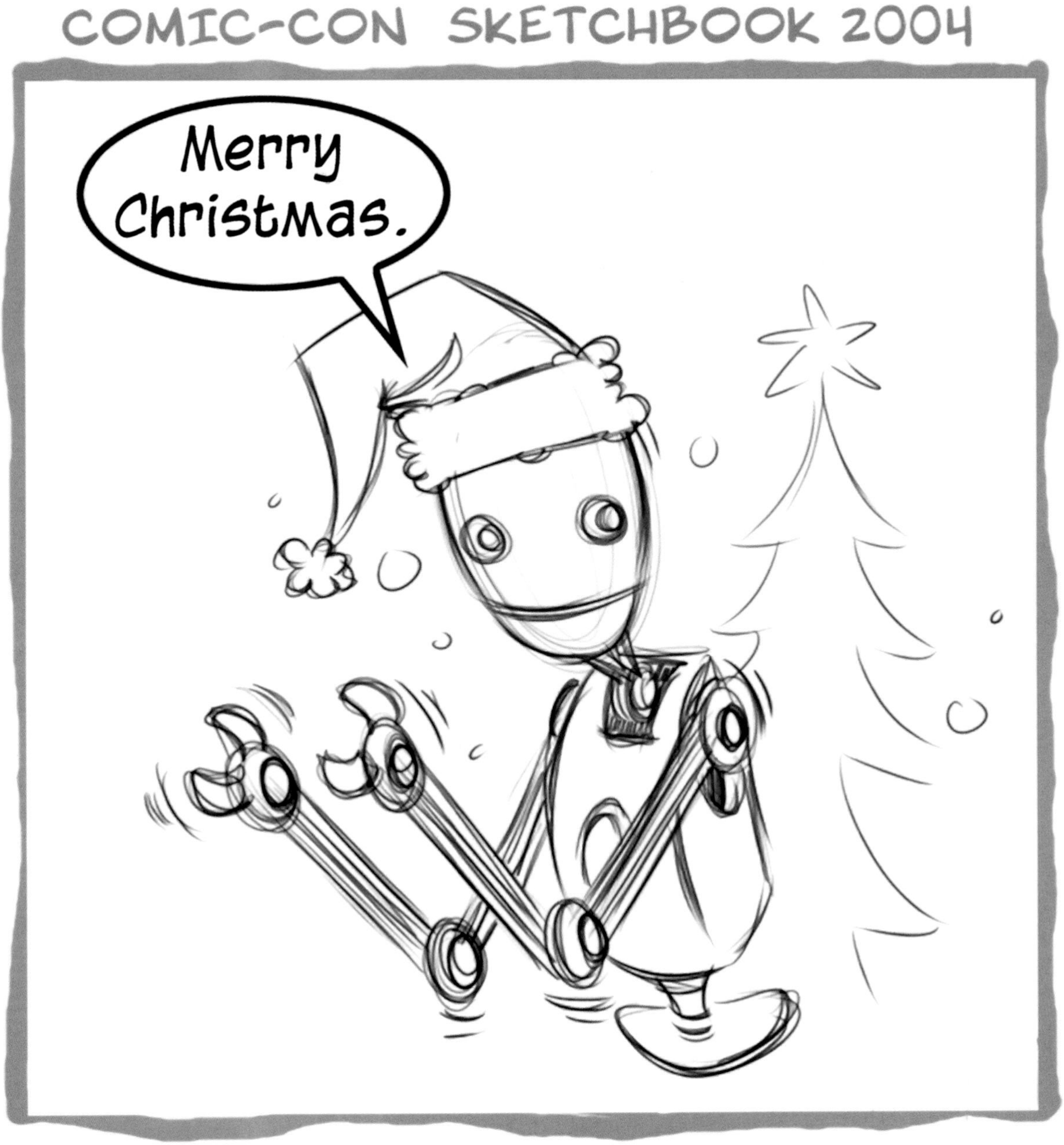
COMIC-CON SKETCHBOOK 2004
Merry Christmas.

SAN DIEGO SKETCHBOOK: LA DANSE DE NOËL

July 24, 2004 And that, friends, is the last of the dancing robot. Thank you, noble droid! You got us out of, like, five strips. Now go do whatever it is droids *do* when they aren't aiding and abetting lazy-ass motherfuckers.

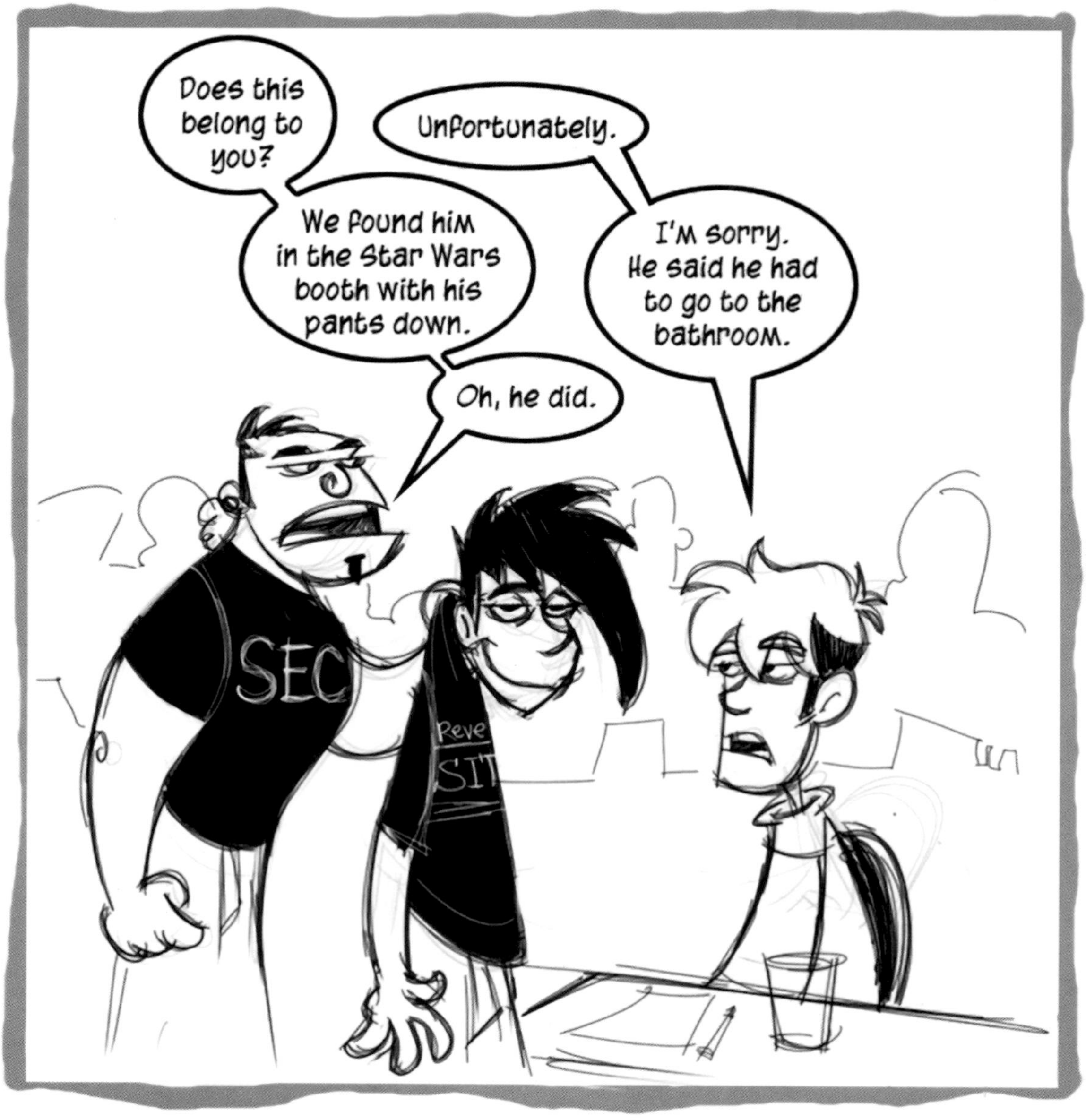
Does this belong to you?
We found him in the Star Wars booth with his pants down.
Oh, he did.
Unfortunately.
I'm sorry. He said he had to go to the bathroom.
SEC

SAN DIEGO SKETCHBOOK: THE PAHD THAI

July 26, 2004 | I often believe that I have moved beyond Stars and the frequent Wars which occur between them, that is until we attend each year's San Diego Comic-Con. There is always ample kindling to reignite the old passions, be they exquisite new collectible busts or seven-foot-tall *wookiees* made entirely of Lego.

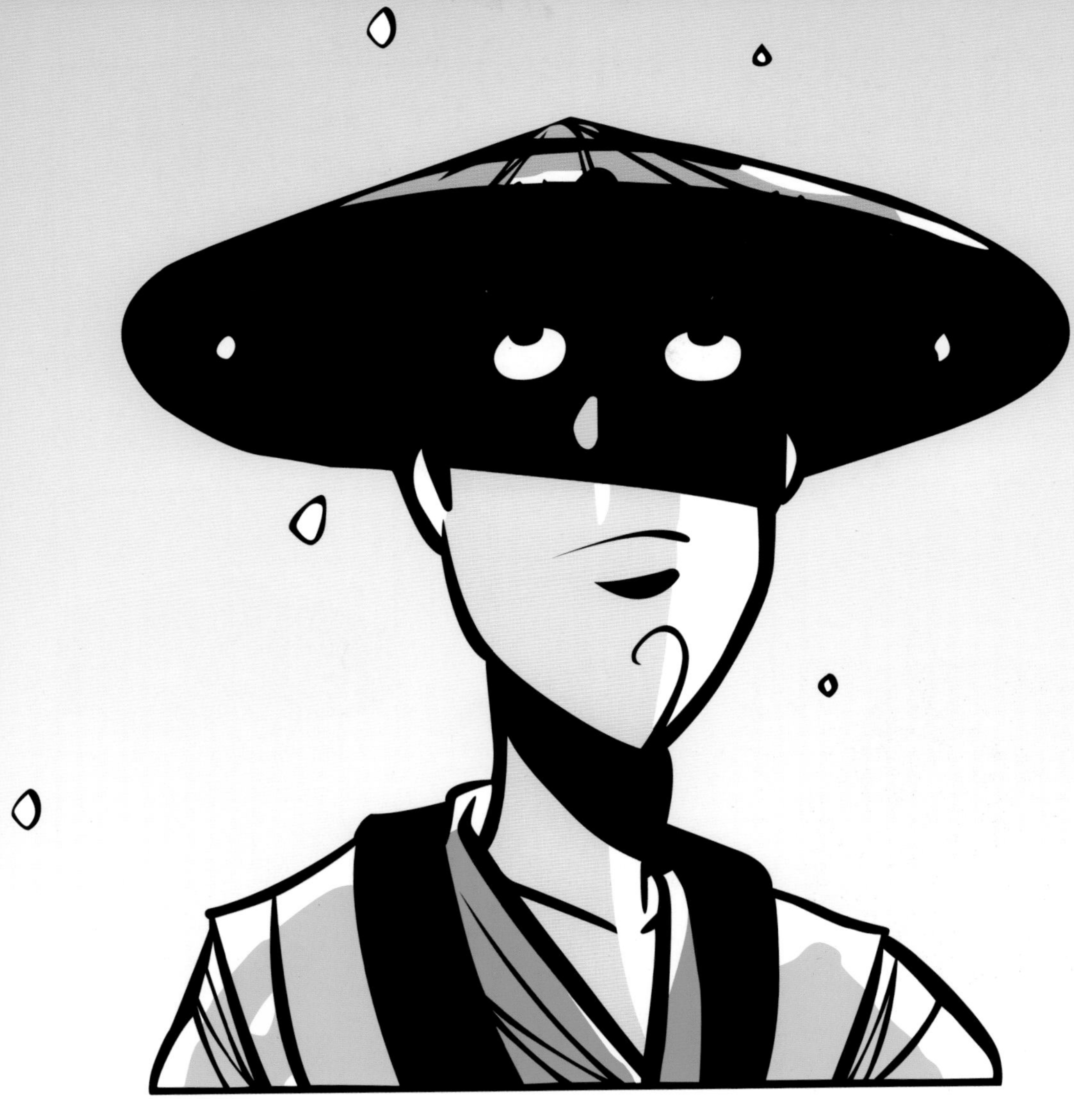

THE WANDERING AGE: LAST RITES

July 21-30, 2004 When we're away from home at a convention, we usually upload sketches instead of full comics—a tradition that started at our first E3. We could certainly do comics ahead of time, but one of the main things we like about *Penny Arcade* is reacting to events in something approaching real-time.

Similar to *The Last Christmas* (whose twelve blasphemous pages are included at the end of this volume), we wanted to poke that tradition and see if there was anything we could do with it. We decided to try and fill in the cracks of the first *Last Rites* comic with hazy recollections about the events leading up to it—while they would still be sketches, they'd be narrative in nature and less stream of consciousness. The laptop we brought to do it on couldn't actually handle it, crashing and losing hours of work. So tradition won out. Once we got back, Gabriel did the other two pages in a much more elaborate style than he could have managed on the road. We had a short animation done of this story, as well—it's not hard to find online.

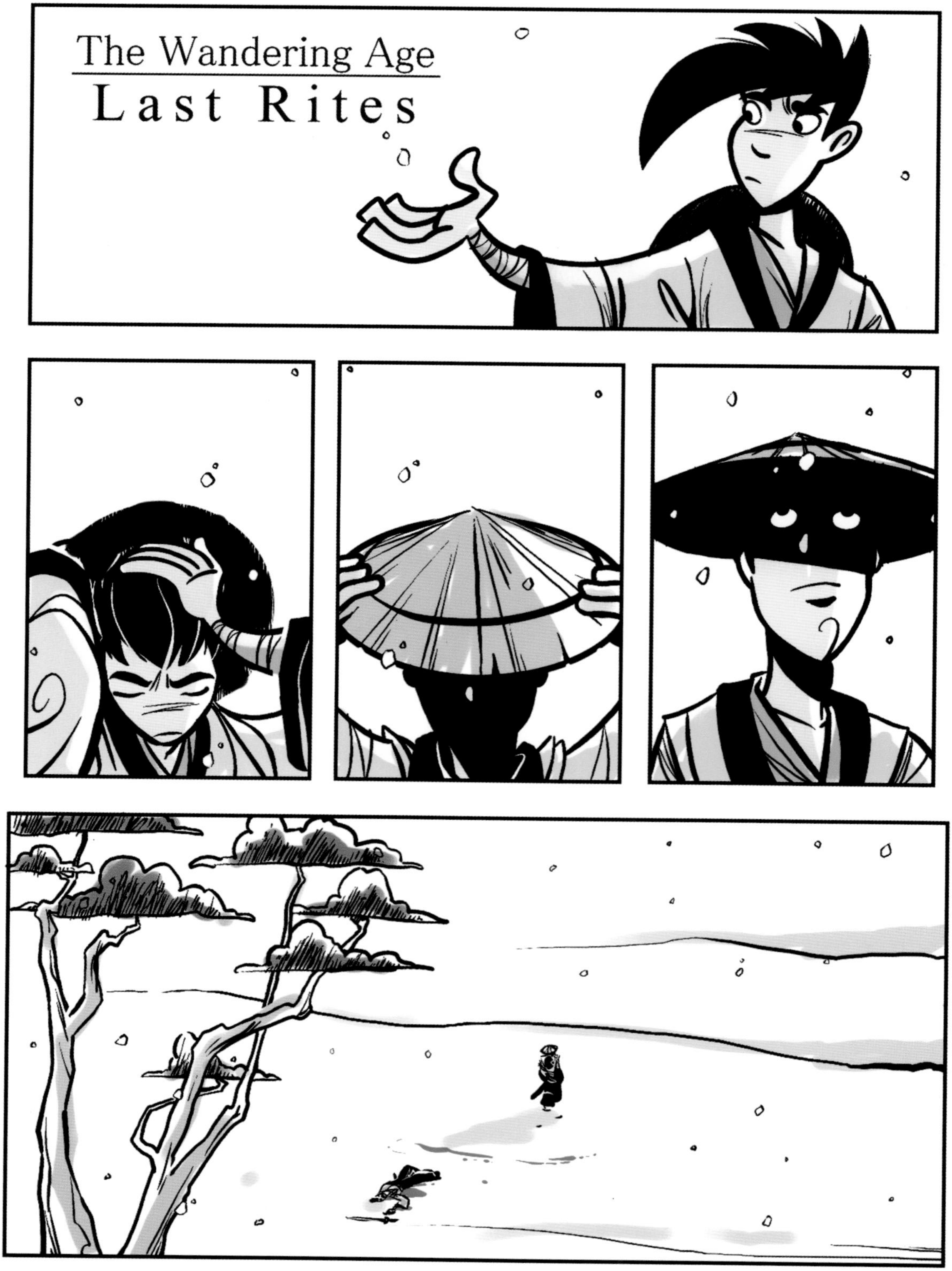
The Wandering Age
Last Rites

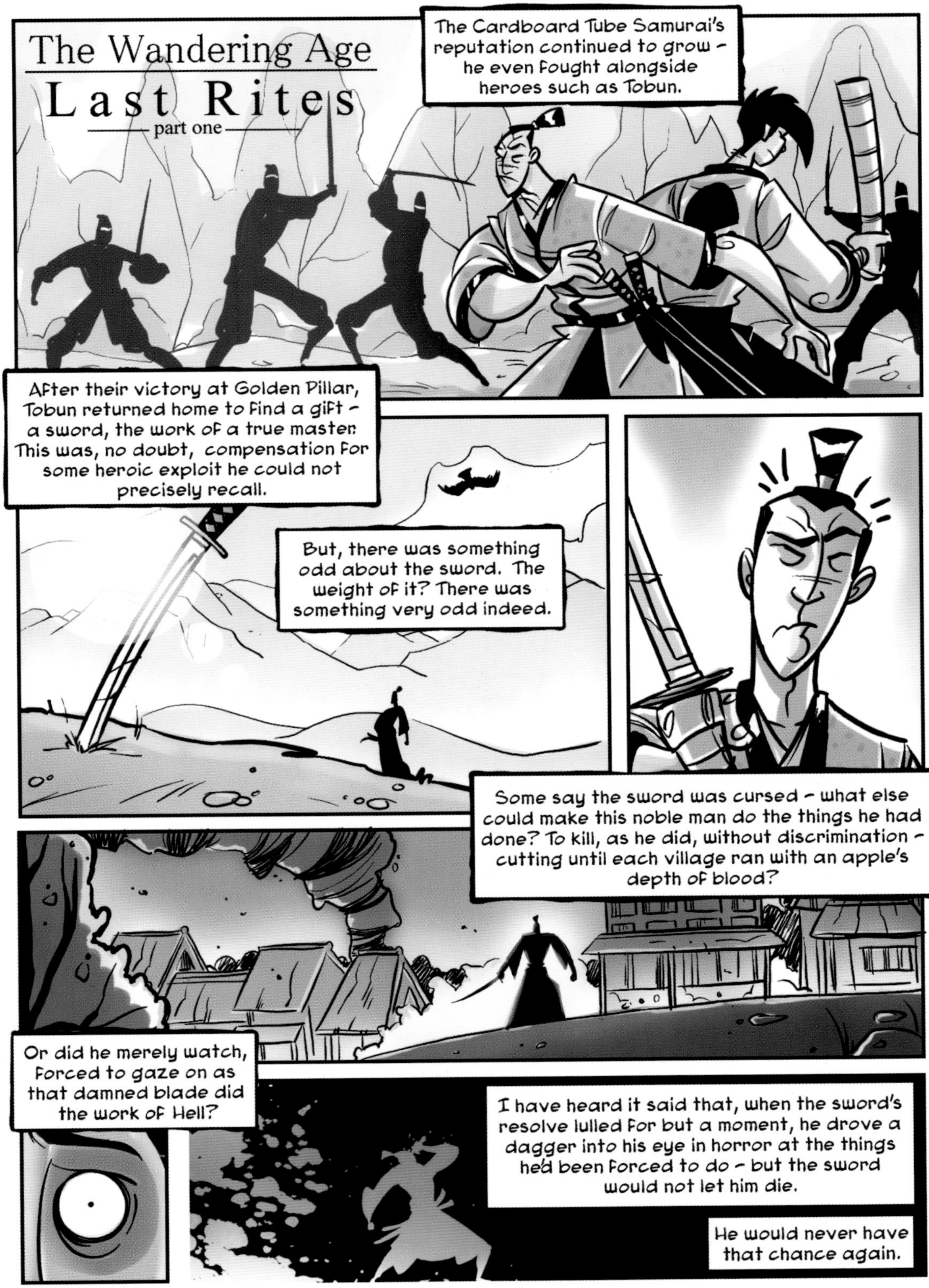
The Wandering Age
Last Rites
part one
The Cardboard Tube Samurai's reputation continued to grow - he even fought alongside heroes such as Tobun.
After their victory at Golden Pillar, Tobun returned home to find a gift - a sword, the work of a true master. This was, no doubt, compensation for some heroic exploit he could not precisely recall.
But, there was something odd about the sword. The weight of it? There was something very odd indeed.
Some say the sword was cursed - what else could make this noble man do the things he had done? To kill, as he did, without discrimination - cutting until each village ran with an apple's depth of blood?
Or did he merely watch, forced to gaze on as that damned blade did the work of Hell?
I have heard it said that, when the sword's resolve lulled for but a moment, he drove a dagger into his eye in horror at the things he'd been forced to do - but the sword would not let him die.
He would never have that chance again.

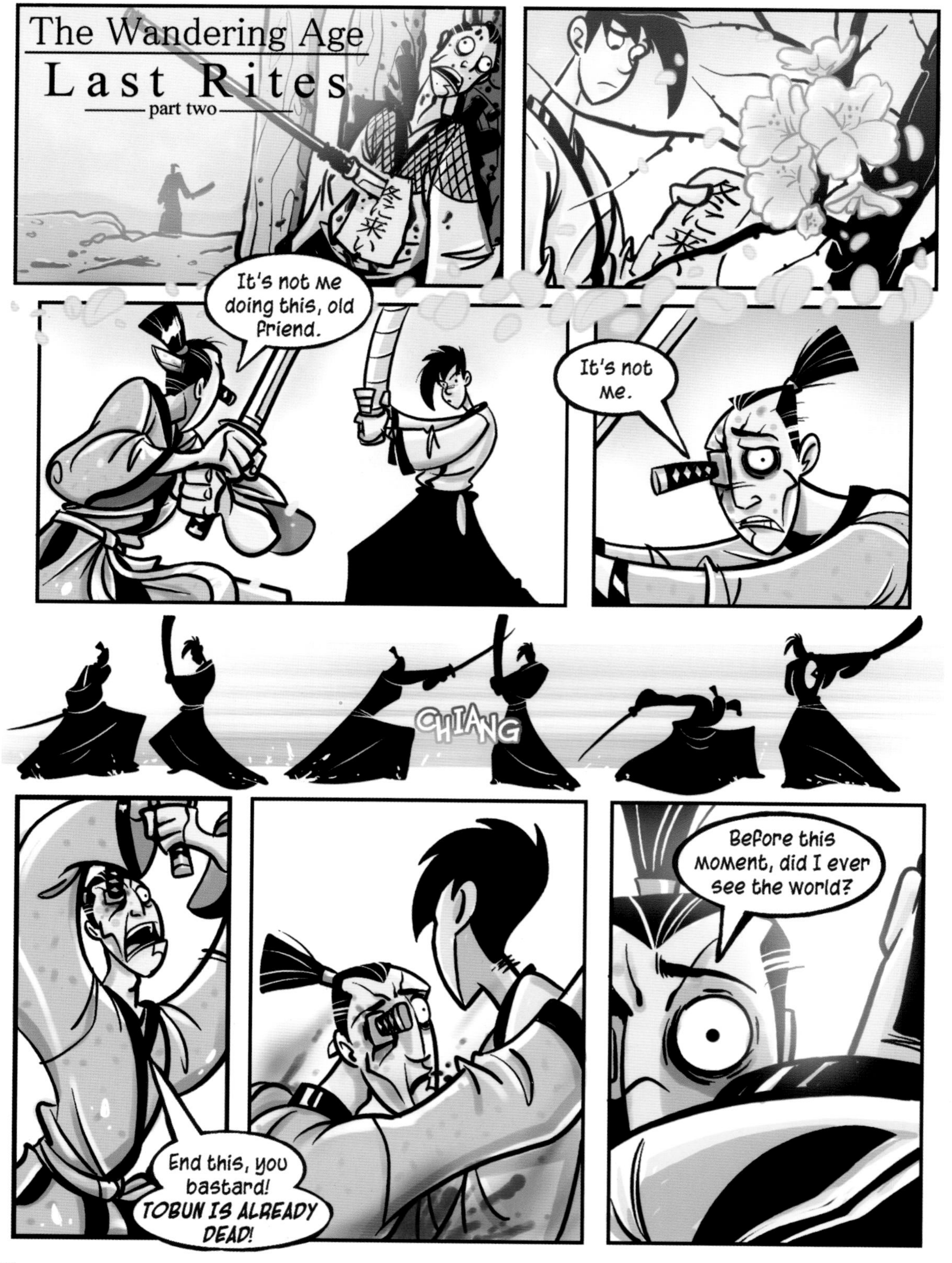
The Wandering Age
Last Rites
part two
冬に来い
It's not me doing this, old friend.
It's not me.
CHIANG
End this, you bastard! TOBUN IS ALREADY DEAD!
Before this moment, did I ever see the world?

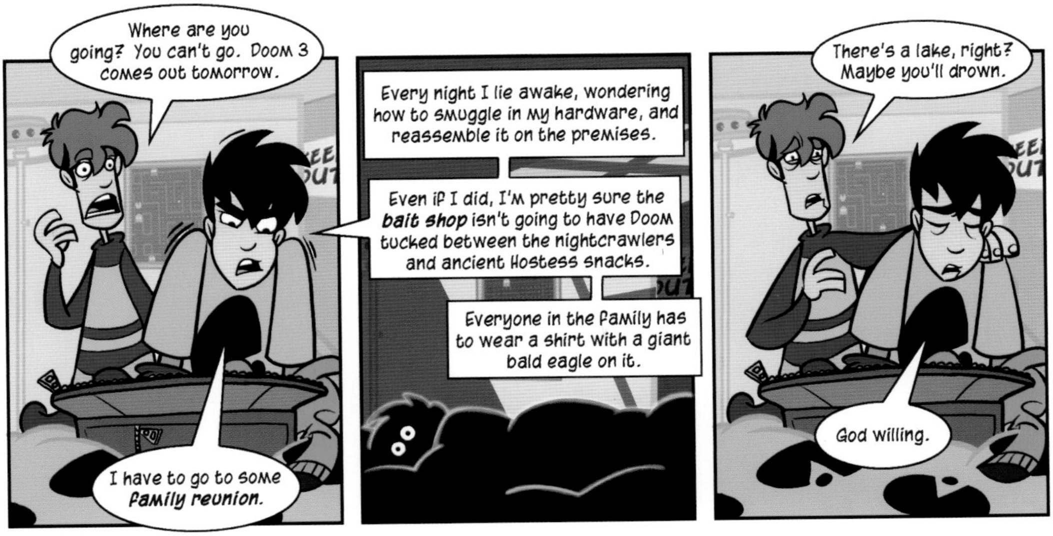
Where are you going? You can't go. Doom 3 comes out tomorrow.
I have to go to some *family reunion.*
Every night I lie awake, wondering how to smuggle in my hardware, and reassemble it on the premises.
Even if I did, I'm pretty sure the **bait shop** isn't going to have Doom tucked between the nightcrawlers and ancient Hostess snacks.
Everyone in the family has to wear a shirt with a giant bald eagle on it.
There's a lake, right? Maybe you'll drown.
God willing.

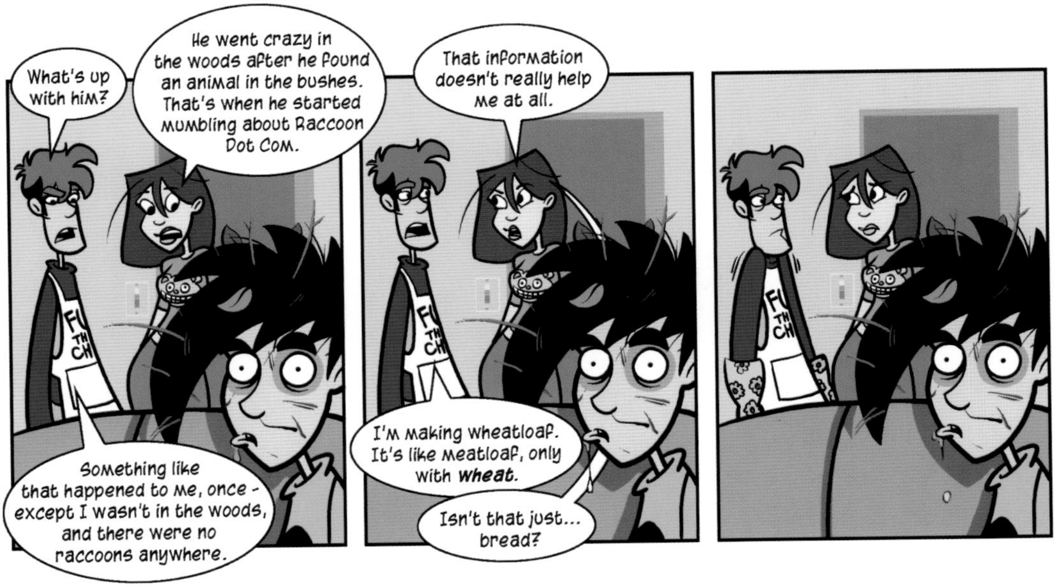
What's up with him?
He went crazy in the woods after he found an animal in the bushes. That's when he started mumbling about Raccoon Dot Com.
Something like that happened to me, once - except I wasn't in the woods, and there were no raccoons anywhere.
That information doesn't really help me at all.
I'm making wheatloaf. It's like meatloaf, only with **wheat.**
Isn't that just... bread?

THAT INAUSPICIOUS EVENT

August 2, 2004 Does anyone actually like these grim exercises in enforced revelry? Are the custom shirts entirely necessary? Does every person attending them do so out of some twisted sense of duty? Is that person even related to us? What is it that Aunts eat or drink that makes them so Goddamned crazy? Do I want to swim out to the dock? Well, we might as well try to glean *some* kind of amusement from OH NO HELP PIRANHAS!

THOSE KINDS OF CONVERSATIONS

August 9, 2004 Eventually, Gabriel returned from his family reunion a different man. Where before he might have called me a cockmonger—literally, a person who sells cocks—this new husk wouldn't move, or couldn't, harrowed by the experience. I had to nurse him back to health on Gogurt, which (as you know) is the yogurt with attitude. I think that stuff is mostly algae, but at any rate it did the trick.

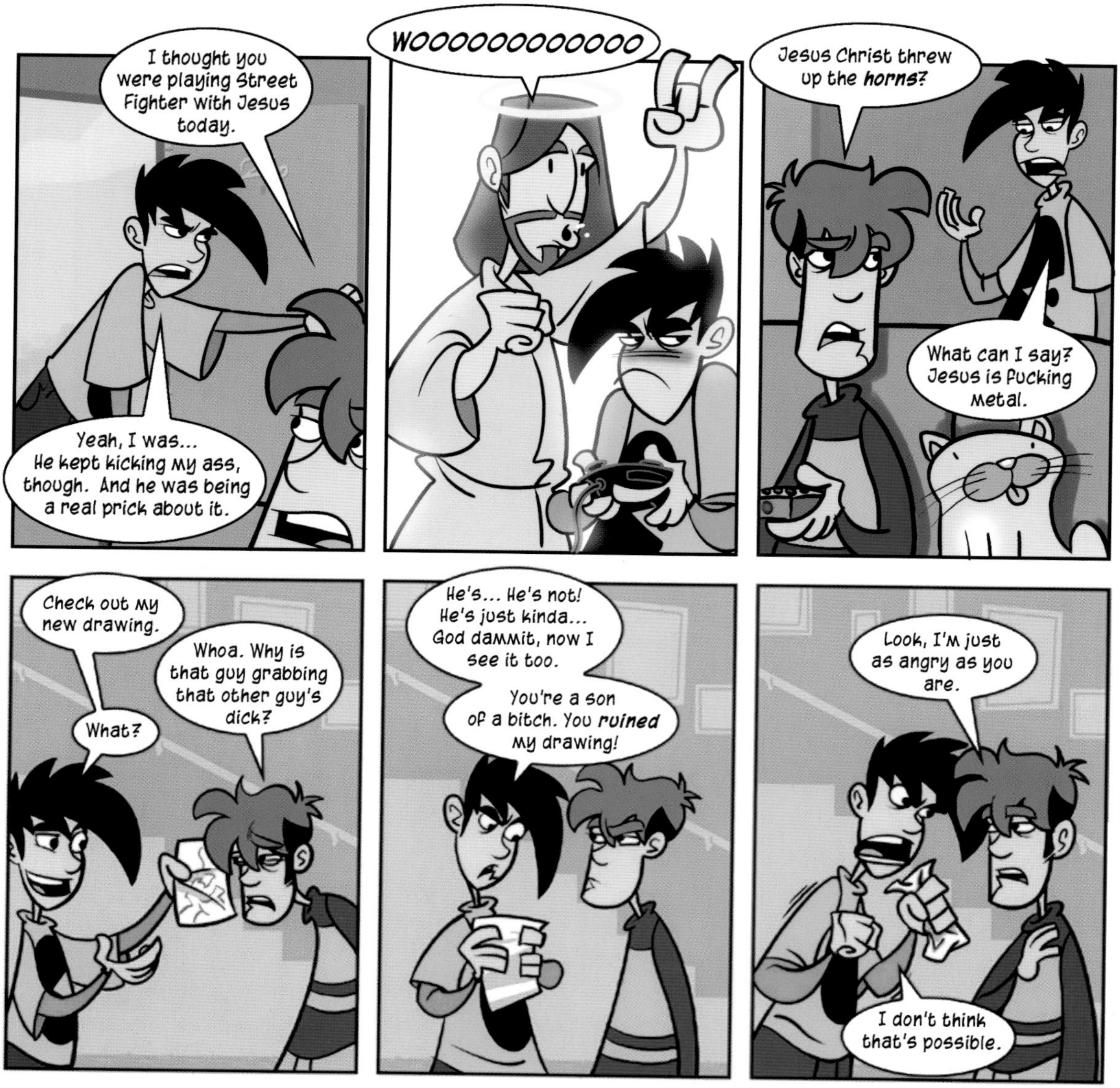
I thought you were playing Street Fighter with Jesus today.
Yeah, I was... He kept kicking my ass, though. And he was being a real prick about it.
WOOOOOOOOOOOO
Jesus Christ threw up the horns?
What can I say? Jesus is fucking metal.
Check out my new drawing.
What?
Whoa. Why is that guy grabbing that other guy's dick?
He's... He's not! He's just kinda... God dammit, now I see it too.
You're a son of a bitch. You ruined my drawing!
Look, I'm just as angry as you are.
I don't think that's possible.

DER HORNEN

August 4, 2004 I believe I've already mentioned it, but since it would be sort of ridiculous to assume you'd read every book, I should reprise it here: Gabriel actually considers our use of Jesus (who is The Christ) maybe not reverent, but in any case not sinful. I think it actually fits in with the mission of his own faith that Jesus is a person you can know personally and who is knowledgeable and relevant to popular culture.

THE EYE OF THE BEHOLDER

August 6, 2004 From that day's post:

While you are digesting today's comic, I have something that might give you a bit of context.

In addition to the other things I have mentioned—and the things I *will* mention—PAX will also have large banners emblazoned with characters from the comic. Of course, there are versions which are particular to each room, as well—but there are also ones with Twisp and Catsby, Div and the Fruit Fucker, etc. There's one of the Cardboard Tube Samurai. And there's one of Gabe, tugging earnestly on Tycho's penis, as a robin would an earthworm. Observe:

I mean, seriously. Look at him go. You'd think that Tycho would appreciate that sort of dedication.

I *told* Gabe as much, which led to the conversation in the comic strip, during and after which he was as angry as I've ever seen him. Why he would be angry at *me* is an absolute mystery—I didn't take some drawing of his and use the "move" tool to nudge Gabe's grasping paw over my character's genitals. With purpose and conviction, he drew a sexually charged encounter that was designed to be printed six feet tall. So now, not only is there a scene of basest fornication being played out, it's being performed by a race of carnal, homosexual giants.

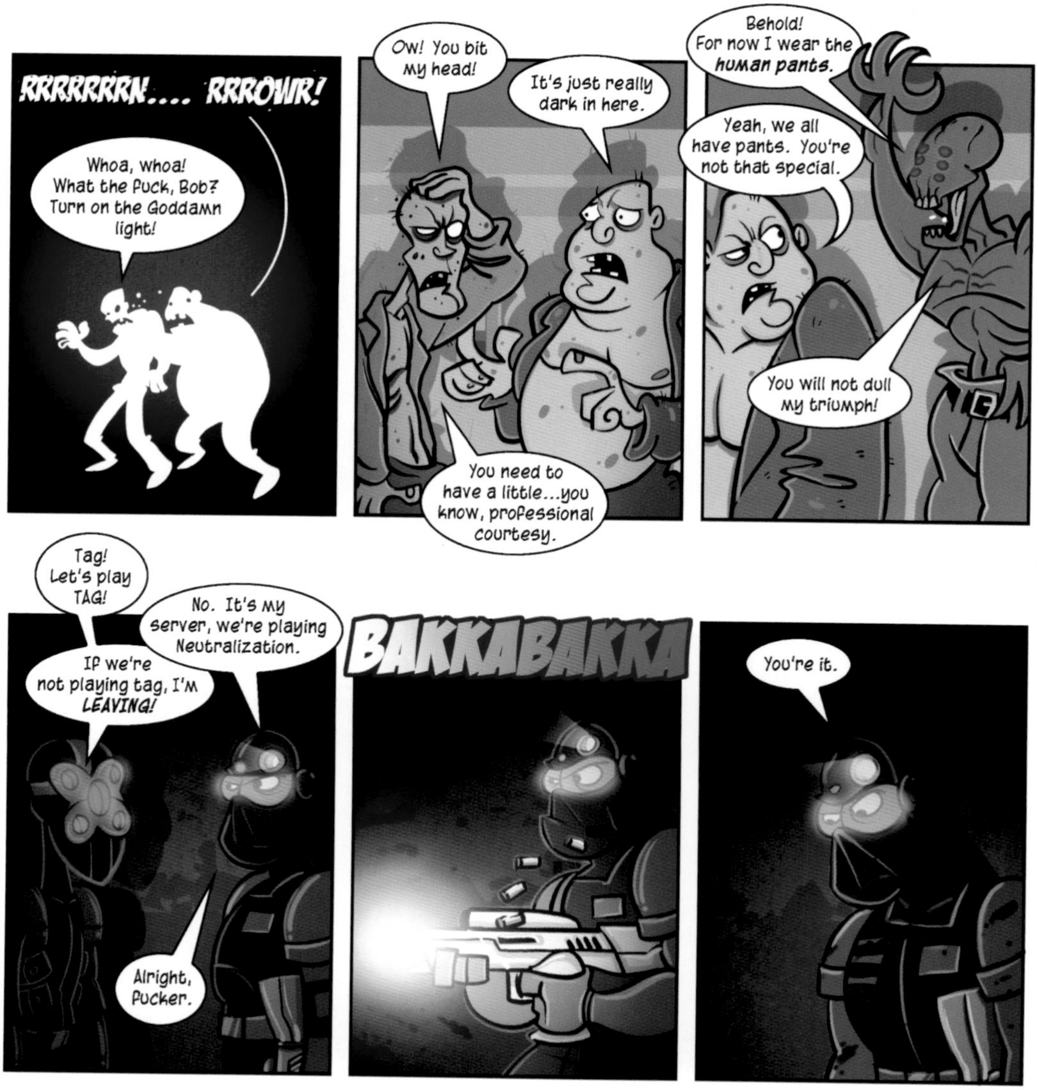
RRRRRRRN.... RRROWR!
Whoa, whoa! What the fuck, Bob? Turn on the Goddamn light!
Ow! You bit my head!
It's just really dark in here.
You need to have a little...you know, professional courtesy.
Behold! For now I wear the human pants.
Yeah, we all have pants. You're not that special.
You will not dull my triumph!
Tag! Let's play TAG!
No. It's my server, we're playing Neutralization.
If we're not playing tag, I'm LEAVING!
Alright, fucker.
BAKKABAKKA
You're it.

THE OTHER SIDE

August 11, 2004 I liked Doom 3 a fair bit more than most people. I even liked the *expansion*, which puts me even further in the corner. It was an extremely dark game, as its real-time lighting was really its crown jewel and they took every opportunity to highlight it. My expectations were very different from other people's; namely, I did not have any. Taken on its own terms—and not as the scion of a great house—it's a very solid product.

A NEW TWIST ON AN OLD FAVORITE

August 13, 2004 It's a subset of a subset of a subset of humanity that would know what is going on here, even among Ultra Hardcore X Gamezors, so let me break it down one time. It got to the point in online Splinter Cell that most of the games you'd join weren't playing the base rules. They would play entirely player-made games, using "honor system" rules. It's kind of cool, unless you like playing the *actual* game.

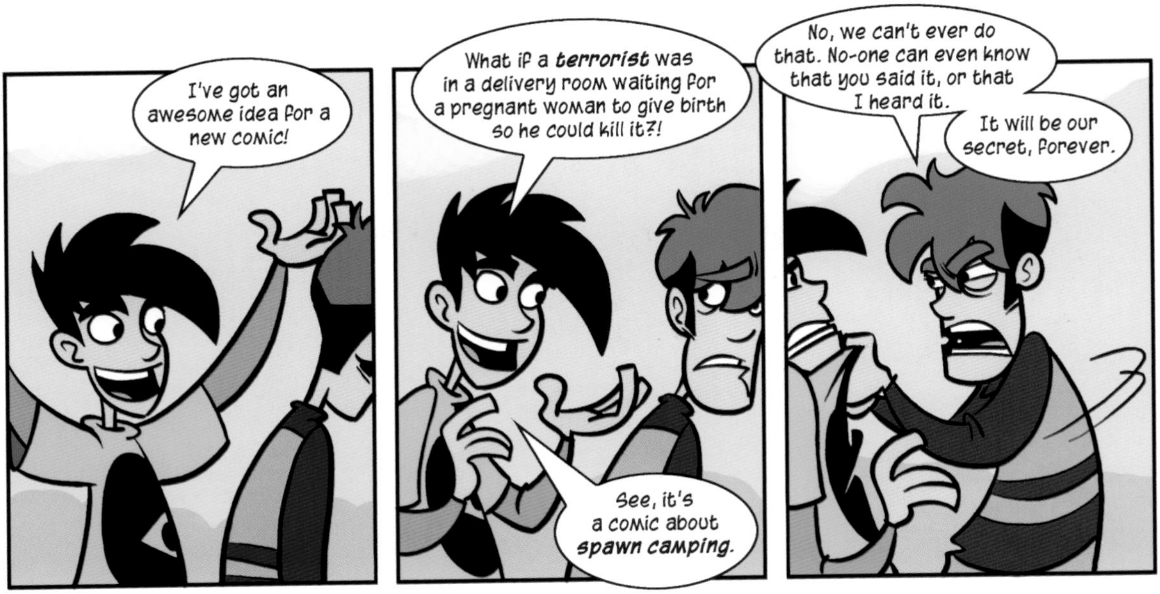
I've got an awesome idea for a new comic!
What if a terrorist was in a delivery room waiting for a pregnant woman to give birth so he could kill it?!
See, it's a comic about spawn camping.
No, we can't ever do that. No-one can even know that you said it, or that I heard it.
It will be our secret, forever.

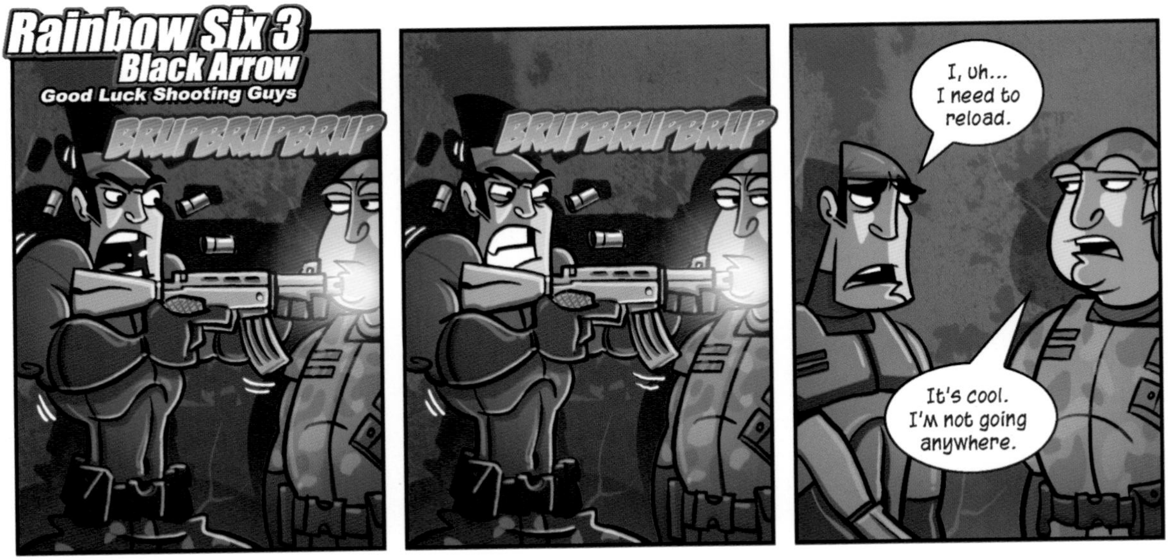
Rainbow Six 3
Black Arrow
Good Luck Shooting Guys
BRUPBRUPBRUP
BRUPBRUPBRUP
I, uh... I need to reload.
It's cool. I'm not going anywhere.

WE DO IN FACT HAVE LIMITS

August 16, 2004 In the days before we did the occasional podcast, there wasn't really a way to show people how bizarre the comic-writing process can be. It starts with a pretty wide net, and the revolting creatures such a net snares are grotesque and wriggling things. You can *hear* some of the things we toss out these days, but we wanted to show people how weird it gets before we reel it back in.

A LIGHT TICKLING SENSATION

August 18, 2004 Black Arrow was a mess in many ways, but they were still spinning the tumbler on how to make a great version of the game on consoles. It took Vegas to really cement it in my opinion, especially after the wrong turns of Rainbow Six: Lockdown. They managed to make a first-person game with a satisfying cover system work, and work well.

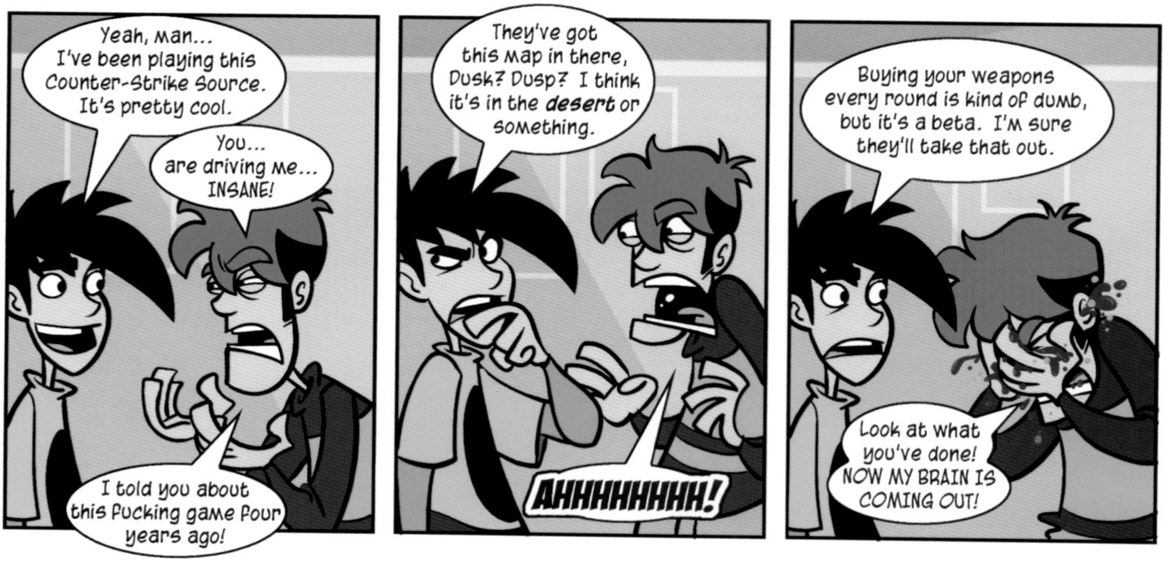
Yeah, man...
I've been playing this Counter-Strike Source. It's pretty cool.
You... are driving me... INSANE!
I told you about this fucking game four years ago!
They've got this map in there, Dusk? Dusp? I think it's in the desert or something.
AHHHHHHHH!
Buying your weapons every round is kind of dumb, but it's a beta. I'm sure they'll take that out.
Look at what you've done! NOW MY BRAIN IS COMING OUT!

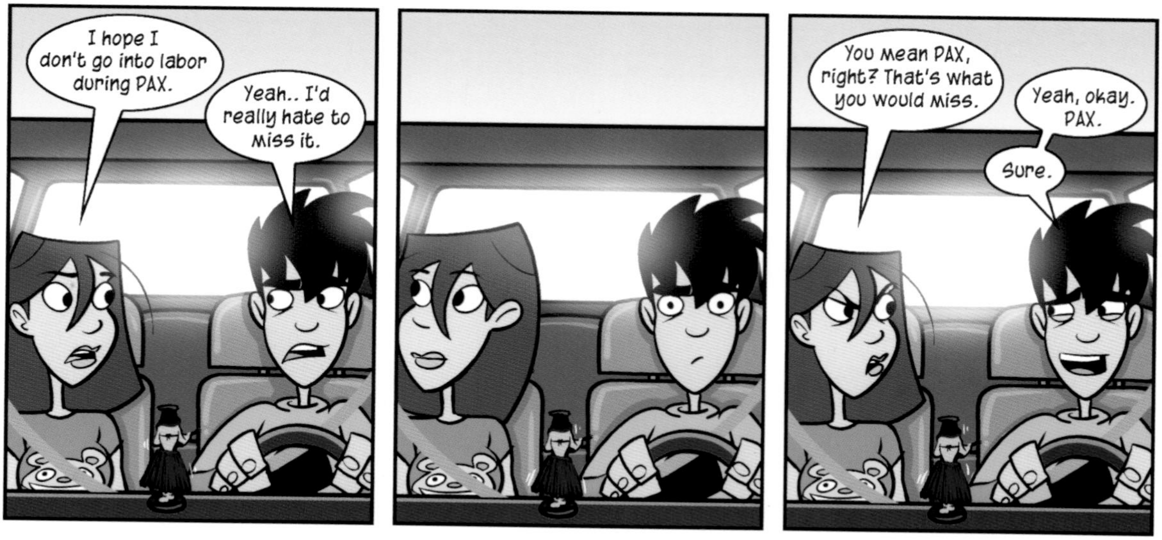
I hope I don't go into labor during PAX.
Yeah.. I'd really hate to miss it.
You mean PAX, right? That's what you would miss.
Yeah, okay. PAX.
Sure.

HE IS LITERALLY TRYING TO KILL ME

August 20, 2004 We have a huge print of this in our room of the office, originally from PAX, and I must have read it a million times but I'm still fond of it. I probably have a very different relationship to these weird things than you do, but who knows: maybe you like the same things? Tycho's mouth in the second panel, stretched far outside its bounds in horror and disgust, really just says "yes" to me.

LARVAE

August 23, 2004 Oh, that's . . . That's right. Gabriel, that is to say the real Gabriel—Gabriel Aden Krahulik—was born this year. Welcome aboard, young man. I shall always endeavor to be the *weirdest uncle possible*.

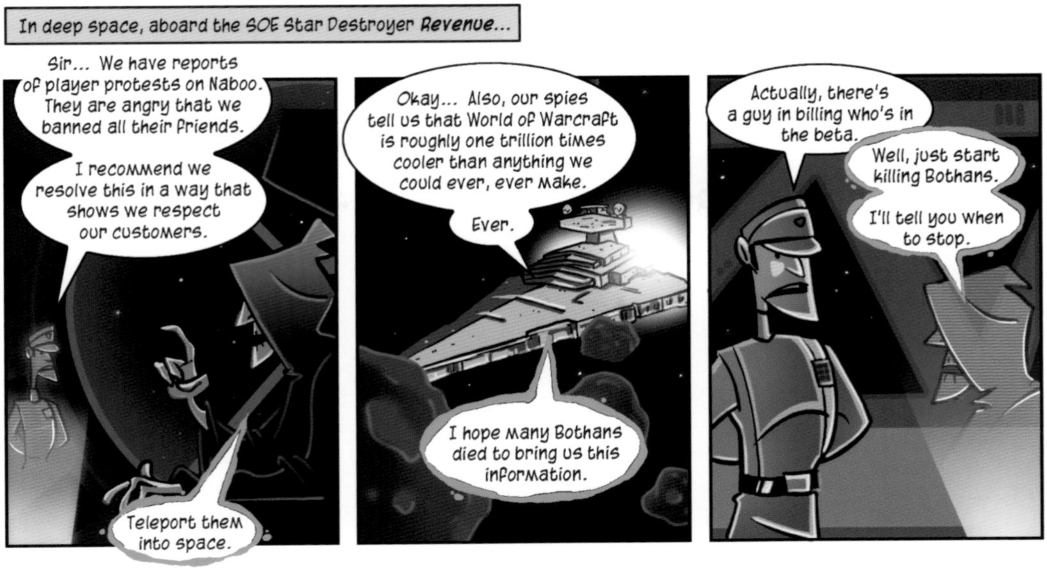
In deep space, aboard the SOE Star Destroyer Revenue...
Sir... We have reports of player protests on Naboo. They are angry that we banned all their friends.
I recommend we resolve this in a way that shows we respect our customers.
Teleport them into space.
Okay... Also, our spies tell us that World of Warcraft is roughly one trillion times cooler than anything we could ever, ever make.
Ever.
I hope many Bothans died to bring us this information.
Actually, there's a guy in billing who's in the beta.
Well, just start killing Bothans.
I'll tell you when to stop.

THIS IS AN ALLEGORY

August 25, 2004 It's really just been championship-level bullshit from day one with these guys. The first insult was the game itself, and each day they have heaped injury upon it further. The terrible thing is that even if it had been better, it wouldn't matter. World of Warcraft would still have caught it by the neck, and like some fierce leopard hauled its still corpse into a tree.

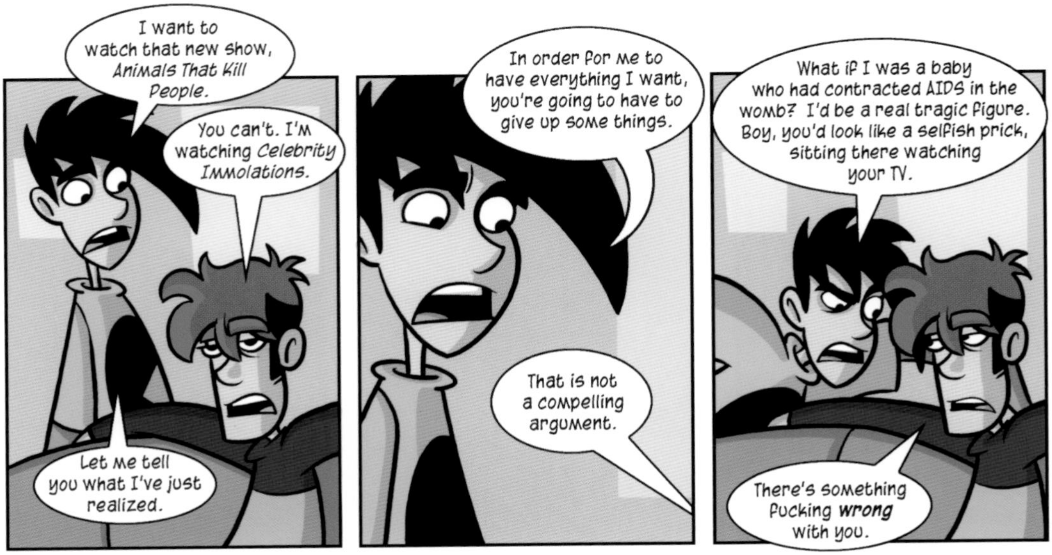
I want to watch that new show, Animals That Kill People.
You can't. I'm watching Celebrity Immolations.
Let me tell you what I've just realized.
In order for me to have everything I want, you're going to have to give up some things.
That is not a compelling argument.
What if I was a baby who had contracted AIDS in the womb? I'd be a real tragic figure. Boy, you'd look like a selfish prick, sitting there watching your TV.
There's something fucking wrong with you.

GABRIEL THE ORATOR

August 27, 2004 Once, while we were arguing, which is *seriously* like every fucking day, I did an autopsy of his argumentation right there for him, free of charge: In order for me to have everything I want, you're going to have to give up some things. It didn't actually help, and the squabble continued. But I felt smart for several hours.

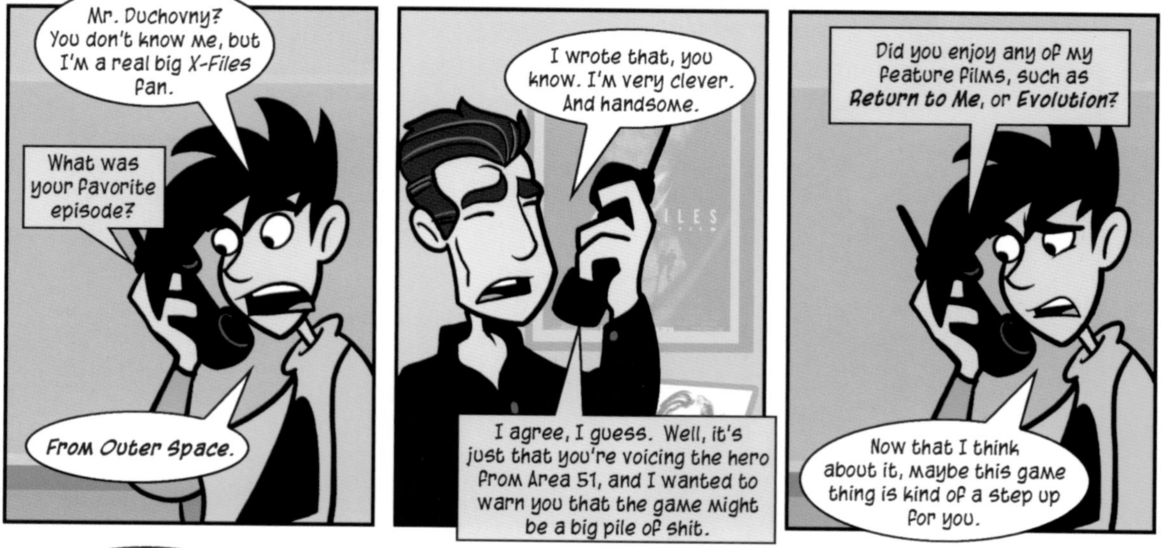
Mr. Duchovny? You don't know me, but I'm a real big X-Files fan.
What was your favorite episode?
From Outer Space.
I wrote that, you know. I'm very clever. And handsome.
I agree, I guess. Well, it's just that you're voicing the hero from Area 51, and I wanted to warn you that the game might be a big pile of shit.
Did you enjoy any of my feature films, such as Return to Me, or Evolution?
Now that I think about it, maybe this game thing is kind of a step up for you.

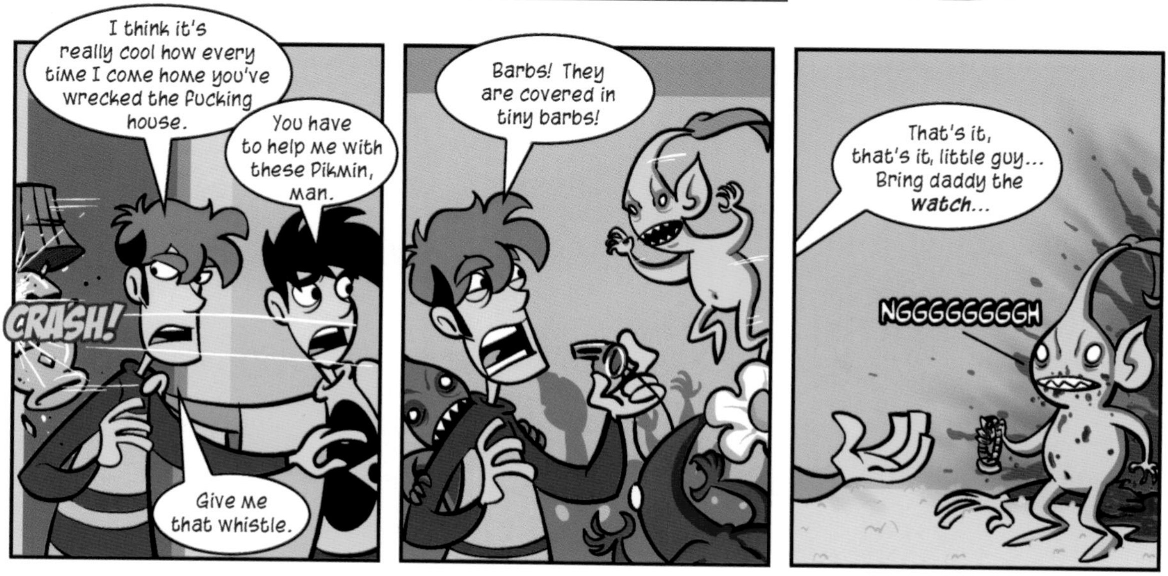
I think it's really cool how every time I come home you've wrecked the fucking house.
You have to help me with these Pikmin, man.
CRASH!
Give me that whistle.
Barbs! They are covered in tiny barbs!
That's it, that's it, little guy... Bring daddy the watch...
NGGGGGGGGH

CHECK ME OUT, I AM DAVID DUCHOVNY

August 30, 2004 Is David Duchovny still alive?

THE BURRS AND BARBS

September 1, 2004 I really liked the idea that Pikmin are only cute because you're seeing them so *small*—that, at greater magnification and under the right circumstances, they are cruel monsters that hunt prey with a savage, collective intellect. Also, this was a *watch* strip, engineered to please that watch strip *fan*. They do exist; I was surprised to learn this.

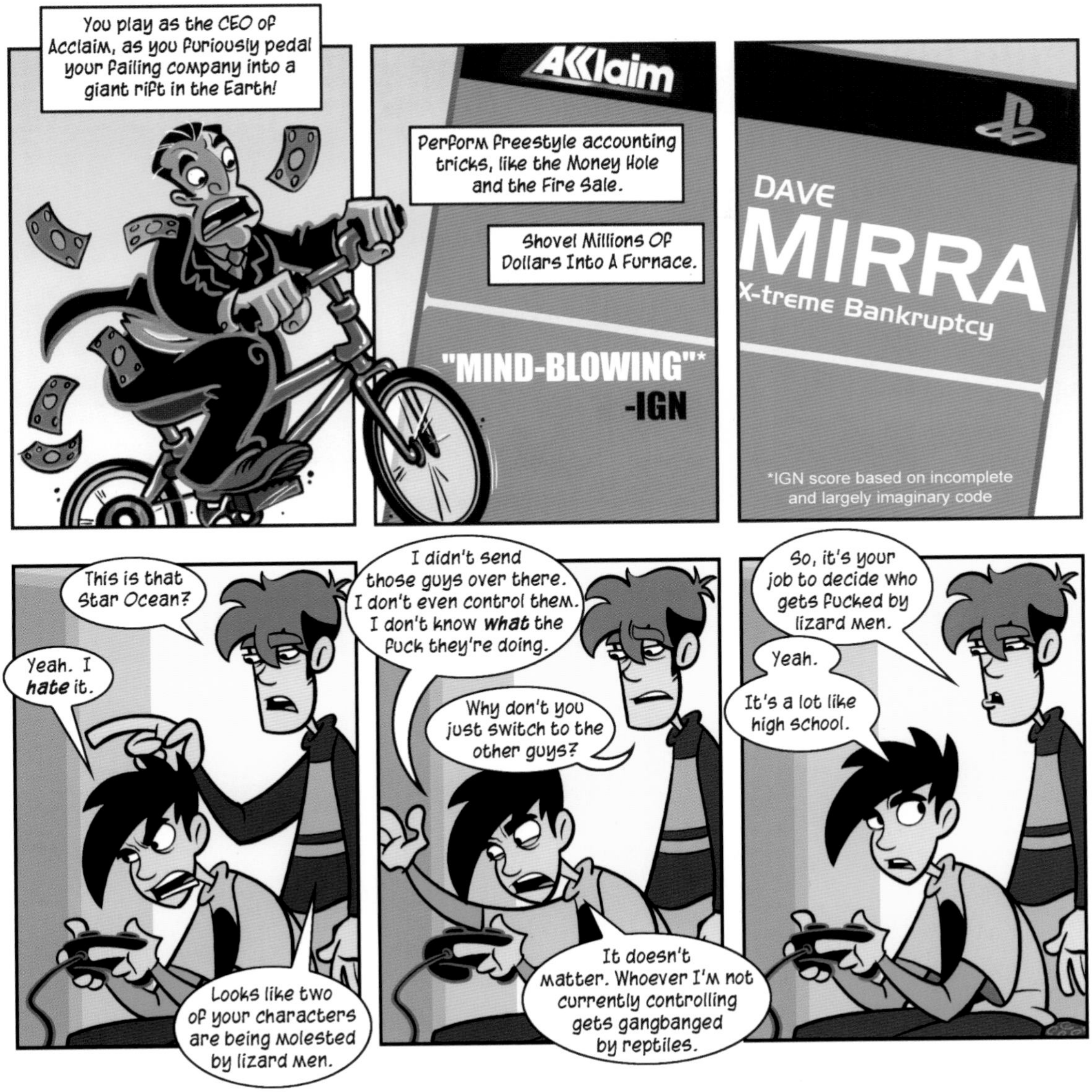
You play as the CEO of Acclaim, as you furiously pedal your failing company into a giant rift in the Earth!
AKKlaim
Perform freestyle accounting tricks, like the Money Hole and the Fire Sale.
Shovel Millions Of Dollars Into A Furnace.
"MIND-BLOWING"* -IGN
DAVE MIRRA
X-treme Bankruptcy
*IGN score based on incomplete and largely imaginary code
This is that Star Ocean?
Yeah. I *hate* it.
Looks like two of your characters are being molested by lizard men.
I didn't send those guys over there. I don't even control them. I don't know *what* the fuck they're doing.
Why don't you just switch to the other guys?
It doesn't matter. Whoever I'm not currently controlling gets gangbanged by reptiles.
So, it's your job to decide who gets fucked by lizard men.
Yeah.
It's a lot like high school.

COMING SOON

September 3, 2004 After years of brutal treatment toward gamers and the public at large, Acclaim was finally dragged to earth. It must be said again that these are the people who offered advertising on headstones, suggesting that it might be especially appealing to the poor. Really just wall-to-wall fucking class.

A UNIQUE CURRICULUM

September 6, 2004 The ending of Star Ocean III is one of the biggest Fuck Yous in the medium. You put a hundred hours into this thing, and then it just flat out fucking mugs you. I don't want to spoil it, even though the ending is already entirely rancid. But it's something like this: imagine that you have just pulled the lever on a Las Vegas slot machine, only to have three buttholes spin up. This arrangement of buttholes causes the coin tray to overflow with diarrhea.

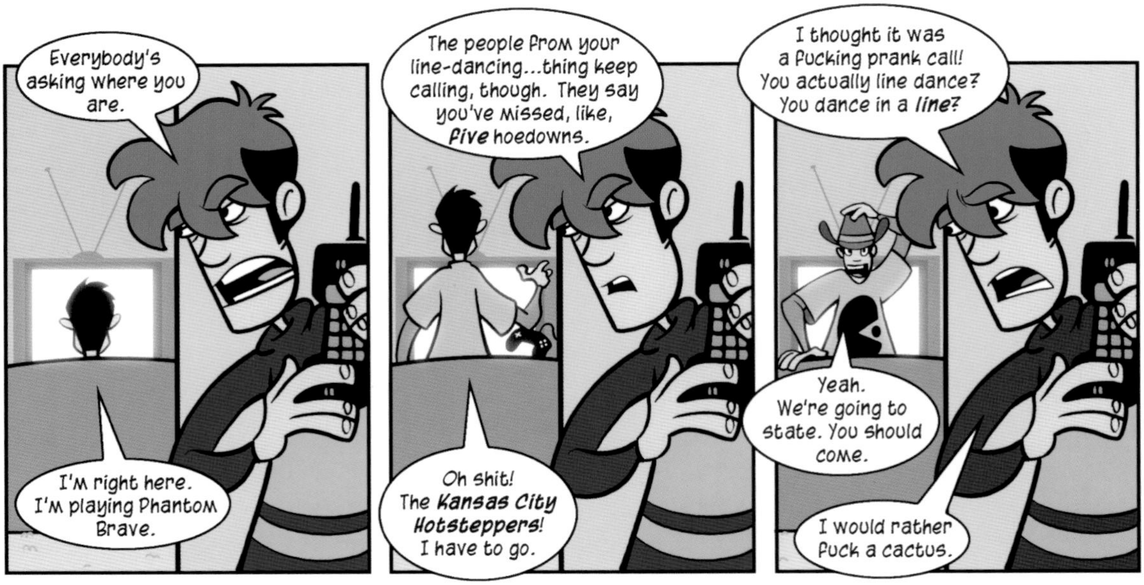

Everybody's asking where you are.
I'm right here. I'm playing Phantom Brave.
The people from your line-dancing...thing keep calling, though. They say you've missed, like, *five* hoedowns.
Oh shit! The ***Kansas City Hotsteppers!*** I have to go.
I thought it was a fucking prank call! You actually line dance? You dance in a ***line?***
Yeah. We're going to state. You should come.
I would rather fuck a cactus.

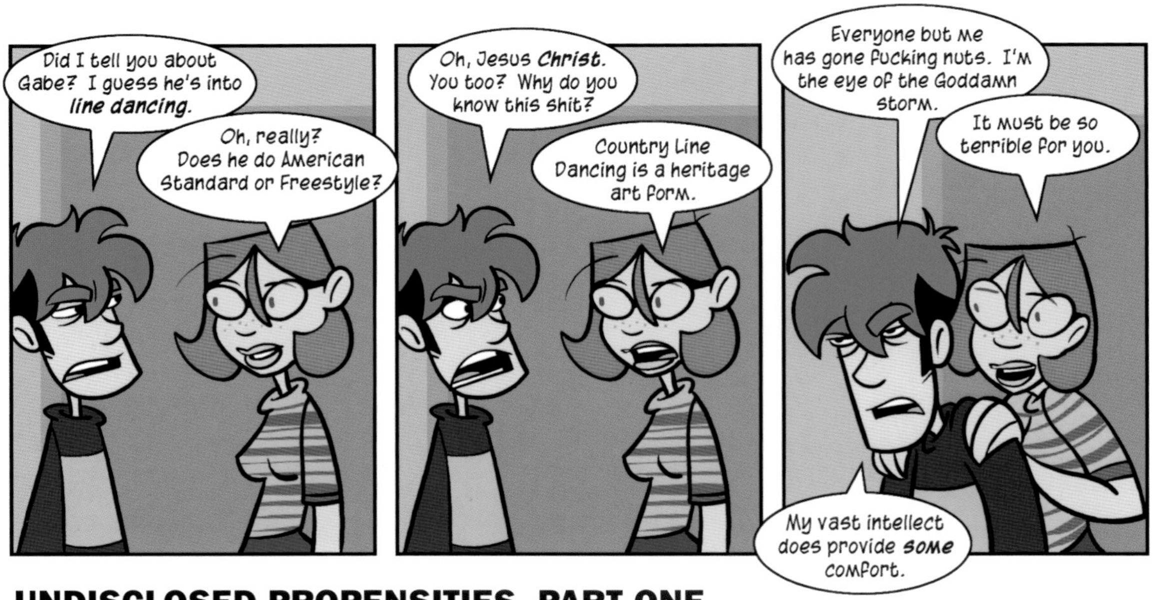

Did I tell you about Gabe? I guess he's into ***line dancing.***
Oh, really? Does he do American Standard or Freestyle?
Oh, Jesus ***Christ.*** You too? Why do you know this shit?
Country Line Dancing is a heritage art form.
Everyone but me has gone fucking nuts. I'm the eye of the Goddamn storm.
It must be so terrible for you.
My vast intellect does provide ***some*** comfort.

UNDISCLOSED PROPENSITIES, PART ONE

September 8, 2004 We had a sense that Gabriel would be a father fairly soon at this point, and armed with knowledge we decided to do this comic a little ahead of time. Once we had done it, it seemed wise to get another one "in the hopper" so to speak, but for some reason I couldn't let go of these good and evil line-dancing troupes, eternally at war.

UNDISCLOSED PROPENSITIES, PART TWO

September 10, 2004 Also, I rarely get a chance to try and model my own relationship in the comic. Our strips are almost always based on some authentic event before they are deep fried in allegory, but the tone presented here is fairly accurate: I constantly believe myself to be under siege by a hostile universe, and via some deep reserve of personal strength she finds the power to endure me.

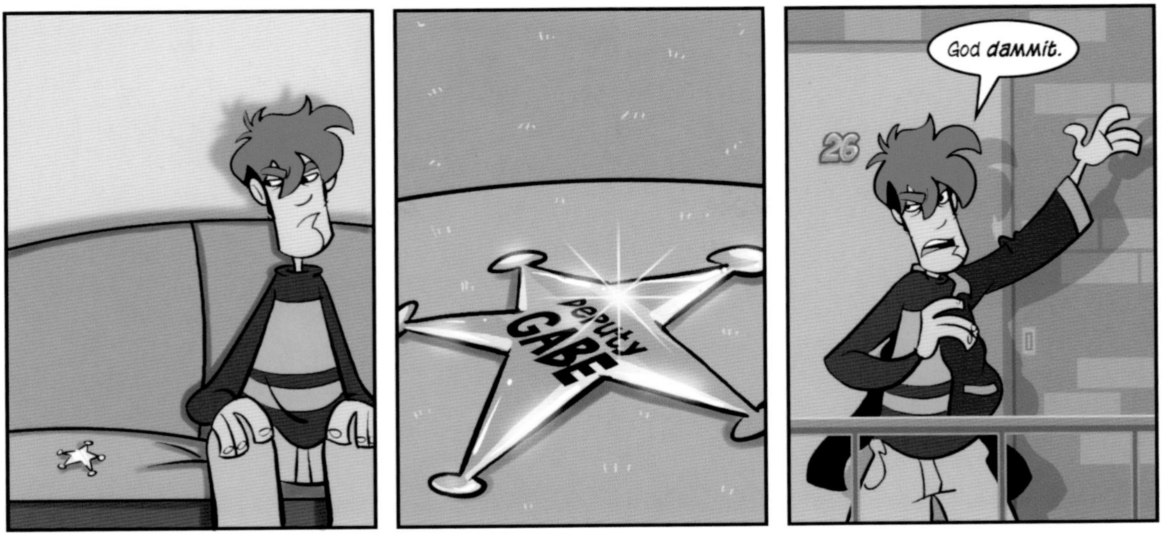
DEPUTY GABE
26
God dammit.

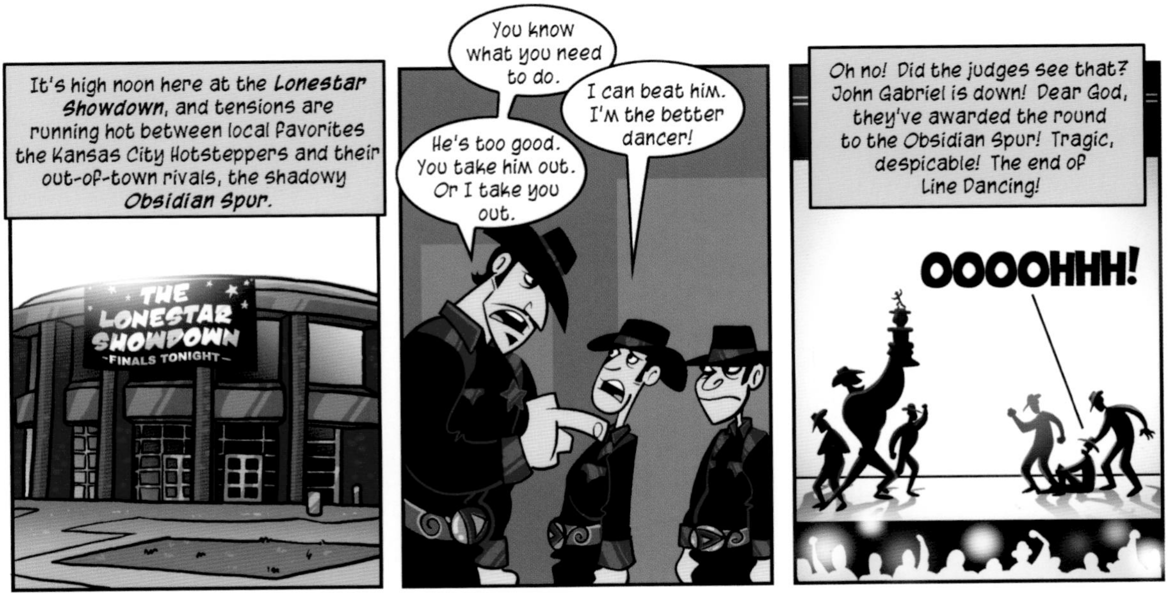
It's high noon here at the Lonestar Showdown, and tensions are running hot between local favorites the Kansas City Hotsteppers and their out-of-town rivals, the shadowy Obsidian Spur.
THE LONESTAR SHOWDOWN
FINALS TONIGHT
You know what you need to do.
He's too good. You take him out. Or I take you out.
I can beat him. I'm the better dancer!
Oh no! Did the judges see that? John Gabriel is down! Dear God, they've awarded the round to the Obsidian Spur! Tragic, despicable! The end of Line Dancing!
OOOOHHH!

UNDISCLOSED PROPENSITIES, PART THREE

September 13, 2004 This strip and the ones before and after it are entirely me, which (even as the supposed "writer") is really quite rare. We're like those two otherwise-good boys who, when together, enable each other in a suite of increasingly depraved behavior. If we weren't making comics together, I think it very unlikely that we would be making them at all.

UNDISCLOSED PROPENSITIES, PART FOUR

September 15, 2004 Ridiculous as it may seem, there is a very complete accounting of this ages-old feud. The D on their belt buckles stands for Darkspur, as in *Weyland* Darkspur, the man you see to your left. He looks sprightly indeed for a man who is over three thousand years old.

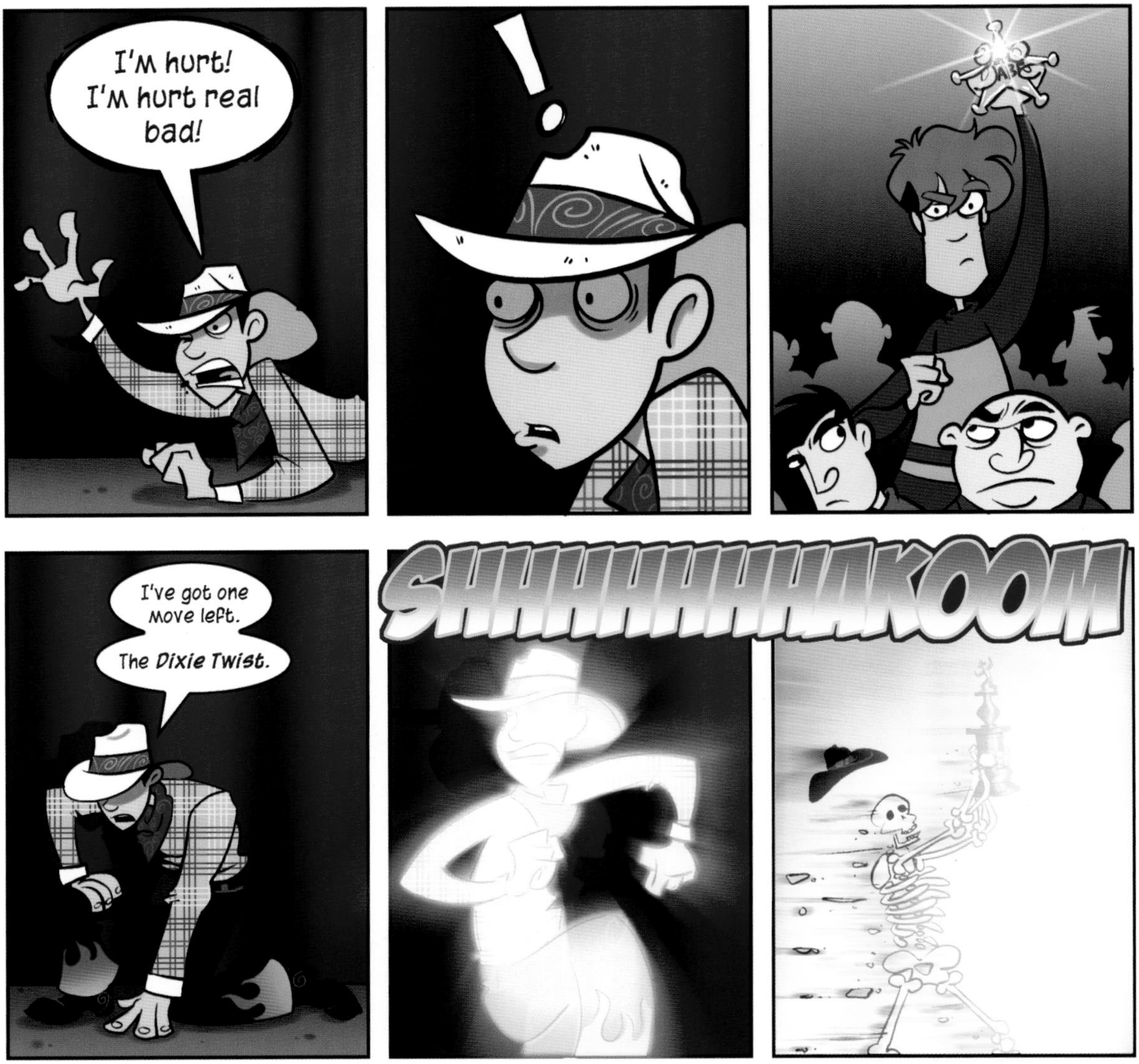
I'M hurt!
I'M hurt real bad!
!
I've got one move left.
The Dixie Twist.
SHHHHHHHHAKOOM

UNDISCLOSED PROPENSITIES, PART FIVE

September 17, 2004 Our exultant hero, or hero *adjunct* perhaps, has brought the icon and all is well. He really understands the spirit of line dancing! At least, for the duration of this comic. The best part about *Penny Arcade*, at least, as a writer, is that everyone always seems to forget the important lessons they learn. They are always perfectly teed up for whatever gruesome fate we concoct next.

UNDISCLOSED PROPENSITIES, PART SIX

September 20, 2004 Seeing a man obliterated by the shock wave generated by a dance technique, was, like the jeweled eye thing earlier, something that I longed for without knowing it. For example, there's a Canadian candy bar called a Caramilk, of which our native Caramello is only a dim shadow. Even without knowledge of this bar, you desire it. This is why you cry.

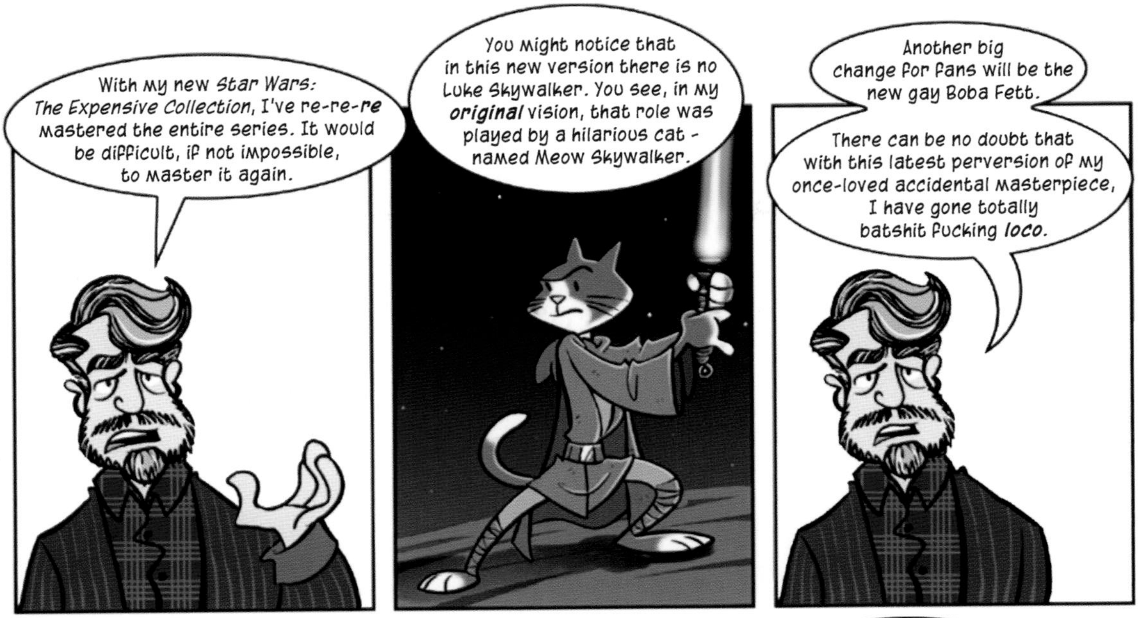
With my new *Star Wars: The Expensive Collection*, I've re-re-**re** mastered the entire series. It would be difficult, if not impossible, to master it again.
You might notice that in this new version there is no Luke Skywalker. You see, in my ***original*** vision, that role was played by a hilarious cat - named Meow Skywalker.
Another big change for fans will be the new gay Boba Fett.
There can be no doubt that with this latest perversion of my once-loved accidental masterpiece, I have gone totally batshit fucking *loco*.

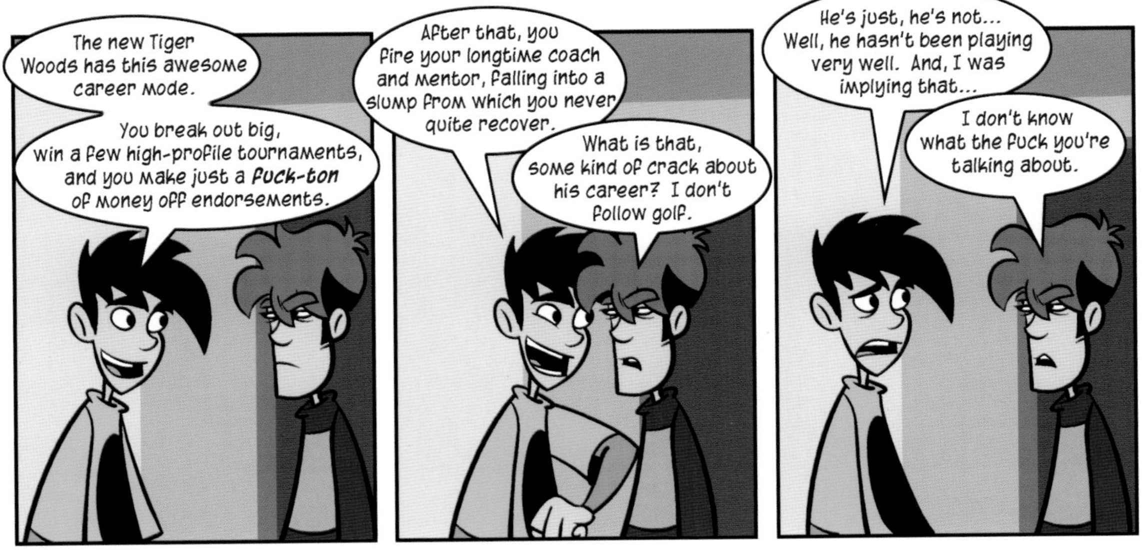
The new Tiger Woods has this awesome career mode.
You break out big, win a few high-profile tournaments, and you make just a ***fuck-ton*** of money off endorsements.
After that, you fire your longtime coach and mentor, falling into a slump from which you never quite recover.
What is that, some kind of crack about his career? I don't follow golf.
He's just, he's not... Well, he hasn't been playing very well. And, I was implying that...
I don't know what the fuck you're talking about.

THIS ISN'T YOUR FATHER'S TRILOGY

September 22, 2004 I sometimes wonder if he understands his terrible crimes, or if he doesn't actually care, or what. What is his actual level of awareness? Were *A New Hope* and *Empire* simply accidents, around which whirl successive acts of mercantile cynicism? Is there anyone, anywhere, in a position to tell him the truth—that he has callously and consistently diluted his own legend?

TIGER WOO, SUPPLEMENTAL

September 24, 2004 Typically he knows better than to engage me with *sporting trivia*, but it may be that our earlier time on the course made him believe that he had found in me some kind of confidant. Best to nip that in the bud, I think.

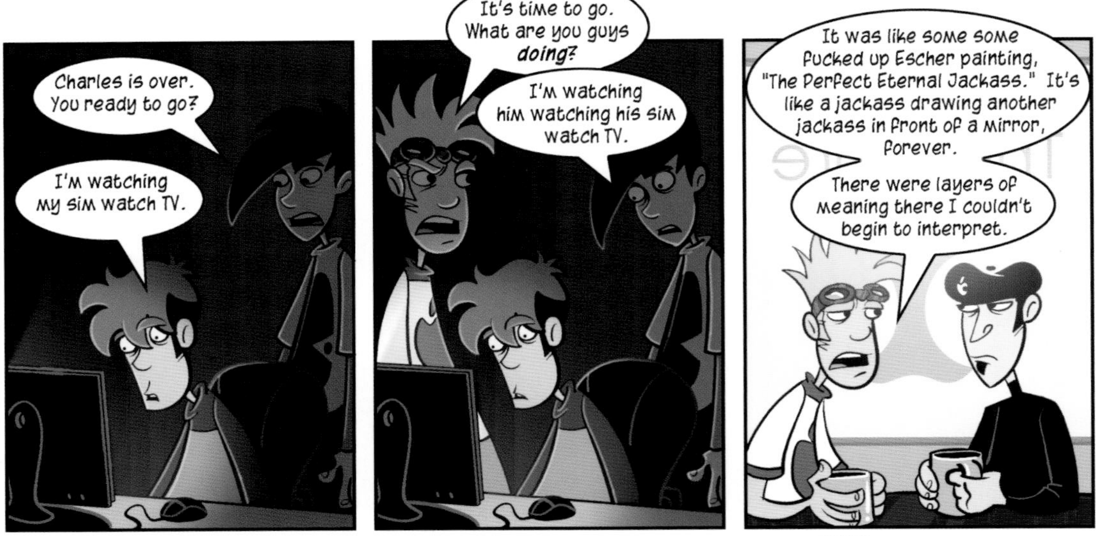

Charles is over. You ready to go?
I'm watching my sim watch TV.
It's time to go. What are you guys doing?
I'm watching him watching his sim watch TV.
It was like some some fucked up Escher painting, "The Perfect Eternal Jackass." It's like a jackass drawing another jackass in front of a mirror, forever.
There were layers of meaning there I couldn't begin to interpret.

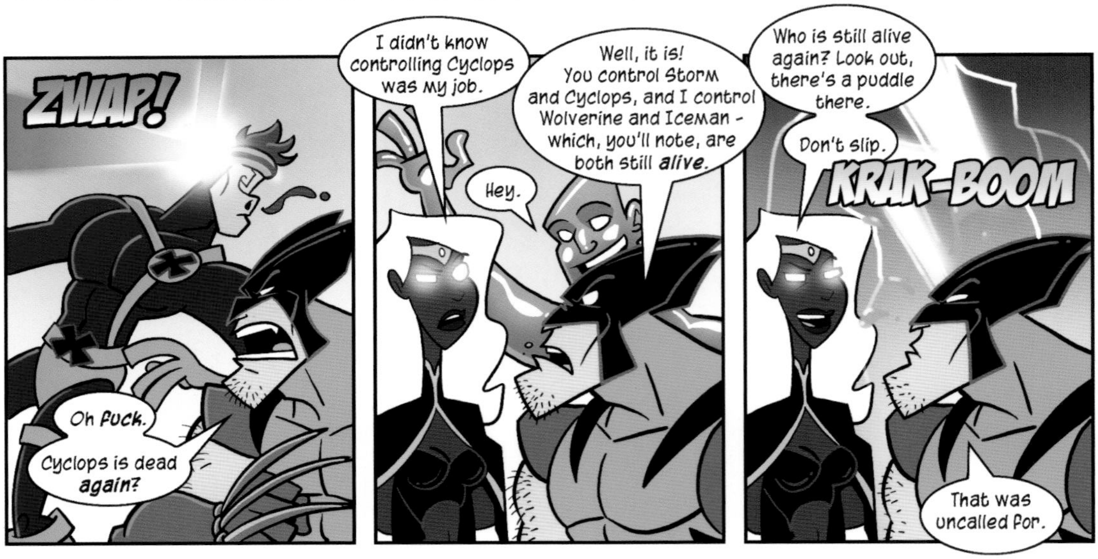

ZWAP!
Oh fuck.
Cyclops is dead again?
I didn't know controlling Cyclops was my job.
Hey.
Well, it is! You control Storm and Cyclops, and I control Wolverine and Iceman - which, you'll note, are both still alive.
Who is still alive again? Look out, there's a puddle there.
Don't slip.
KRAK-BOOM
That was uncalled for.

AD INFINITUM

September 27, 2004 The television programs that your Sims could watch in the sequel were more elaborate, and featured those weird but appropriate Simlish voiceovers. Simlish is that goofy made-up language that they all speak in those games if you didn't know, or didn't *care*, which I would absolutely understand. I should probably accept that not every person finds that element of the series as fascinating as I do.

AN ALL-STAR CAST

September 29, 2004 Raven tried their hand at the console market, and must have generated a fair bit of success—there's one sequel to the X-Men game you see here, in addition to an expanded take on the setting with Marvel: Ultimate Alliance. They're all decent games, but if you want to see them at their best you really need to get a friend on board. It should be a pretty easy sell.

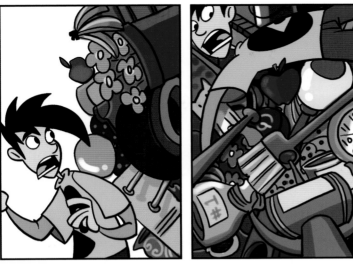

> Hey.
>
> Hey.
>
> I'm hoping this thing rolls over a liquor store.

> In Shadow Hearts: Covenant, you collect gay pornography which you can trade to a homosexual tailor. In exchange, he will produce fabulous, tiny dresses for your living doll.
>
> That's not the joke.
>
> This is something you actually do.

> You find yourself hoping that each character you meet is actually a **closet queen** sitting on a stockpile of queer smut.
>
> Hang on a second, Mom.
>
> Check his flower pot. Check his flower pot for **gay porn.**

> We desperately need those new dresses.
>
> No, Mom — we're not.
>
> Yes, I know you worry about that.

KATAHADA DAMAHOOCHA

October 1, 2004 The surreal delights of Katamari Damacy are still being savored by gamers the world over. After completing the first one on the PS2, and then the portable version on the PSP, I felt confident that future iterations of the game would involve *rolling*—I didn't really need to buy it again. As these books are essentially an archive of gaming trivia, I want to remind people that the first game was only twenty dollars.

THE UTILITY OF RARE EROTICA

October 4, 2004 I don't speak or write Japanese, so I don't know if the original version of Shadow Hearts: Covenant is as funny as the U.S. version. What I'm trying to say is that it is *extremely funny*. It's serious, too—when it needs to be—but there're jokes sticking out all over this thing. Some of the game systems even appeared to be jokes, at the expense of other JRPGs.

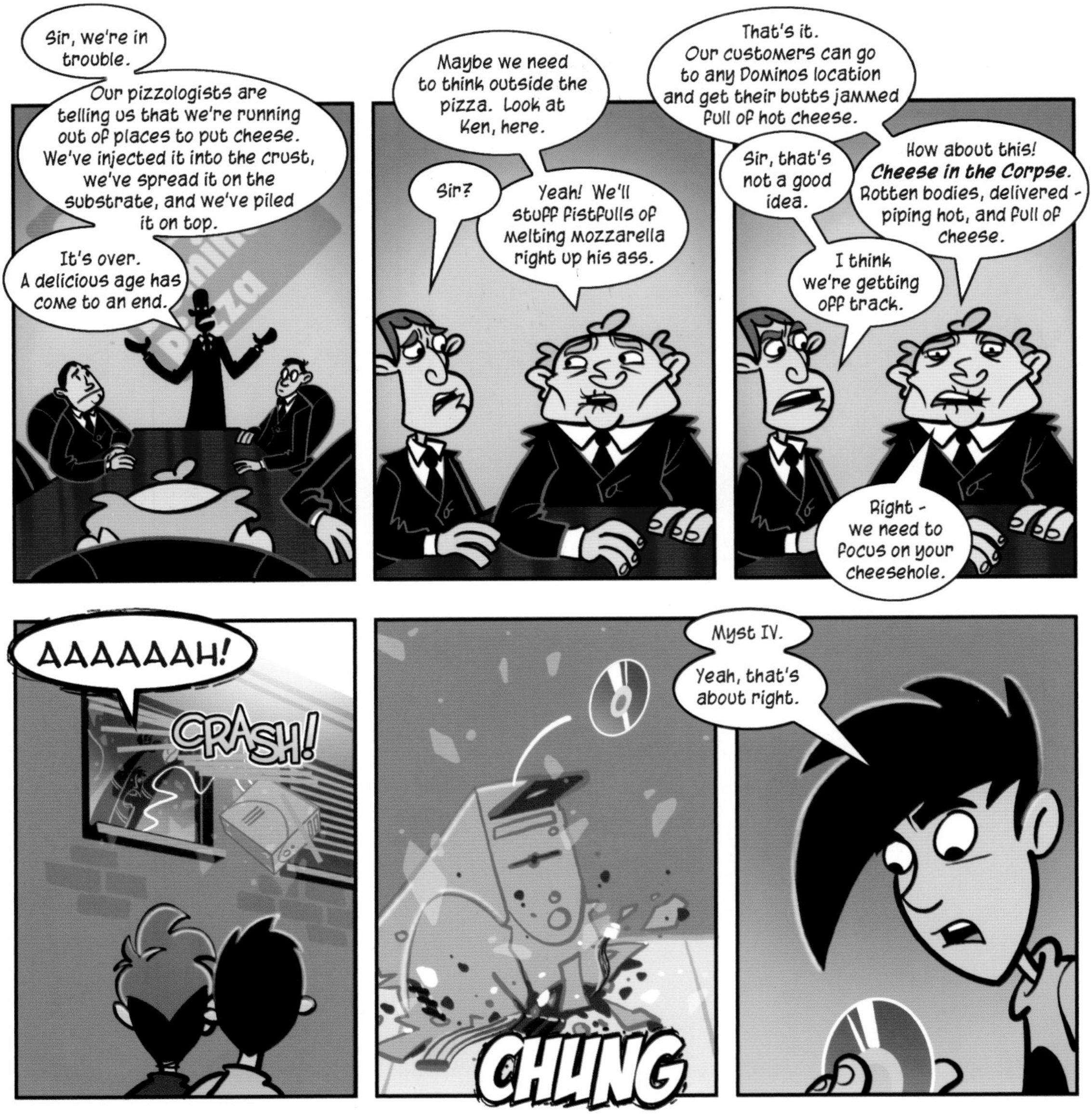
Sir, we're in trouble.
Our pizzologists are telling us that we're running out of places to put cheese. We've injected it into the crust, we've spread it on the substrate, and we've piled it on top.
It's over. A delicious age has come to an end.
Maybe we need to think outside the pizza. Look at Ken, here.
Sir?
Yeah! We'll stuff fistfulls of melting mozzarella right up his ass.
That's it. Our customers can go to any Dominos location and get their butts jammed full of hot cheese.
Sir, that's not a good idea.
How about this! Cheese in the Corpse. Rotten bodies, delivered - piping hot, and full of cheese.
I think we're getting off track.
Right - we need to focus on your cheesehole.
AAAAAAH!
CRASH!
CHUNG
Myst IV.
Yeah, that's about right.

THE VISIONARY

October 6, 2004 I don't even have cable, such is my loathing for commercials. I won't endure them, and I certainly won't pay to endure them. But, as I suggested in that day's post, Gabriel sees commercials as a kind of *art form*, and so even without television service I am still exposed to a moment-by-moment breakdown of the lures I have arranged my ENTIRE LIFE to AVOID.

TRAJECTORY

October 8, 2004 Myst IV was frustrating, like all puzzle games, but the release of that tension upon discovering the solution was a whole body experience. I liked four much better than three, or five, and maybe even two. It had a couple mechanisms that were hard to manipulate, falsely increasing their difficulty, but the story being told resolved the first game with symmetry, savvy, and elegance.

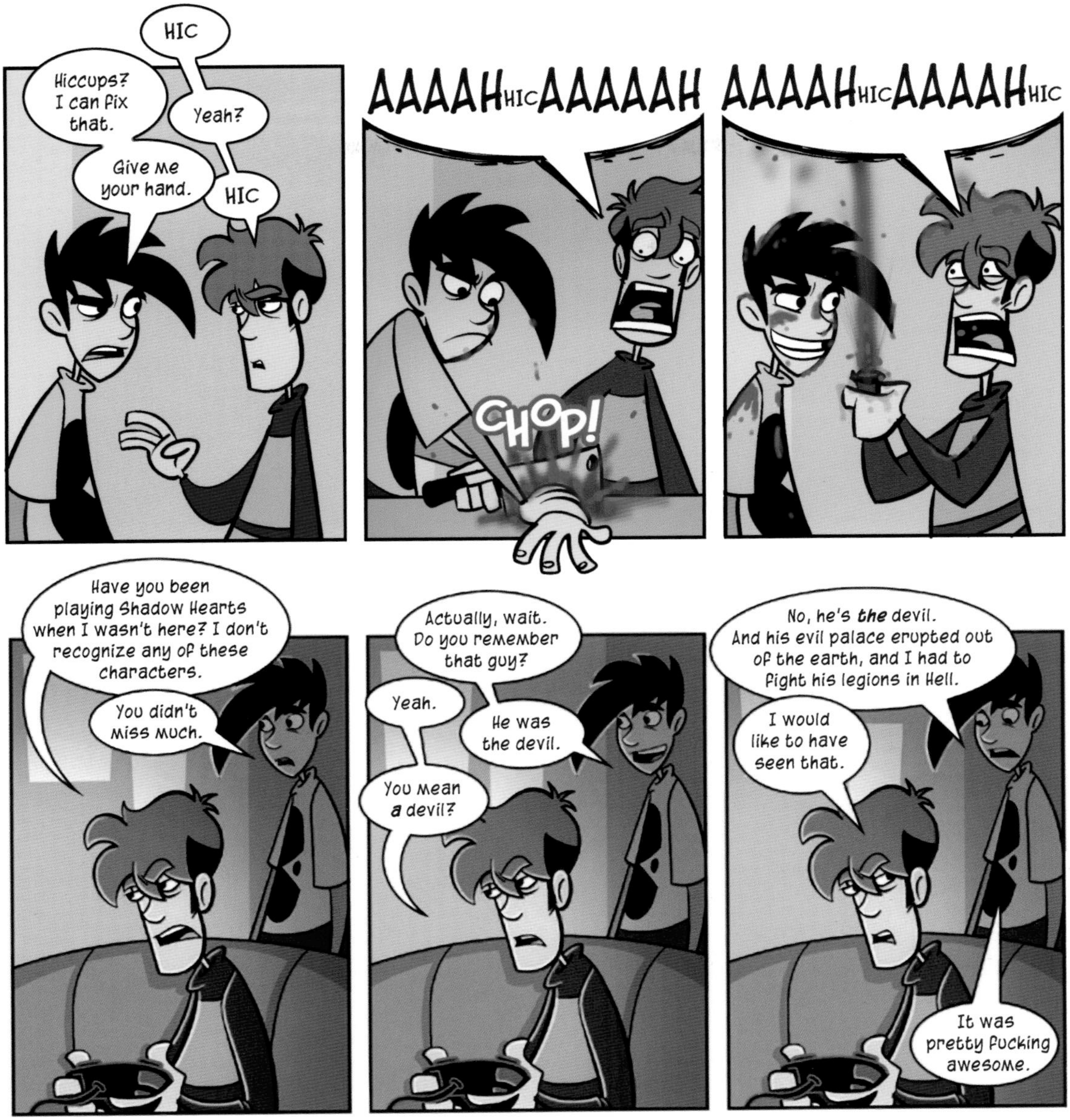
Hiccups? I can fix that.
HIC
Yeah?
Give me your hand.
HIC
AAAAHhicAAAAAH
CHOP!
AAAAHhicAAAAHhic
Have you been playing Shadow Hearts when I wasn't here? I don't recognize any of these characters.
You didn't miss much.
Actually, wait. Do you remember that guy?
Yeah.
He was the devil.
You mean a devil?
No, he's the devil. And his evil palace erupted out of the earth, and I had to fight his legions in Hell.
I would like to have seen that.
It was pretty fucking awesome.

THE HICCOUGH, SCOURGE OF MAN

October 11, 2004 For some reason he thinks of the hiccups as some kind of personal assault. Whenever an attack comes on, I can sense him winding up inside. He has a technique which he claims resolves hiccups one hundred percent of the time, so if you do have them and don't avail yourself of his method, he believes you are only hiccupping to spite *him*, and not because of a physical process that is occurring in your body.

RANK BETRAYAL

October 13, 2004 The system we have in place now is that if something awesome is about to happen, you had damned well better save the game so you can share that shit with the rest of the class.

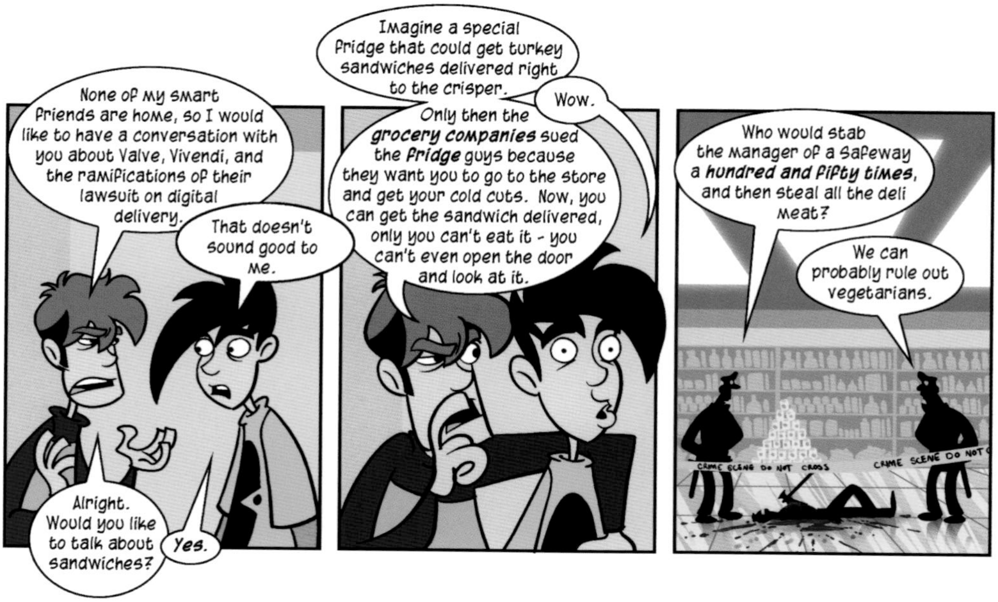
None of my smart friends are home, so I would like to have a conversation with you about Valve, Vivendi, and the ramifications of their lawsuit on digital delivery.
That doesn't sound good to me.
Alright. Would you like to talk about sandwiches?
Yes.
Imagine a special fridge that could get turkey sandwiches delivered right to the crisper.
Wow.
Only then the grocery companies sued the fridge guys because they want you to go to the store and get your cold cuts. Now, you can get the sandwich delivered, only you can't eat it - you can't even open the door and look at it.
Who would stab the manager of a Safeway a hundred and fifty times, and then steal all the deli meat?
We can probably rule out vegetarians.
CRIME SCENE DO NOT CROSS
CRIME SCENE DO NOT C

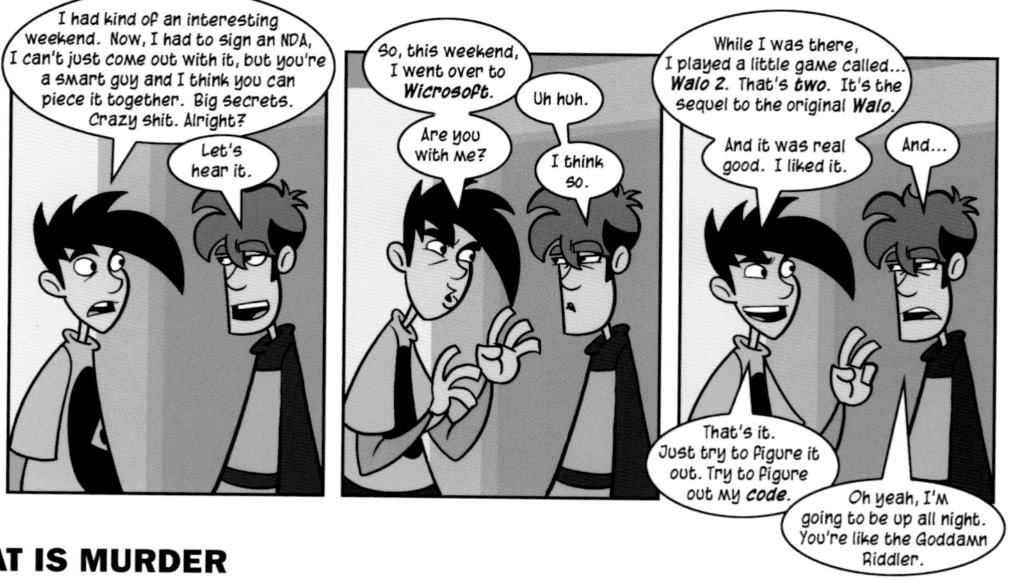
I had kind of an interesting weekend. Now, I had to sign an NDA, I can't just come out with it, but you're a smart guy and I think you can piece it together. Big secrets. Crazy shit. Alright?
Let's hear it.
So, this weekend, I went over to Wicrosoft.
Uh huh.
Are you with me?
I think so.
While I was there, I played a little game called... Walo 2. That's two. It's the sequel to the original Walo.
And it was real good. I liked it.
And...
That's it. Just try to figure it out. Try to figure out my code.
Oh yeah, I'm going to be up all night. You're like the Goddamn Riddler.

MEAT IS MURDER

October 15, 2004 I think that, like most people, I imagined that the age of digital delivery would allow me to download games once they had been completed, and for less money, as opposed to waiting for physical boxes to be delivered and then paying the same Goddamned amount. Its power is severely restrained by the retail outlets, who essentially have the entire industry by the "mean beans."

HIGH ENCRYPTION

October 18, 2004 Halo 2 brought with it the automatic matchmaking that others have since tried to implement. PC gamers tend to like browsing for servers, they find that act liberating, but if I'm always choosing the "best ping" with the "right number of slots," I don't mind if a computer somewhere in Redmond does that for me.

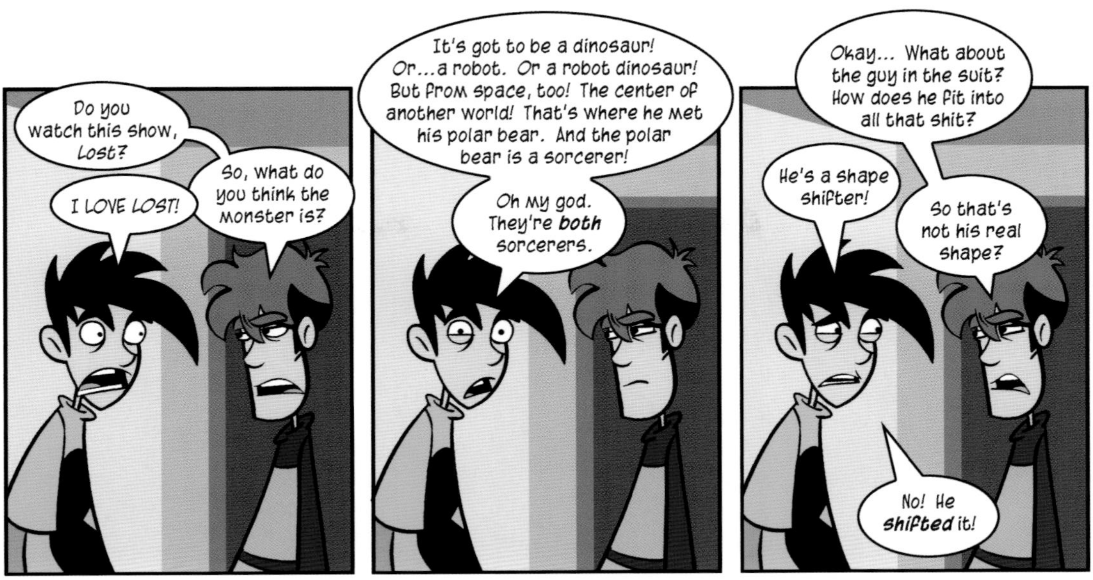
Do you watch this show, Lost?
I LOVE LOST!
So, what do you think the monster is?
It's got to be a dinosaur! Or...a robot. Or a robot dinosaur! But from space, too! The center of another world! That's where he met his polar bear. And the polar bear is a sorcerer!
Oh my god. They're both sorcerers.
Okay... What about the guy in the suit? How does he fit into all that shit?
He's a shape shifter!
So that's not his real shape?
No! He shifted it!

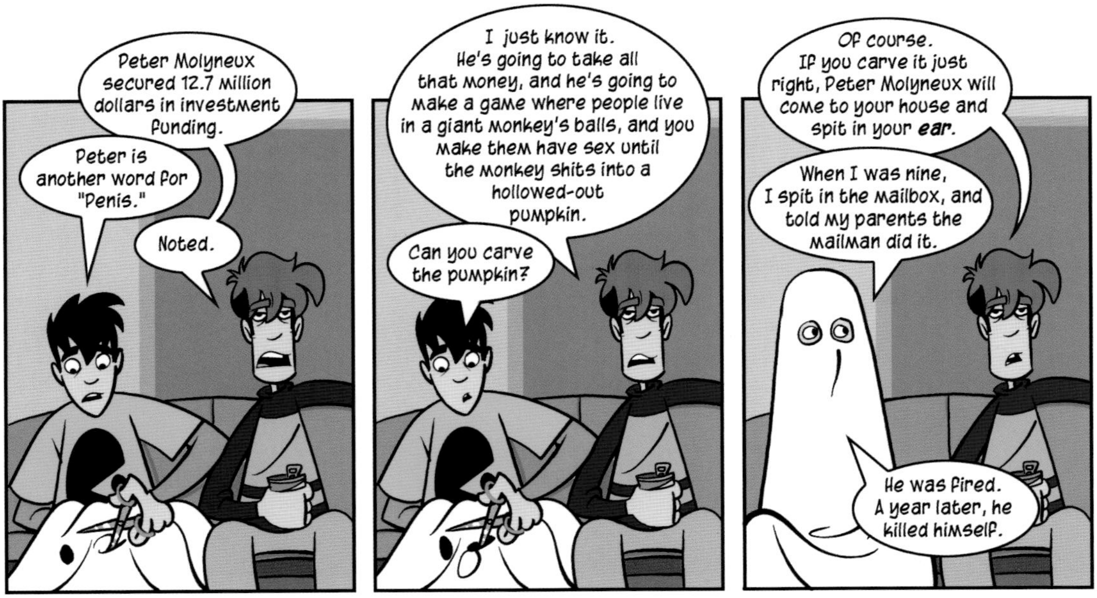
Peter Molyneux secured 12.7 million dollars in investment funding.
Peter is another word for "Penis."
Noted.
I just know it. He's going to take all that money, and he's going to make a game where people live in a giant monkey's balls, and you make them have sex until the monkey shits into a hollowed-out pumpkin.
Can you carve the pumpkin?
Of course. If you carve it just right, Peter Molyneux will come to your house and spit in your ear.
When I was nine, I spit in the mailbox, and told my parents the mailman did it.
He was fired. A year later, he killed himself.

DON'T FORGET DOPPELGANGERS!

October 20, 2004 *Lost* wasn't able to maintain its incredible momentum, at least not with our local contingent. People are continually telling Gabriel (who "LOVES *LOST*," or *did* love it, see above) that the show is *back*, or that it has begun to pay out on some of its drunken promises, but he is beyond this sort of entreaty. He has recovered from the show's grip, and is now attempting to lead a normal life.

THE GAME IS CALLED "FUMPKIN"

October 22, 2004 Did you hear that Fable 2 is going to have a dog in it? That's really all anyone knows. I have a bad feeling that they're only letting you have a dog in order to murder it later, leaving players devastated.

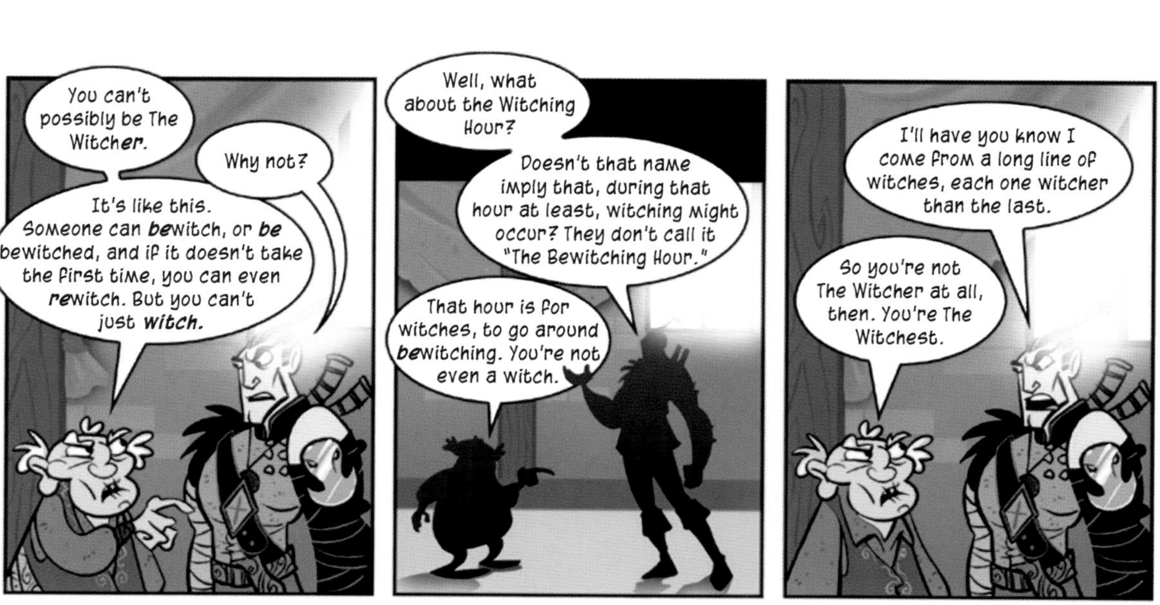
You can't possibly be The Witcher.
Why not?
It's like this. Someone can bewitch, or be bewitched, and if it doesn't take the first time, you can even rewitch. But you can't just witch.
Well, what about the Witching Hour?
Doesn't that name imply that, during that hour at least, witching might occur? They don't call it "The Bewitching Hour."
That hour is for witches, to go around bewitching. You're not even a witch.
I'll have you know I come from a long line of witches, each one witcher than the last.
So you're not The Witcher at all, then. You're The Witchest.

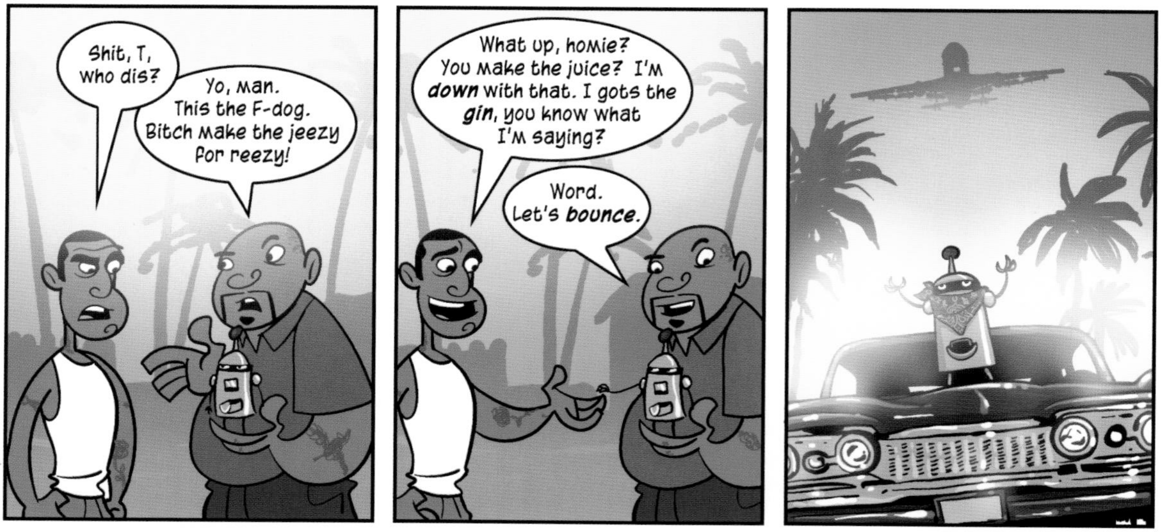
Shit, T, who dis?
Yo, man. This the F-dog. Bitch make the jeezy for reezy!
What up, homie? You make the juice? I'm down with that. I gots the gin, you know what I'm saying?
Word. Let's bounce.

THIRD BASE!

October 24, 2004 This is the comic I refer to when I say that people don't like "word comics." At any rate, most people seem not to. But there are those who are *only* pleased by them, and we must serve that contingent in our small way. We saw the game year after year at E3, always improving slightly, but never imagined that it would actually see release. Imagine my surprise when it was not only released, but *excellent*.

FRUIT FUCKER: SAN ANDREAS

October 27, 2004 I live for third panels like this. One can almost *feel* the seismic bass and warbling synth.

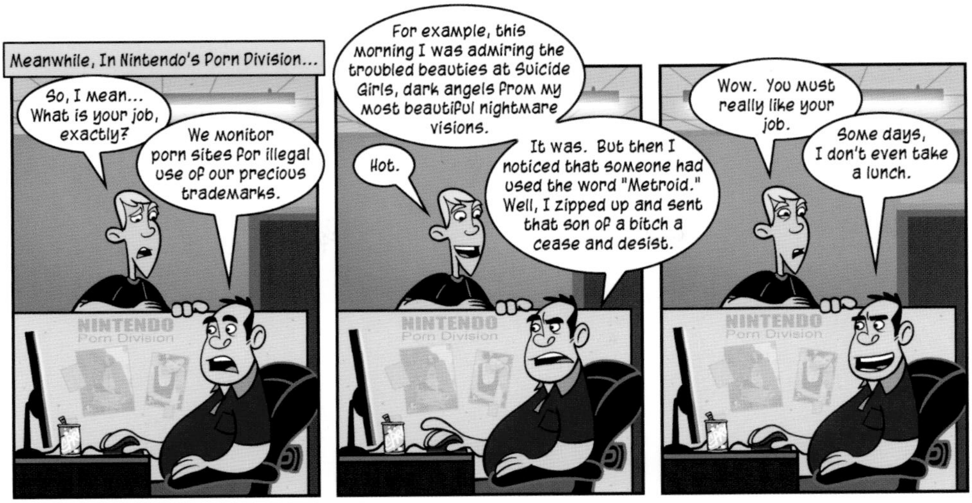
Meanwhile, In Nintendo's Porn Division...
So, I mean... What is your job, exactly?
We monitor porn sites for illegal use of our precious trademarks.
NINTENDO Porn Division
For example, this morning I was admiring the troubled beauties at Suicide Girls, dark angels from my most beautiful nightmare visions.
Hot.
It was. But then I noticed that someone had used the word "Metroid." Well, I zipped up and sent that son of a bitch a cease and desist.
Wow. You must really like your job.
Some days, I don't even take a lunch.

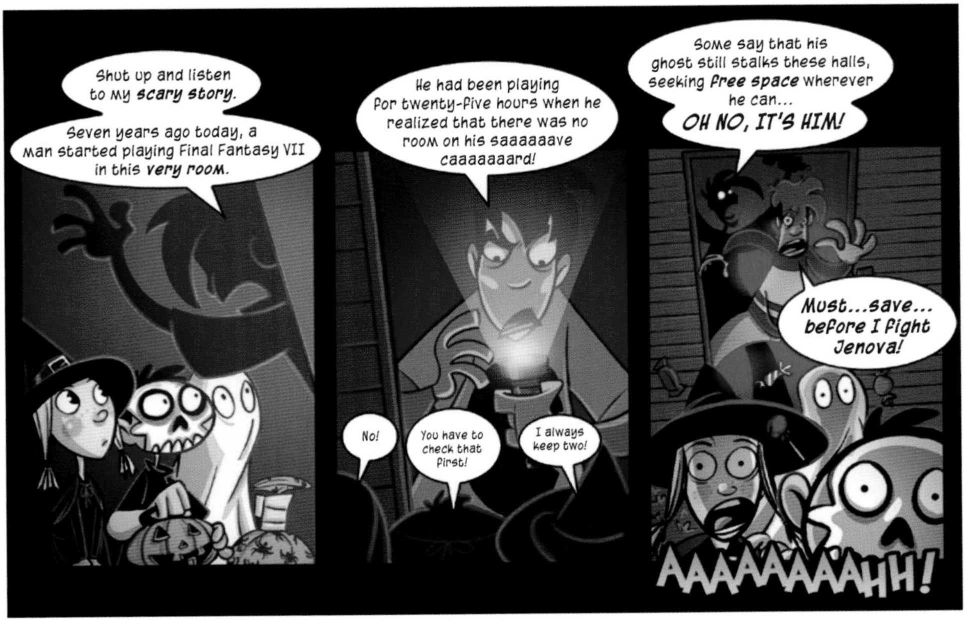
Shut up and listen to my *scary story.*
Seven years ago today, a man started playing Final Fantasy VII in this *very room.*
He had been playing for twenty-five hours when he realized that there was no room on his saaaaaave caaaaaaard!
No!
You have to check that first!
I always keep two!
Some say that his ghost still stalks these halls, seeking *free space* wherever he can...
OH NO, IT'S HIM!
Must...save... before I fight Jenova!
AAAAAAAAAHH!

HOOCHIE COOCHIE MAN

October 29, 2004 Nintendo quickly recanted, of course—it was some automatic process that had snared the aforementioned *Girls*. There was eventually a pictorial based on *Penny Arcade* at that site, but I did not enjoy it! There was *zero* titillation. The entire time I was perusing it—a period spanning six and a half solid days—I thought *only* of mathematics and agriculture.

HARROWEEN!

October 31, 2004 It would actually take twenty minutes to tell a story like this—first, you'd need a slide show detailing the major systems and average file sizes. Then, you'd have to detail the omnipresent dangers of removing the *card* while saving, which every game's stern placards make out to be the end of the known universe.

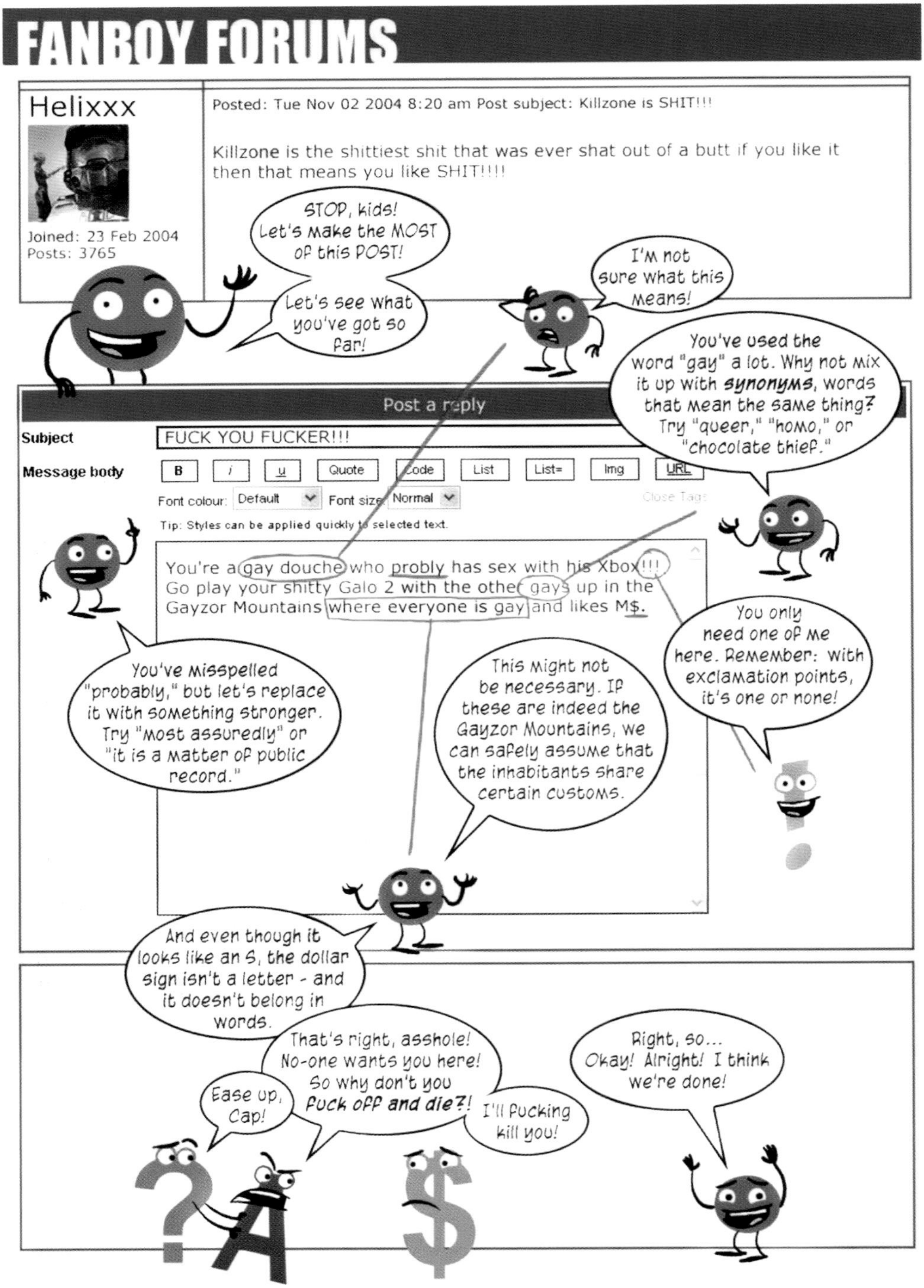
FANBOY FORUMS
Helixxx
Joined: 23 Feb 2004
Posts: 3765
Posted: Tue Nov 02 2004 8:20 am Post subject: Killzone is SHIT!!!
Killzone is the shittiest shit that was ever shat out of a butt if you like it then that means you like SHIT!!!!
STOP, kids! Let's make the MOST of this POST!
Let's see what you've got so far!
I'm not sure what this means!
You've used the word "gay" a lot. Why not mix it up with synonyms, words that mean the same thing? Try "queer," "homo," or "chocolate thief."
Post a reply
Subject
FUCK YOU FUCKER!!!
Message body
B i u Quote Code List List= Img URL
Font colour: Default Font size: Normal
Tip: Styles can be applied quickly to selected text.
You're a gay douche who probly has sex with his Xbox!!! Go play your shitty Galo 2 with the other gays up in the Gayzor Mountains where everyone is gay and likes M$.
You've misspelled "probably," but let's replace it with something stronger. Try "most assuredly" or "it is a matter of public record."
This might not be necessary. If these are indeed the Gayzor Mountains, we can safely assume that the inhabitants share certain customs.
You only need one of me here. Remember: with exclamation points, it's one or none!
And even though it looks like an S, the dollar sign isn't a letter - and it doesn't belong in words.
That's right, asshole! No-one wants you here! So why don't you fuck off and die?!
Ease up, Cap!
I'll fucking kill you!
Right, so... Okay! Alright! I think we're done!

MR. PERIOD RETURNS

November 3, 2004 Mr. Period seems to give this anonymous young man the benefit of the doubt, which is rather charitable given the raw content of his barrage.

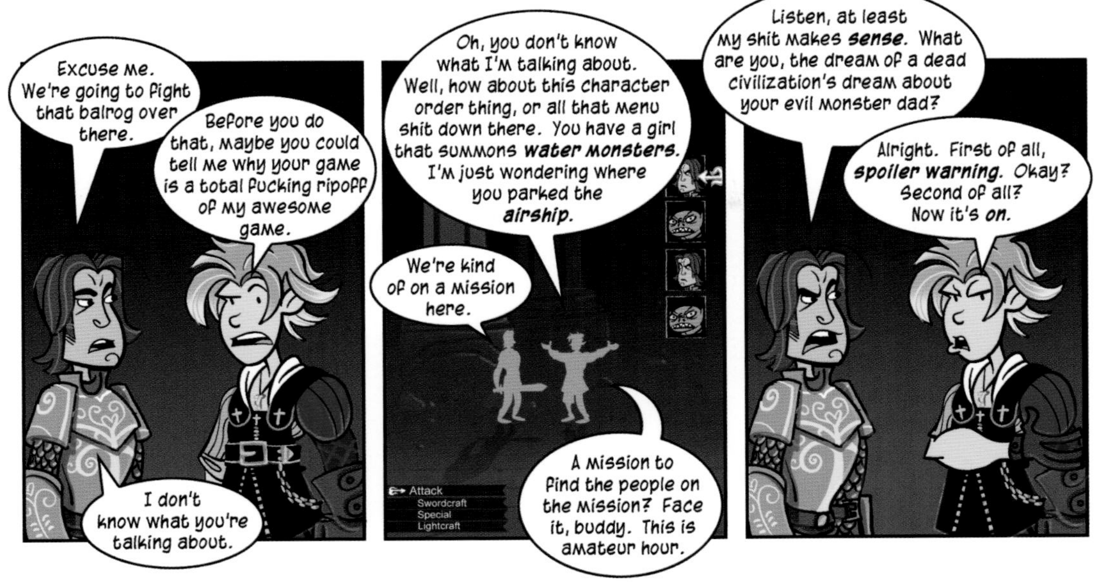
Excuse me. We're going to fight that balrog over there.
Before you do that, maybe you could tell me why your game is a total fucking ripoff of my awesome game.
I don't know what you're talking about.
Oh, you don't know what I'm talking about. Well, how about this character order thing, or all that menu shit down there. You have a girl that summons **water monsters**. I'm just wondering where you parked the ***airship***.
We're kind of on a mission here.
Attack
Swordcraft
Special
Lightcraft
A mission to find the people on the mission? Face it, buddy. This is amateur hour.
Listen, at least my shit makes ***sense***. What are you, the dream of a dead civilization's dream about your evil monster dad?
Alright. First of all, ***spoiler warning***. Okay? Second of all? Now it's ***on***.

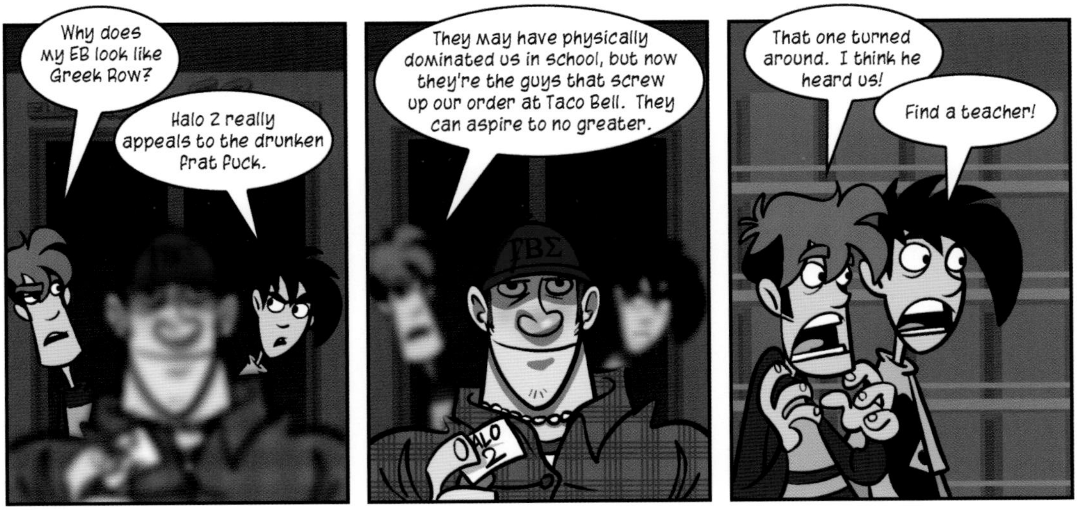
Why does my EB look like Greek Row?
Halo 2 really appeals to the drunken frat fuck.
They may have physically dominated us in school, but now they're the guys that screw up our order at Taco Bell. They can aspire to no greater.
HALO 2
That one turned around. I think he heard us!
Find a teacher!

SOMETHING BORROWED

November 5, 2004 This was back when EA was still experimenting with RPGs set in the Lord of the Rings continuity, before they cancelled The White Council, which was looking pretty cool. They've really made good use of the license, I think—delivering a couple really sharp action games and some RTS entries with great ideas. I really wonder if the time an RPG needs to bake is even compatible with the frenzied, often annual pace of Western development.

THE NIGHTLIFE

November 8, 2004 We played Halo 2, and enjoyed it, but we were never deeply invested and we soon dropped out. Our Halo experiences were always at hastily mounted LAN events, wild, bacchanalian things, and I think playing Halo online just made us miss them. We apparently got over it for Halo 3, but by then our LAN days were largely gone.

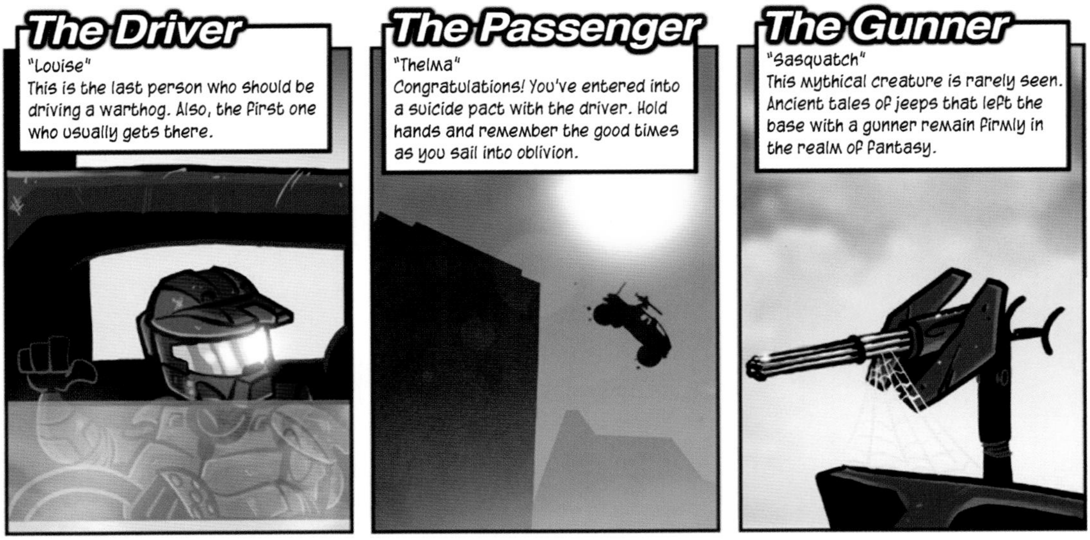
The Driver
"Louise"
This is the last person who should be driving a warthog. Also, the first one who usually gets there.
The Passenger
"Thelma"
Congratulations! You've entered into a suicide pact with the driver. Hold hands and remember the good times as you sail into oblivion.
The Gunner
"Sasquatch"
This mythical creature is rarely seen. Ancient tales of jeeps that left the base with a gunner remain firmly in the realm of fantasy.

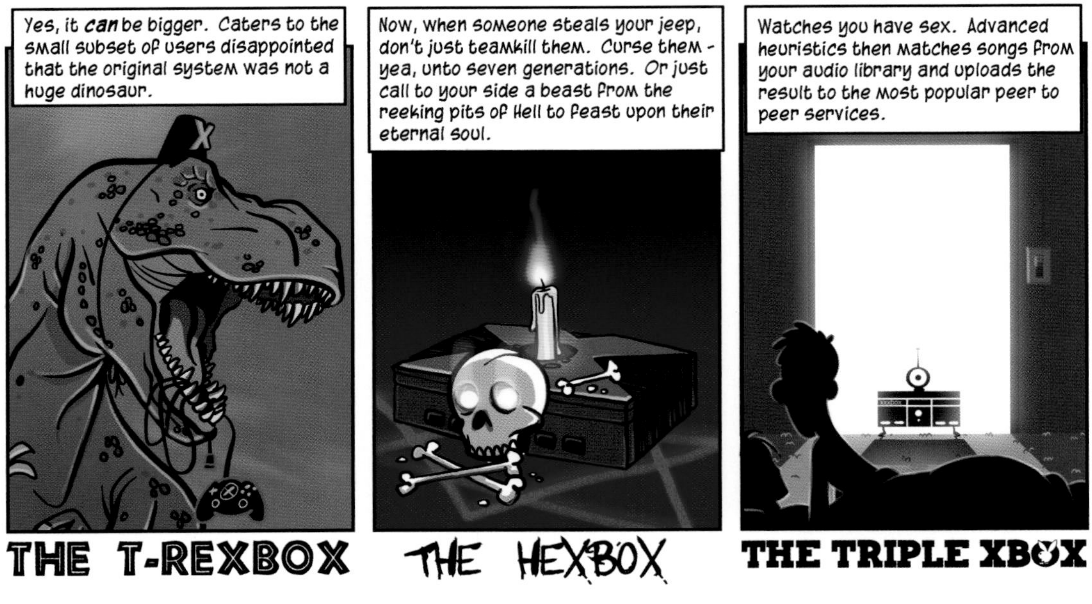
Yes, it *can* be bigger. Caters to the small subset of users disappointed that the original system was not a huge dinosaur.
THE T-REXBOX
Now, when someone steals your jeep, don't just teamkill them. Curse them - yea, unto seven generations. Or just call to your side a beast from the reeking pits of Hell to feast upon their eternal soul.
THE HEXBOX
Watches you have sex. Advanced heuristics then matches songs from your audio library and uploads the result to the most popular peer to peer services.
THE TRIPLE XBOX

THE LAWS

November 10, 2004 This was probably the other thing that kept us from falling absolutely in love with the second Halo—all the human beings out there who played it. The tools to manage the behavior of others have gotten much more sophisticated in the third installment, to be sure. But we also know better than to ever, *ever* play without a team made up of known quantities.

THE OTHER THREE

November 12, 2004 The rumors about the second Xbox have begun to whirl at a fever pitch here, a year before its eventual release, with the revelation that there would be three versions of the device: one without a hard disc, one *with* one, and then a third box which was a home computer *compatible* with the 360. We saw no reason to stop at three, as evidenced here.

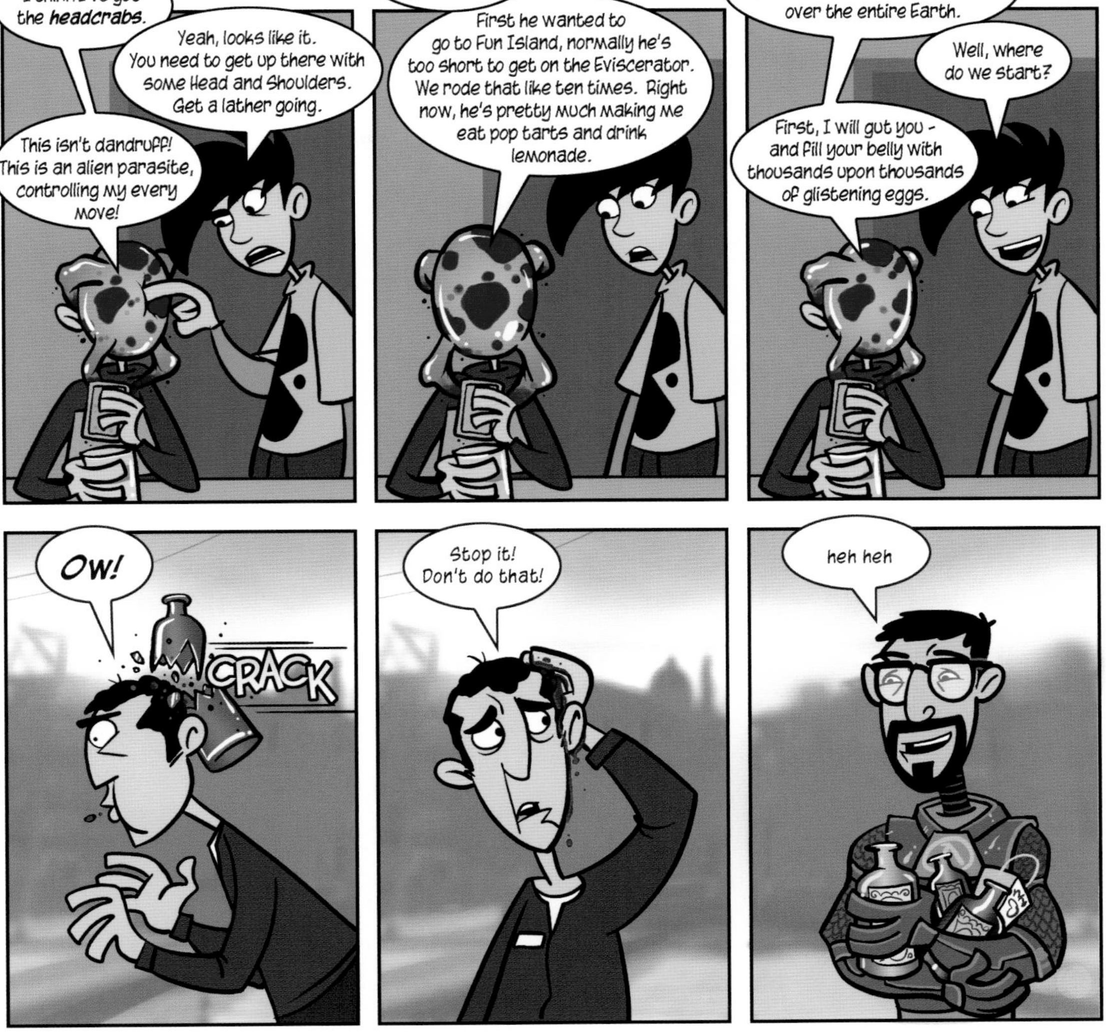
I think I've got the headcrabs.
Yeah, looks like it. You need to get up there with some Head and Shoulders. Get a lather going.
This isn't dandruff! This is an alien parasite, controlling my every move!
What kind of stuff does he want you to do?
First he wanted to go to Fun Island, normally he's too short to get on the Eviscerator. We rode that like ten times. Right now, he's pretty much making me eat pop tarts and drink lemonade.
After that, I think he wants to extend his dominion over the entire Earth.
Well, where do we start?
First, I will gut you - and fill your belly with thousands upon thousands of glistening eggs.
OW!
CRACK
Stop it! Don't do that!
heh heh

THE COMMON HEADCRAB

November 15, 2004 The headcrab is tremendously iconic, and though it's been years now since Half-Life 2 I've spent time with them recently in the episodic continuations. The first time I saw—and *heard*—the men shredded and ravaged by these things in the sequel, I had to take my headphones off and stand up from the machine. I hadn't done that since System Shock 2.

99 BOTTLES

November 17, 2004 Physics were part of the experience even before you obtained the now iconic gravity gun, as throwing garbage and glass at strangers unlocked incredible new gameplay opportunities. As the anointed savior of humanity, I tried to tamp down my aggressive and antisocial tendencies—understanding the gravity of my task. Pray, friends, *pray* that the earth never needs Gabriel to protect it.

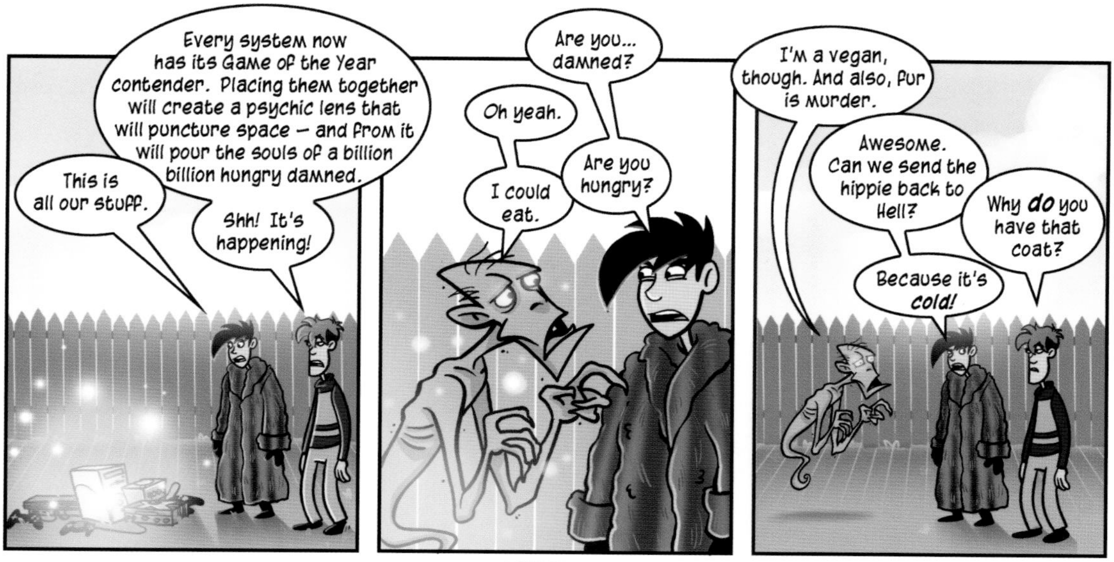
Every system now has its Game of the Year contender. Placing them together will create a psychic lens that will puncture space — and from it will pour the souls of a billion billion hungry damned.
This is all our stuff.
Shh! It's happening!
Are you... damned?
Oh yeah.
Are you hungry?
I could eat.
I'm a vegan, though. And also, fur is murder.
Awesome. Can we send the hippie back to Hell?
Why *do* you have that coat?
Because it's *cold!*

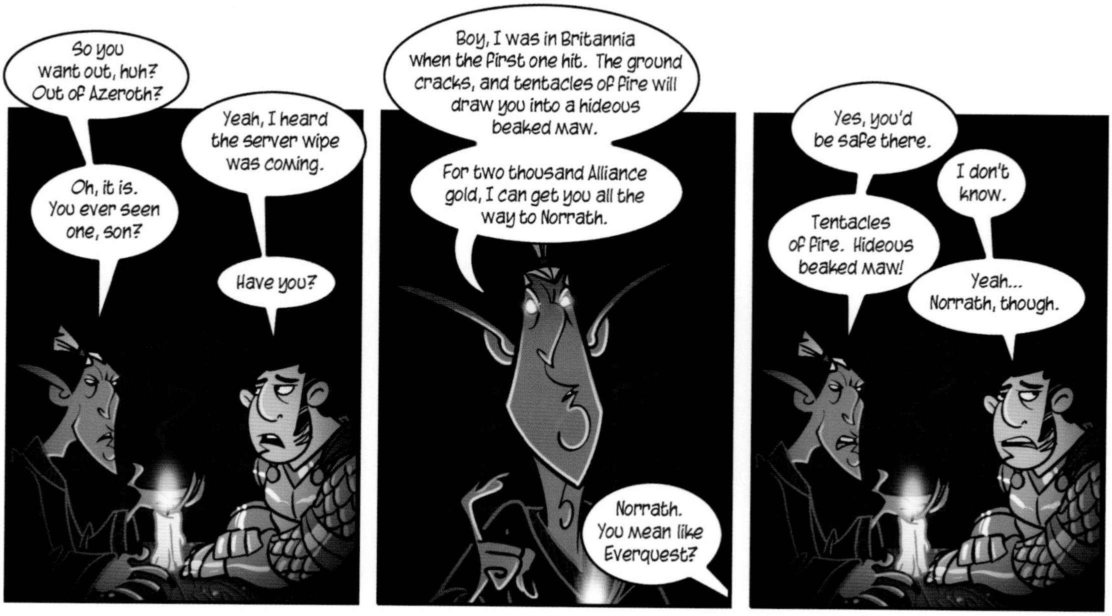
So you want out, huh? Out of Azeroth?
Yeah, I heard the server wipe was coming.
Oh, it is. You ever seen one, son?
Have you?
Boy, I was in Britannia when the first one hit. The ground cracks, and tentacles of fire will draw you into a hideous beaked maw.
For two thousand Alliance gold, I can get you all the way to Norrath.
Norrath. You mean like Everquest?
Yes, you'd be safe there.
I don't know.
Tentacles of fire. Hideous beaked maw!
Yeah... Norrath, though.

A LITERAL SPIGOT OF RAVENOUS DEAD

November 19, 2004 We were talking about toys before, right? Okay, so if the Tycho figure gets the helmet and gloves, maybe Gabe gets the coat? Or would you prefer the Dreamcast? Certainly, there should be a tiny *watch*, over which great battles could be fought.

DEVIL'S BARGAIN

November 22, 2004 Of course, leave it up to *me* to generate a way in which even server wipes can be considered canonical. The idea that characters can go and be anywhere is probably a relic from Planescape, the extraordinary D&D expansion that gave you a means of connecting any two places, *anywhere*, in addition to being a breathtaking setting in its own right.

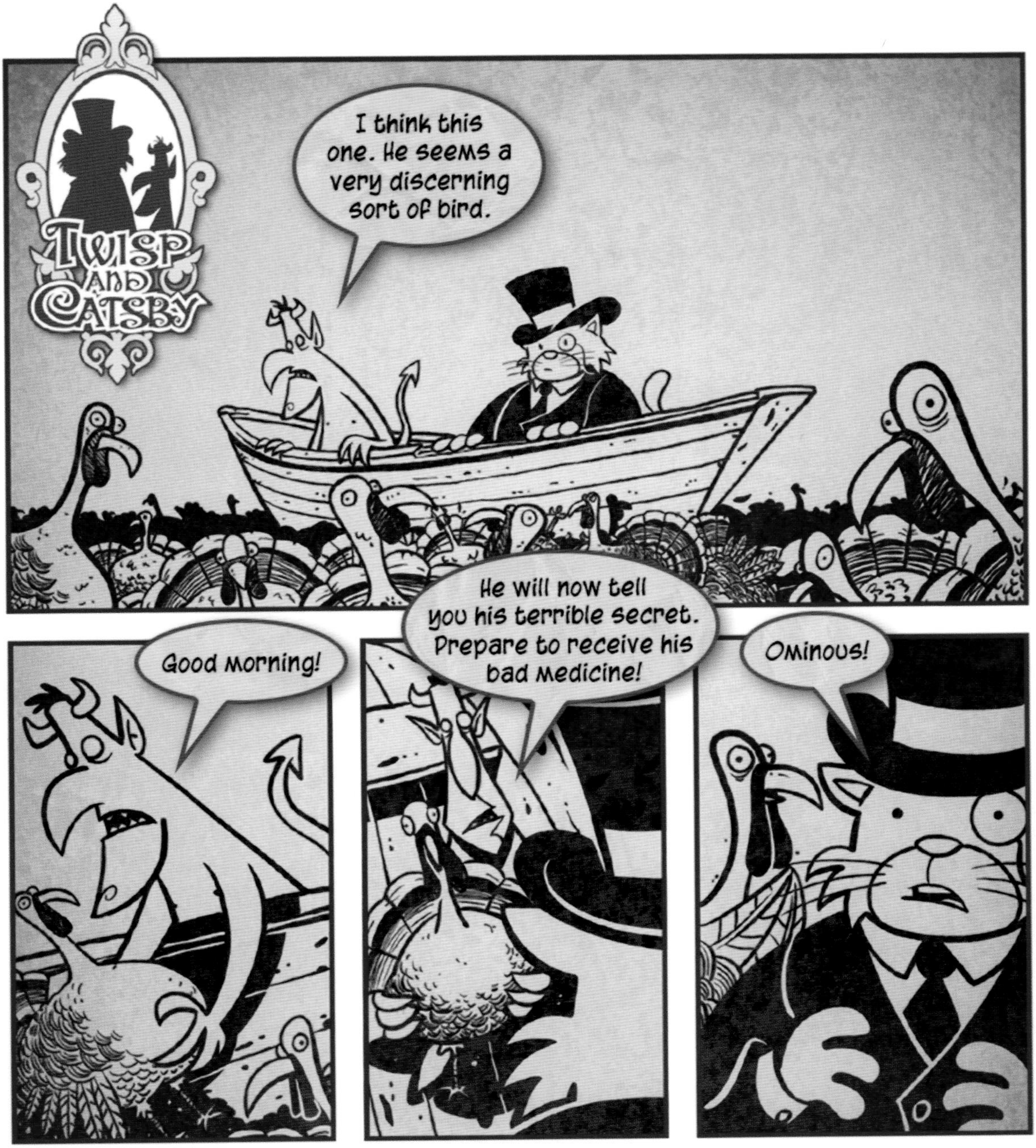
TWISP AND CATSBY
I think this one. He seems a very discerning sort of bird.
Good Morning!
He will now tell you his terrible secret. Prepare to receive his bad medicine!
Ominous!

TWISP & CATSBY IN: THE BIRDSEA

November 24, 2004 Every Twisp & Catsby strip is an interpretation of something very, very specific. Obviously, this is Thanksgiving. *Obviously.*

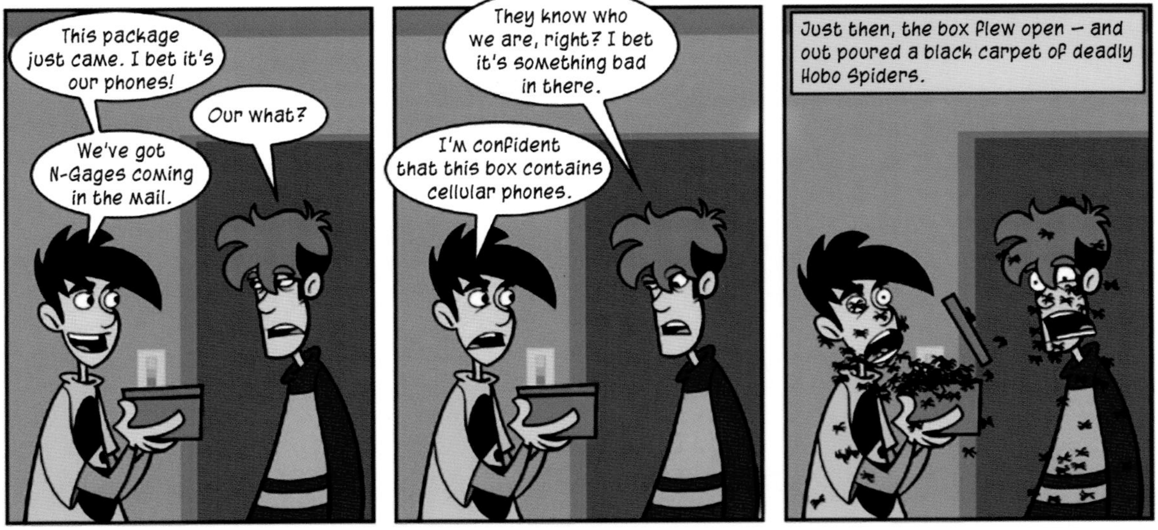
This package just came. I bet it's our phones!
We've got N-Gages coming in the mail.
Our what?
They know who we are, right? I bet it's something bad in there.
I'm confident that this box contains cellular phones.
Just then, the box flew open – and out poured a black carpet of deadly Hobo Spiders.

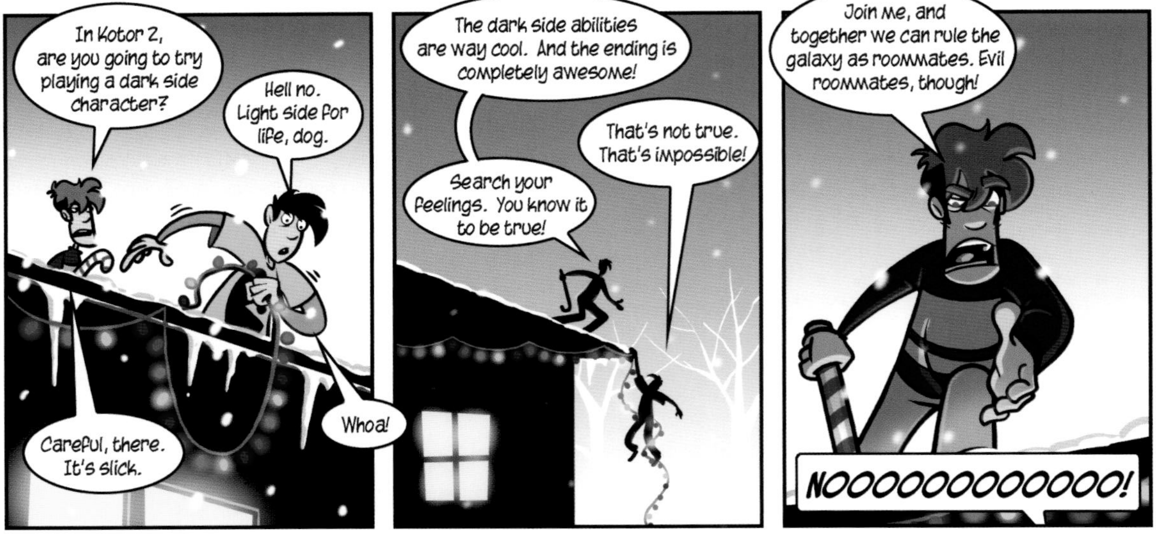
In Kotor 2, are you going to try playing a dark side character?
Hell no. Light side for life, dog.
Careful, there. It's slick.
Whoa!
The dark side abilities are way cool. And the ending is completely awesome!
Search your feelings. You know it to be true!
That's not true. That's impossible!
Join me, and together we can rule the galaxy as roommates. Evil roommates, though!
NOOOOOOOOOOOO!

SPIDER SURPRISE

November 26, 2004 After month upon month of brutality, Nokia *still* sent us review copies of a game along with two phones in what I described as a "strange self-flagellation ritual." What was even *stranger* is the fact that I actually liked the game they sent along. It's an asynchronous strategy game, which is a perfect fit for a cellular handheld. It wasn't some port from a home console, trying to make the phone something it wasn't.

PARALLELS

November 29, 2004 The same thing happened again with Mass Effect, of course. I was a bad, bad man. Or woman, in this case. But I was bad! Elysia Shepard was an engine of cruel battlefield efficiency who felt that the only way to be sure was to nuke the site from orbit. I still think they should have made that an option.

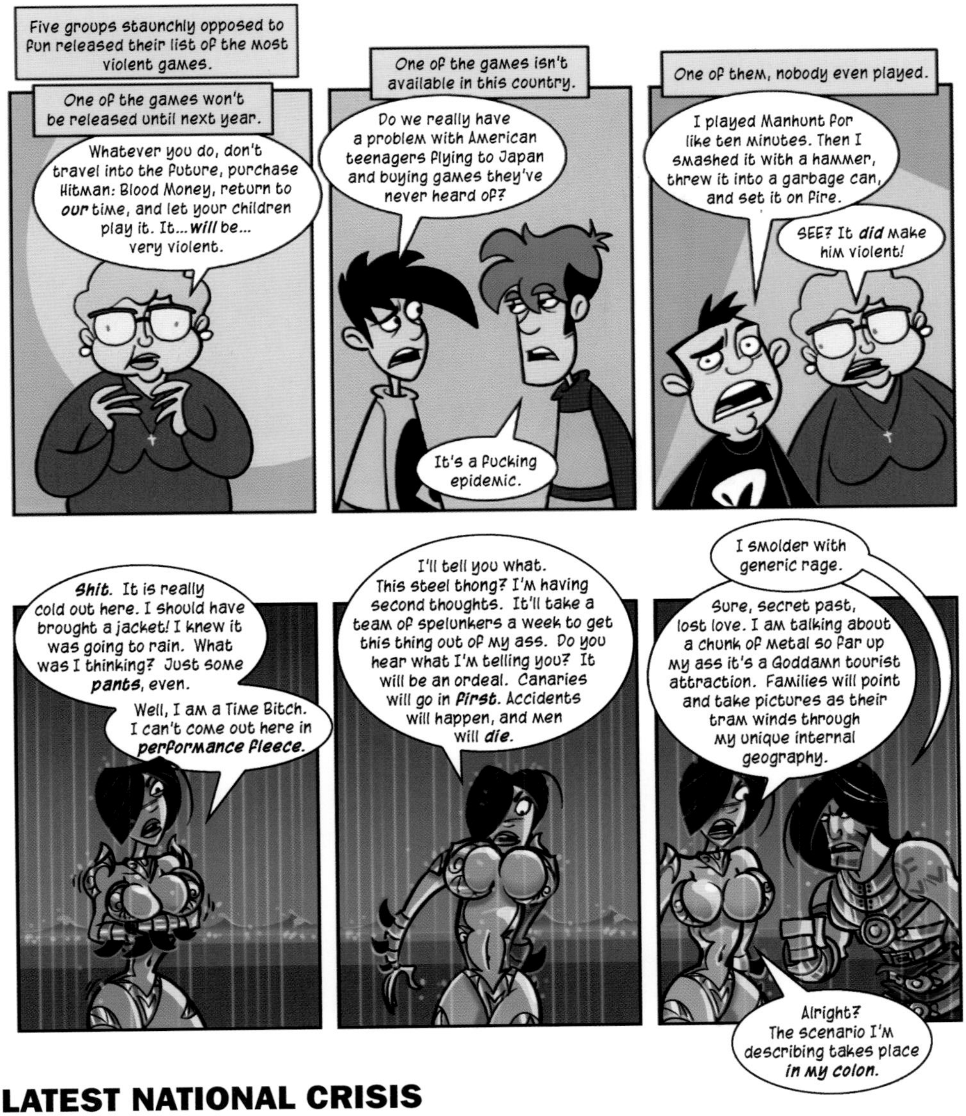
Five groups staunchly opposed to fun released their list of the most violent games.
One of the games won't be released until next year.
Whatever you do, don't travel into the future, purchase Hitman: Blood Money, return to *our* time, and let your children play it. It... *will* be... very violent.
One of the games isn't available in this country.
Do we really have a problem with American teenagers flying to Japan and buying games they've never heard of?
It's a fucking epidemic.
One of them, nobody even played.
I played Manhunt for like ten minutes. Then I smashed it with a hammer, threw it into a garbage can, and set it on fire.
SEE? It *did* make him violent!
Shit. It is really cold out here. I should have brought a jacket! I knew it was going to rain. What was I thinking? Just some *pants*, even.
Well, I am a Time Bitch. I can't come out here in *performance fleece.*
I'll tell you what. This steel thong? I'm having second thoughts. It'll take a team of spelunkers a week to get this thing out of my ass. Do you hear what I'm telling you? It will be an ordeal. Canaries will go in *first.* Accidents will happen, and men will *die.*
I smolder with generic rage.
Sure, secret past, lost love. I am talking about a chunk of metal so far up my ass it's a Goddamn tourist attraction. Families will point and take pictures as their tram winds through my unique internal geography.
Alright? The scenario I'm describing takes place *in my colon.*

THE LATEST NATIONAL CRISIS

December 1, 2004 There are always groups that make those scary annual lists of the games that will corrode our youth on contact, but this year was an especially bad one, with games that would never see release in the West and games that wouldn't be out for months. Plus, I don't think parents need any help knowing what goes on in a game which is entitled "Hitman." Odds are good you aren't going to bake any fucking pies.

ON DISCOMFORT

December 3, 2004 We ran ads for the second Prince of Persia based on our enjoyment of the first one, but something happened between these two games to turn the prince we knew into a kind of nu-metal hard rock vocalist. Since then, except in rare cases, we either demand something playable or verify that a demo will be made available. Sometimes our intuition steers us wrong, but we do try our best.

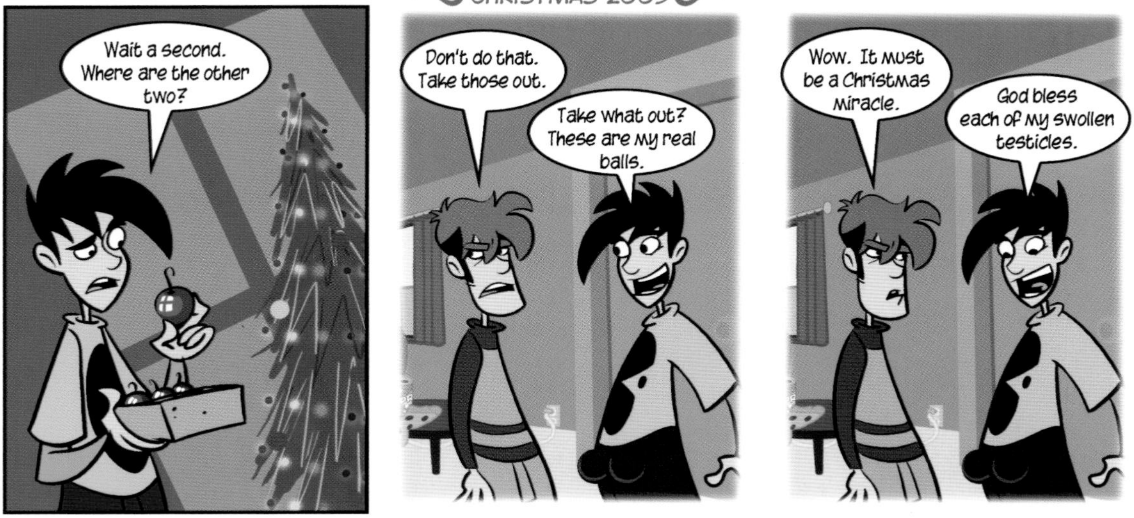
Wait a second. Where are the other two?
Don't do that. Take those out.
Take what out? These are my real balls.
Wow. It must be a Christmas miracle.
God bless each of my swollen testicles.

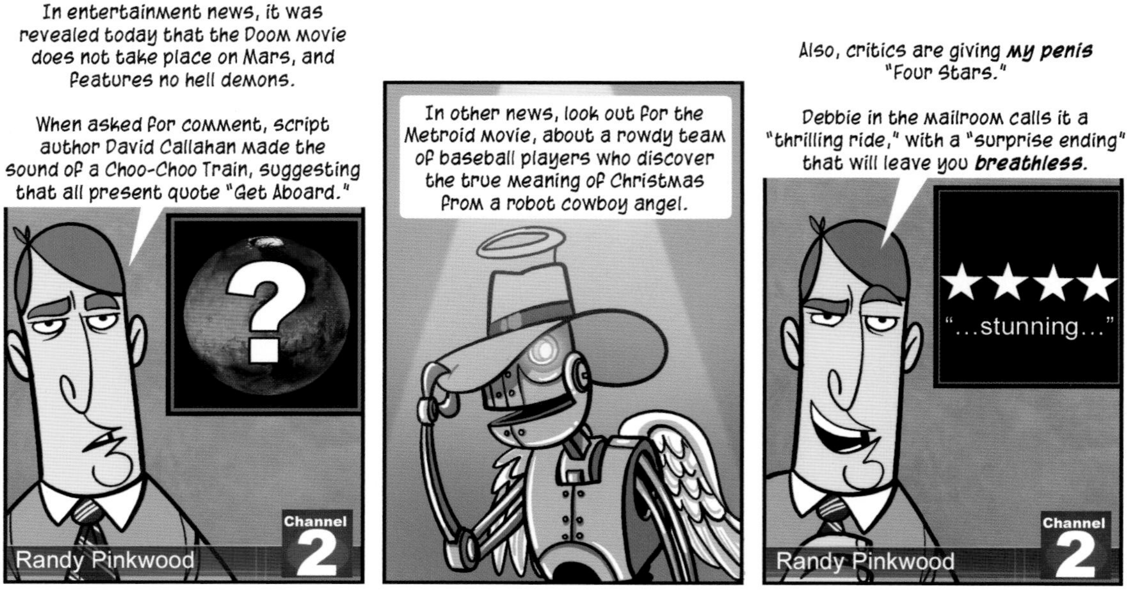
In entertainment news, it was revealed today that the Doom movie does not take place on Mars, and features no hell demons.
When asked for comment, script author David Callahan made the sound of a Choo-Choo Train, suggesting that all present quote "Get Aboard."
Randy Pinkwood
Channel 2
In other news, look out for the Metroid movie, about a rowdy team of baseball players who discover the true meaning of Christmas from a robot cowboy angel.
Also, critics are giving my penis "Four Stars."
Debbie in the mailroom calls it a "thrilling ride," with a "surprise ending" that will leave you breathless.
"...stunning..."
Randy Pinkwood
Channel 2

OSTENTATIOUS ORNAMENTATION

December 6, 2004 He doesn't even *know* when he pulls this kind of crap. We don't go into what happens immediately after that exchange in the strip. But those bulbs are notoriously fragile, and they invariably burst into razor sharp shrapnel at the slightest provocation, so I assume this story ends at or near the emergency room.

AS IT HAPPENS, WITH RANDY PINKWOOD

December 8, 2004 So, here's Randy again. I must occasionally throw a bone in his direction, but it's hard to feel bad about it when he offers up a robot cowboy angel in exchange. Also, that Doom movie thing begged to be mentioned. Doom is only about Hell and demons. Seriously, that's it. There *is* nothing else. If you don't want demons or Hell, then . . . Maybe Doom isn't the best choice?

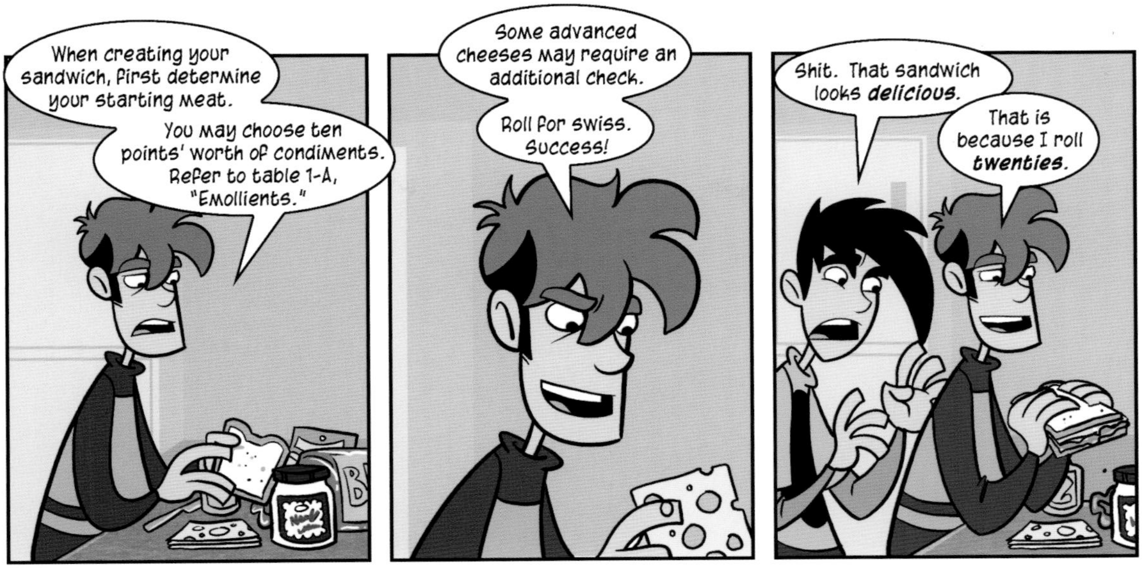
When creating your sandwich, first determine your starting meat.
You may choose ten points' worth of condiments. Refer to table 1-A, "Emollients."
Some advanced cheeses may require an additional check.
Roll for swiss. Success!
Shit. That sandwich looks *delicious.*
That is because I roll *twenties.*

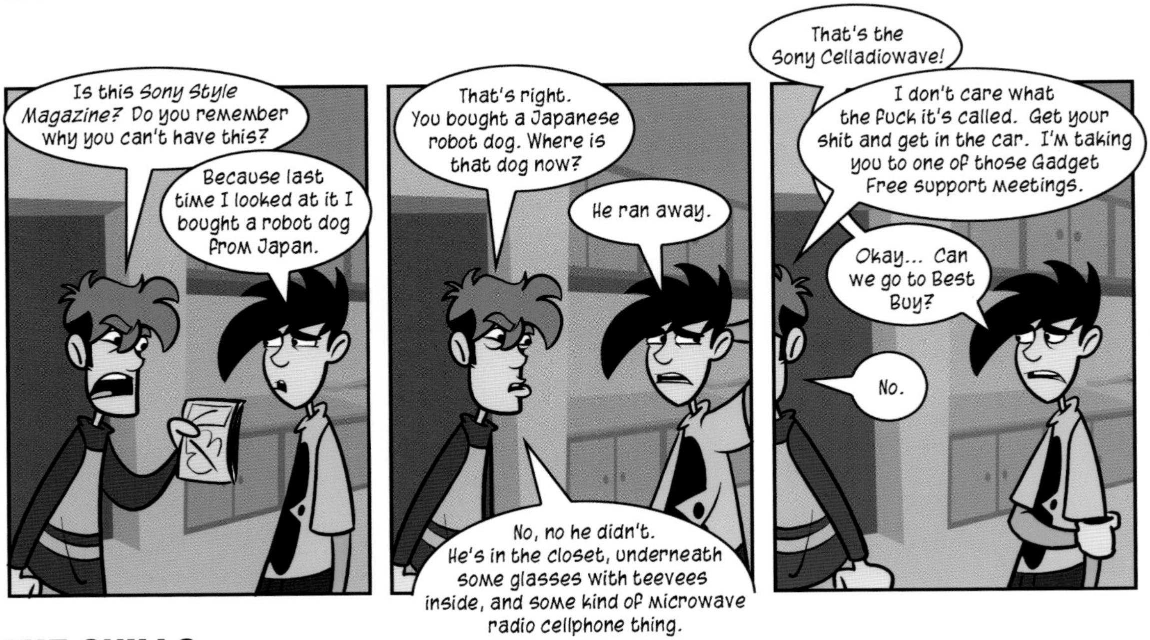
Is this *Sony Style Magazine?* Do you remember why you can't have this?
Because last time I looked at it I bought a robot dog from Japan.
That's right. You bought a Japanese robot dog. Where is that dog now?
He ran away.
No, no he didn't. He's in the closet, underneath some glasses with teevees inside, and some kind of microwave radio cellphone thing.
That's the Sony Celladiowave!
I don't care what the fuck it's called. Get your shit and get in the car. I'm taking you to one of those Gadget Free support meetings.
Okay... Can we go to Best Buy?
No.

THE SKILLS

December 10, 2004 I really want to see the rest of that table—specifically, the rules for critical sandwich failure. I should just crack open OpenOffice and whip that up right now. Not that *I* would ever need it, on account of the *twenties rolling*. This would be for, like, if an *NPC* wanted to make one.

SONY SYNDROME, PART ONE

December 13, 2004 *Sony Style* magazine had ceased publication by this point, which we weren't aware of—we just imagined it floating on forever, emitting its dangerous rays and making people buy dogbots and head-mounted "Hatellites" that look great while they receive data. He hungers for tech deep down in his soul, and the publication was a kind of pornography for him.

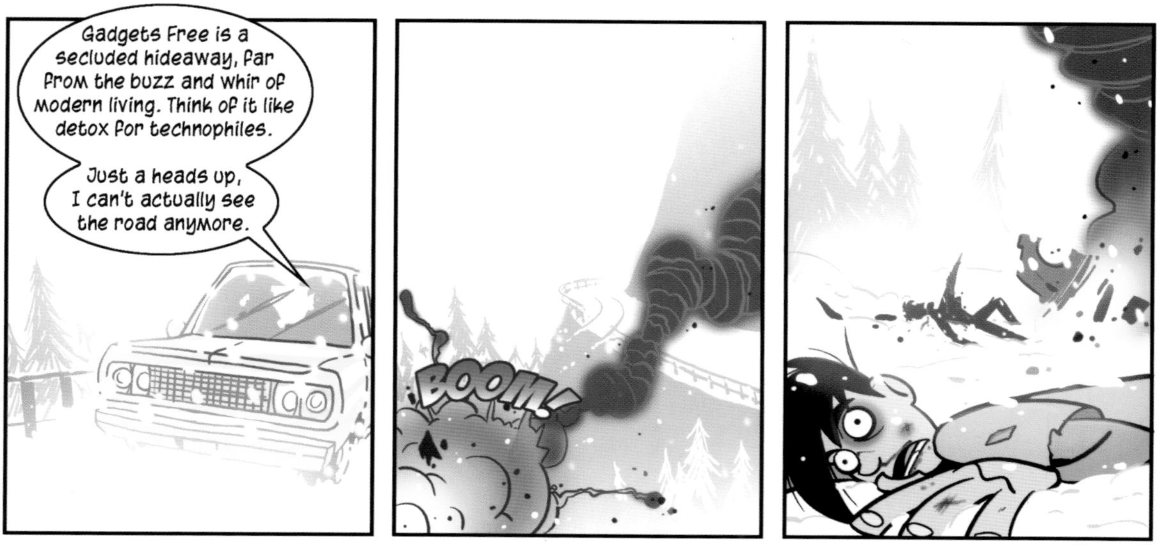
Gadgets Free is a secluded hideaway, far from the buzz and whir of modern living. Think of it like detox for technophiles.
Just a heads up, I can't actually see the road anymore.
BOOM!

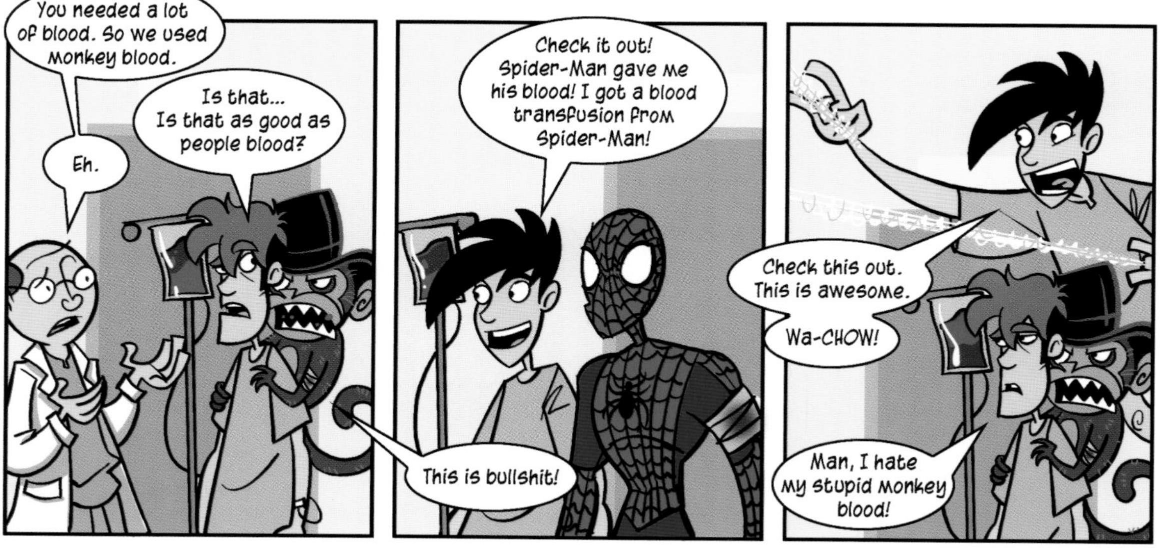
You needed a lot of blood. So we used monkey blood.
Is that... Is that as good as people blood?
Eh.
Check it out! Spider-Man gave me his blood! I got a blood transfusion from Spider-Man!
This is bullshit!
Check this out. This is awesome.
Wa-CHOW!
Man, I hate my stupid monkey blood!

SONY SYNDROME, PART TWO

December 15, 2004 This is actually how the strip ended, basically for the year. We went immediately into a Cthulhu storyline afterward so that it wasn't entirely clear what was going on. Again, we don't really have firm, linear time in the strip, so everyone was *probably* fine, but when things like this happen it's because one of them killed the other. We don't just leave the reader with a big pile of corpses and then turn on our heel.

SONY SYNDROME, FINAL

December 29, 2004 See? They're fine! Everybody's *fine*. In fact, Gabe is even better than he was! Though I guess Tycho sorta got boned.

I thought you said we were going to level up together!
Well... We did, mostly. I just played a little bit while you were at work!
A little bit? You're riding a huge cat! And stars are falling all around you!
What are you, like, level two hundred? Million?
It would be difficult to express my level with mundane numbers. I am partially fused with infinity.
Well, *great*. That must be really nice for you.

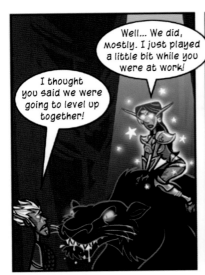

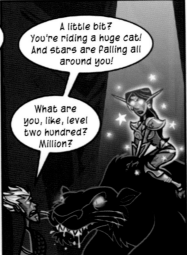

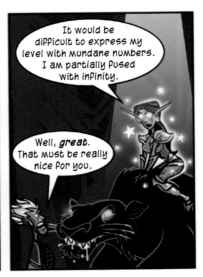

A BEING OF INDESCRIBABLE POWER

December 31, 2004 It's precisely these disparities that instigated my most recent departure from WoW and from the genre in general. There's simply too much enjoyment to be had in the breadth of this medium to play a single game, but every time you play a game that is *not* World of Warcraft you're severely punished for it. These gulfs grow and grow until you and your friends might as well be playing different games.

THE CHRISTMAS SPECIAL THAT SHOULD NOT BE

December 16-27, 2004 We'd done the We're Right Awards for three or so years at this point, and though we hoped that people would find them interesting it always struck me as a little bit of a cop-out. I don't know that it was, necessarily—we spent just as much time arguing about which games were extraordinary as we would have writing ordinary comics. Even so, if we were going to try and write a couple comics ahead, why not try to execute on something truly ridiculous? I think that's an accurate description of what happened next.

Ladies and gentlemen, I give to you . . .

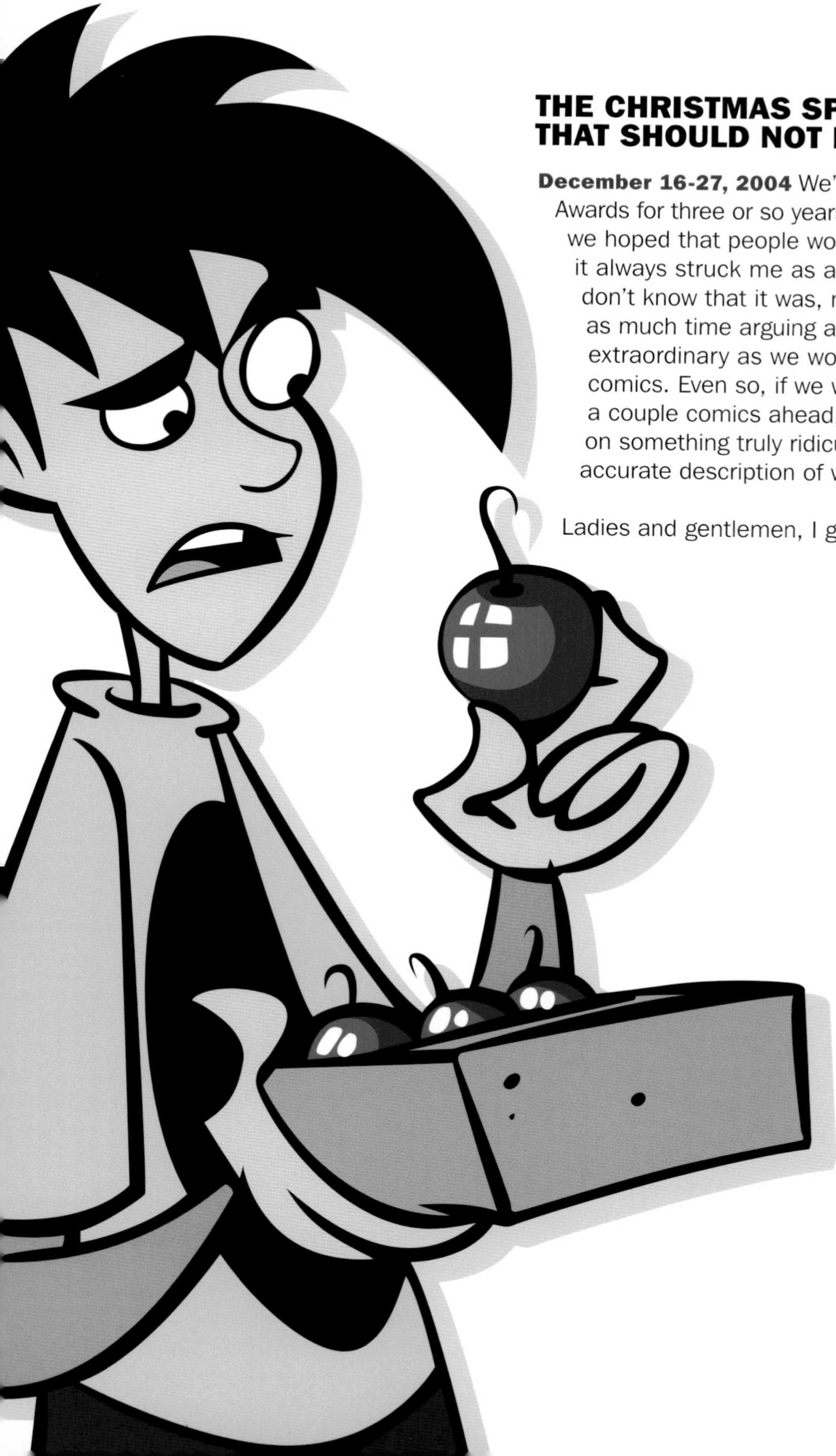

THE LAST CHRISTMAS

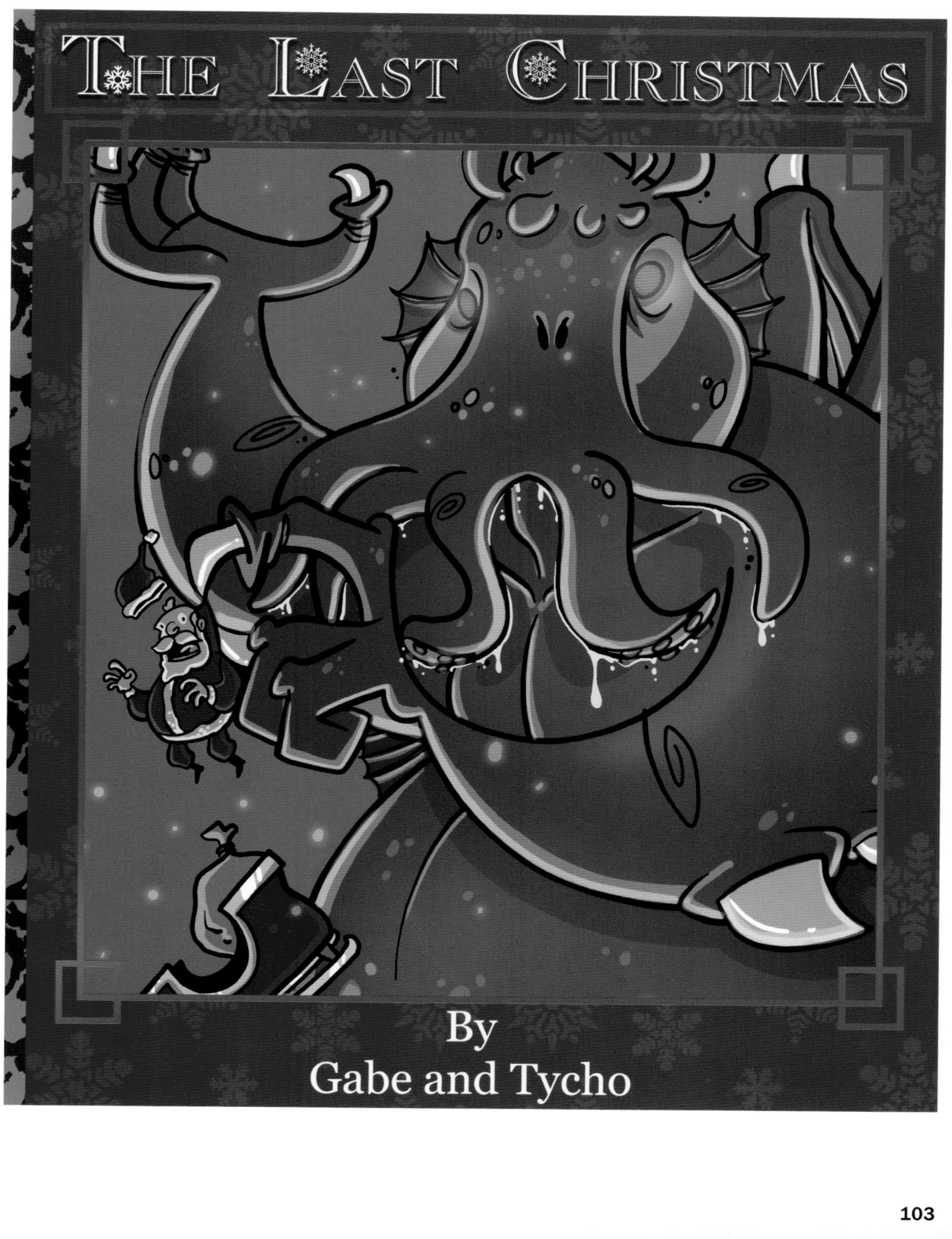

By
Gabe and Tycho

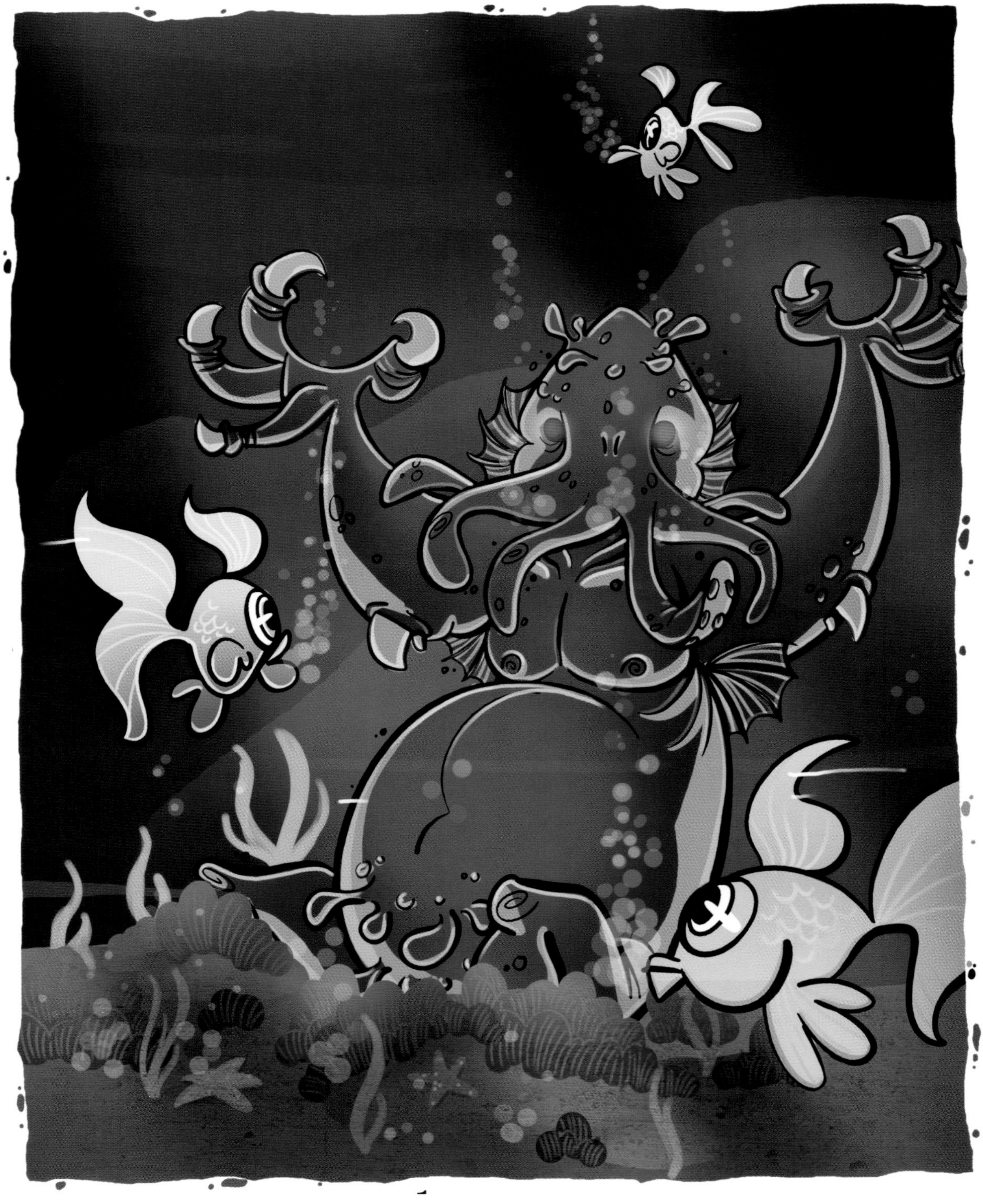

Just as was written in black books of dread

The end of the world came in green and then red

The stars in their sockets, their secrets unfurled

Loosed an alien howl from the womb of the world

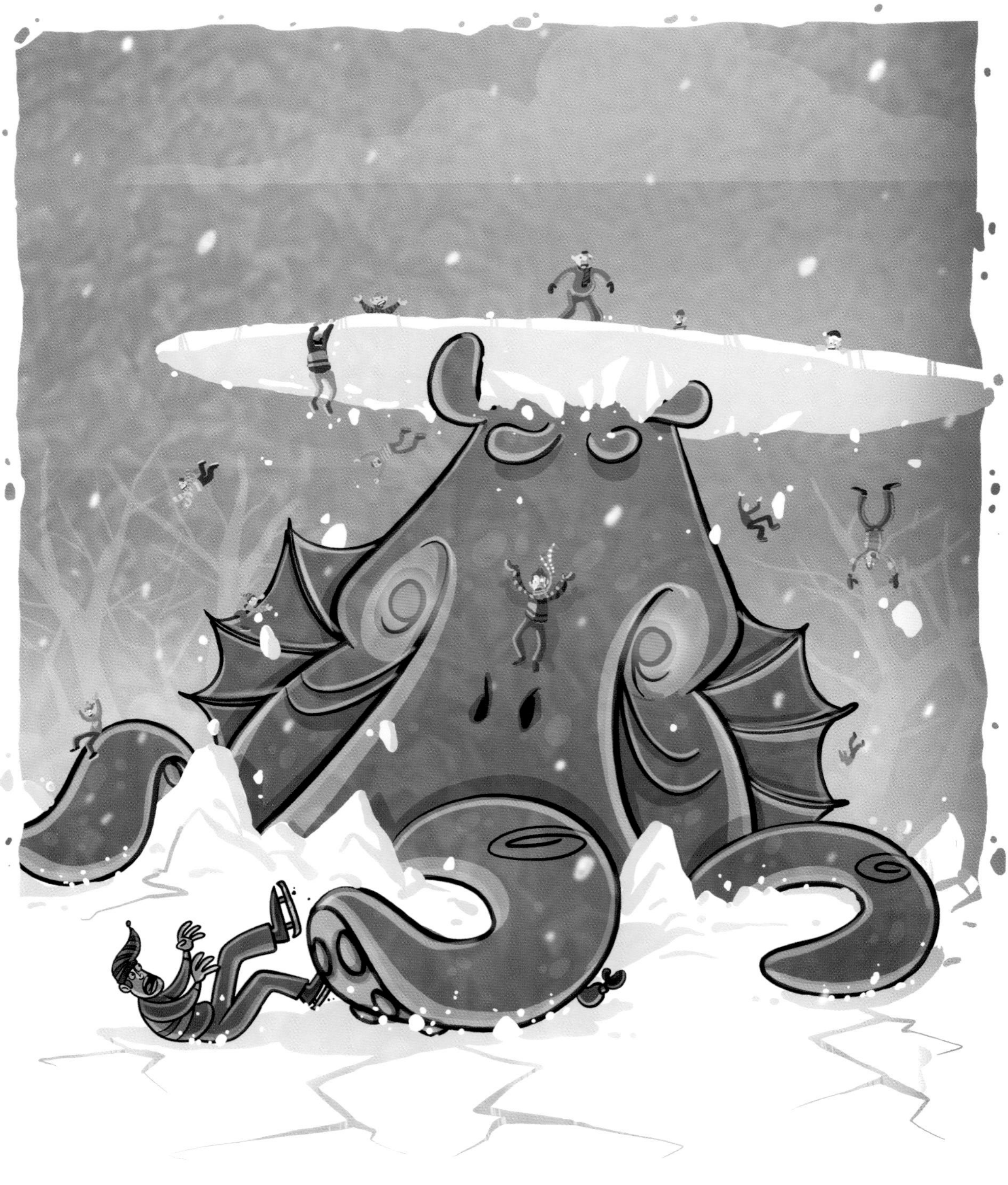

Attractive young couples all laugh as they skate

While under the rink seeds of horror gestate

Everything seemed to be going so nice

'Til the end of all beings punched right through the ice

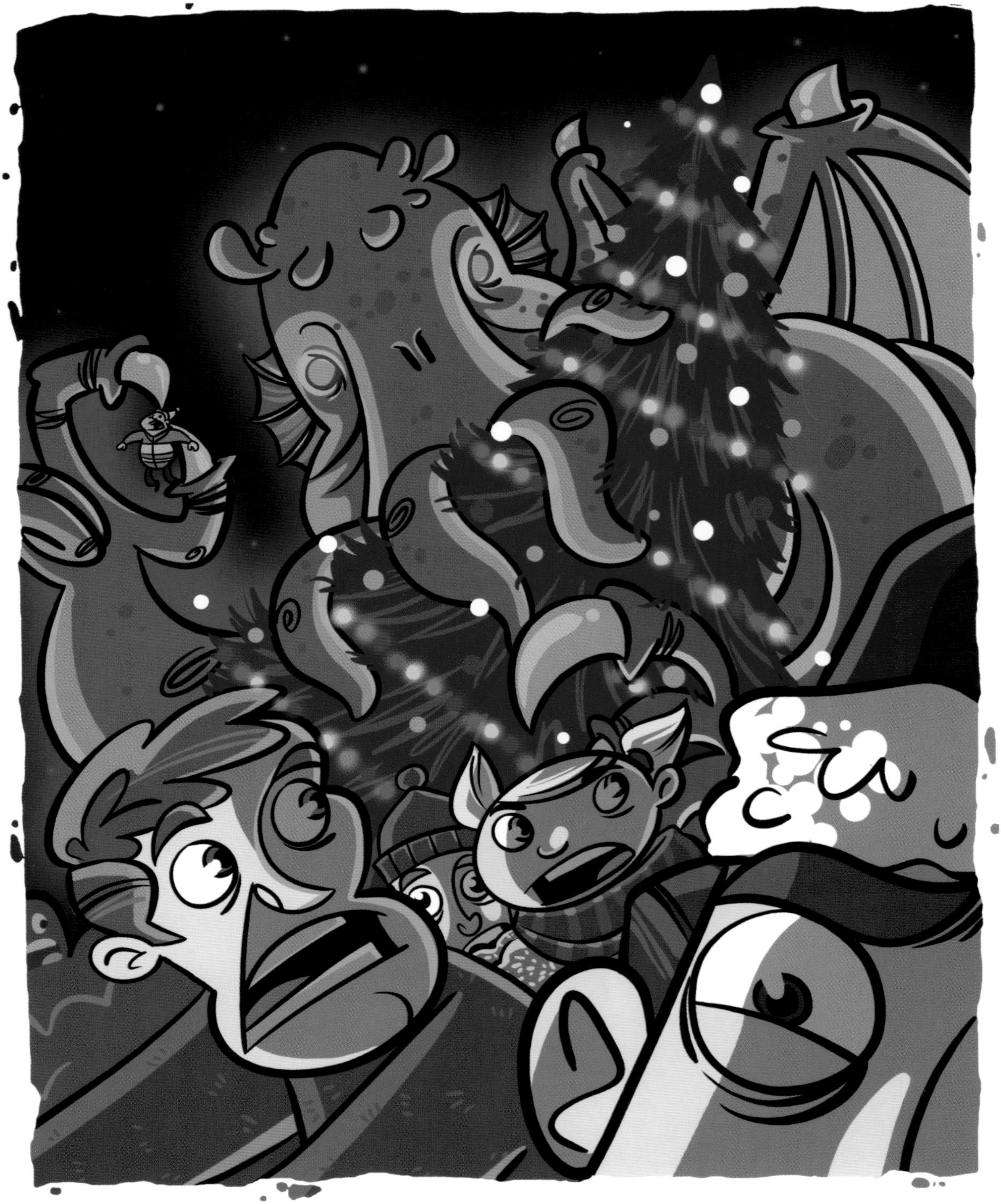

A roar beyond sanity pealed through the air

As grey waves of madness washed over the square

Great Lord Cthulhu munched needle and stem

Chewed benches, ate buildings, crunched women and men

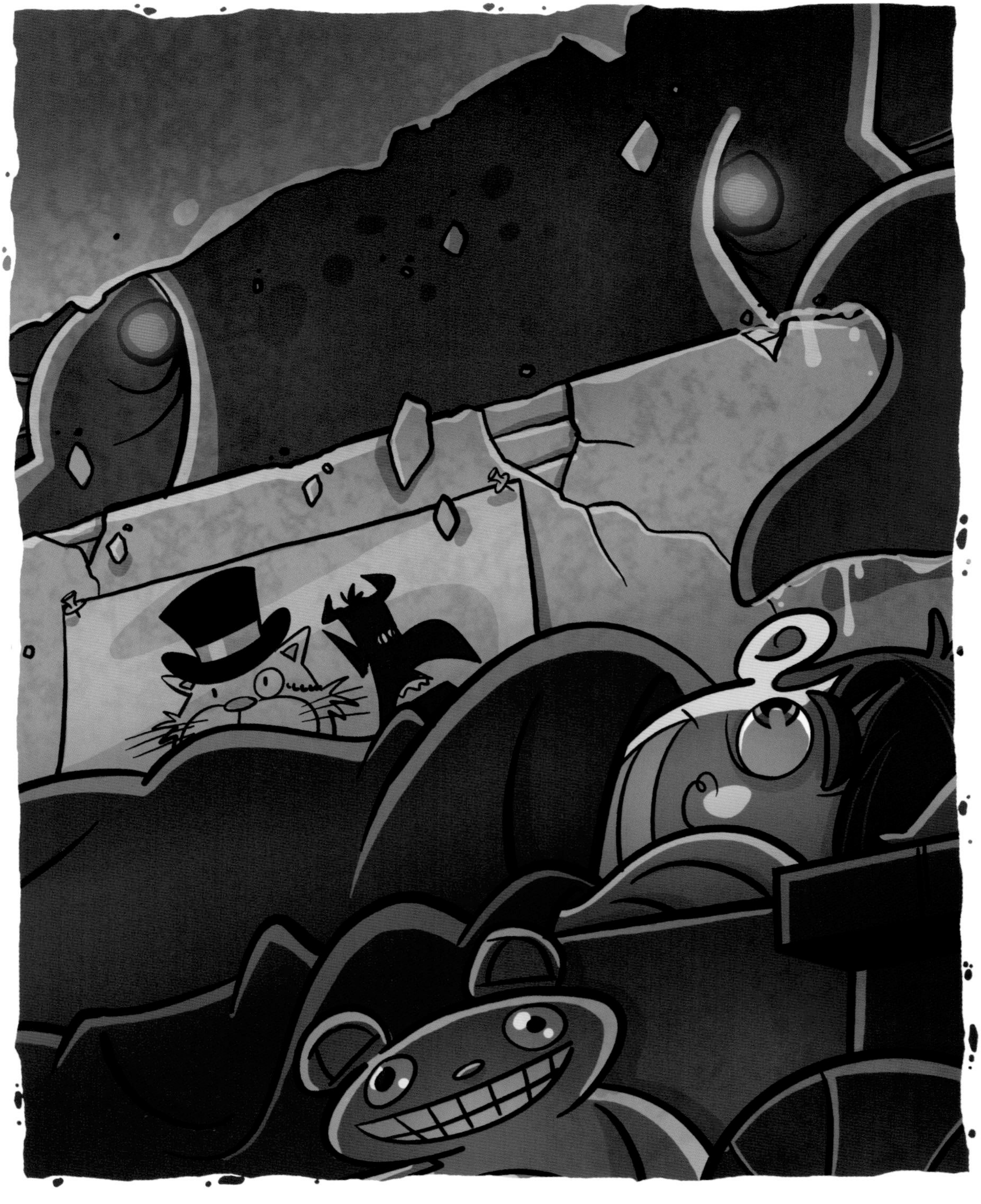

Children were nestled all snug in their beds

When raising the roof came a clammy green head

Young Timmy is actually happy. You see,

The monster he wanted is under the tree!

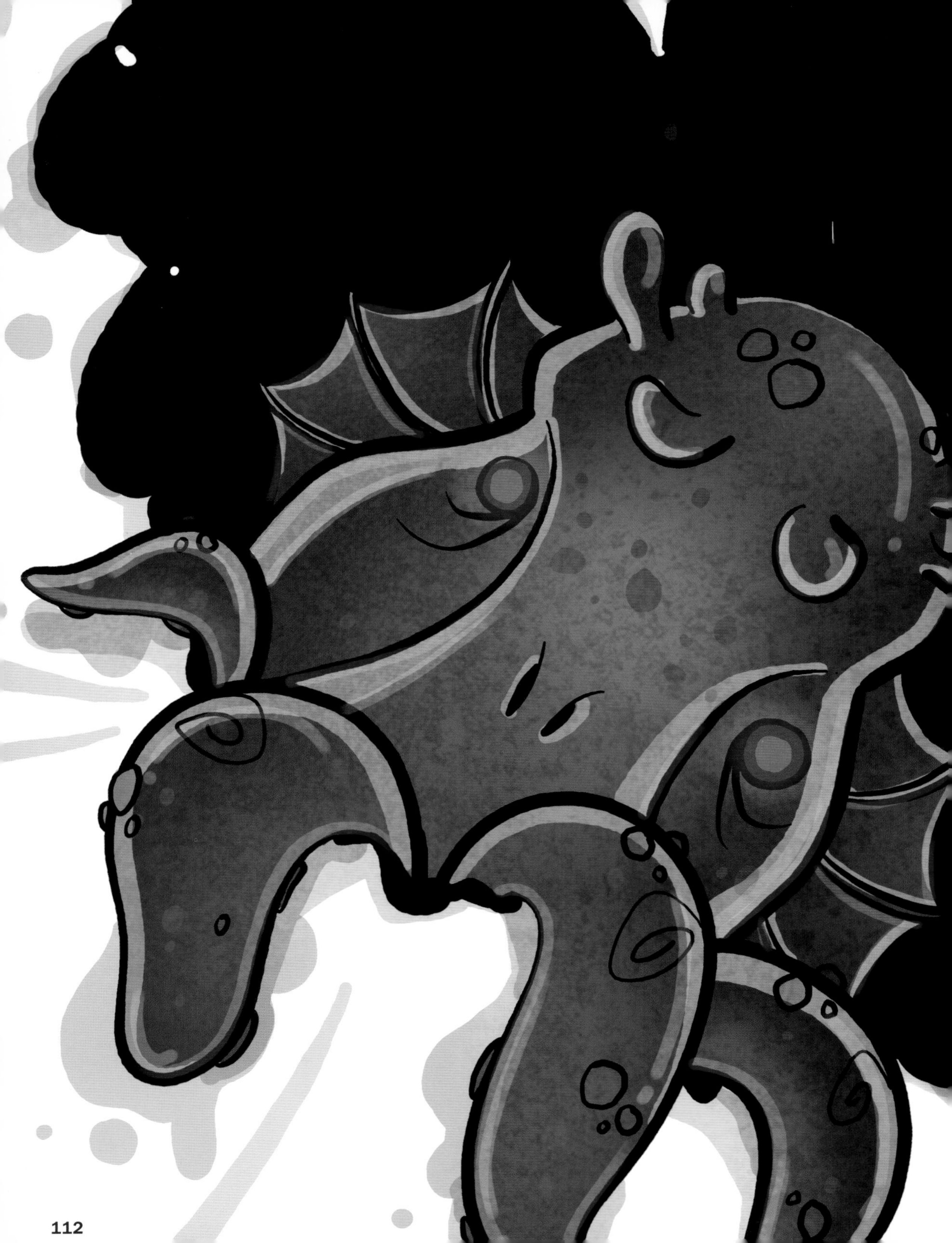

You've read the dire warnings in old pages cryptic,

And seen them play out in ways apocalyptic.

All that exists was devoured, and look!

That hideous horror has eaten the book!

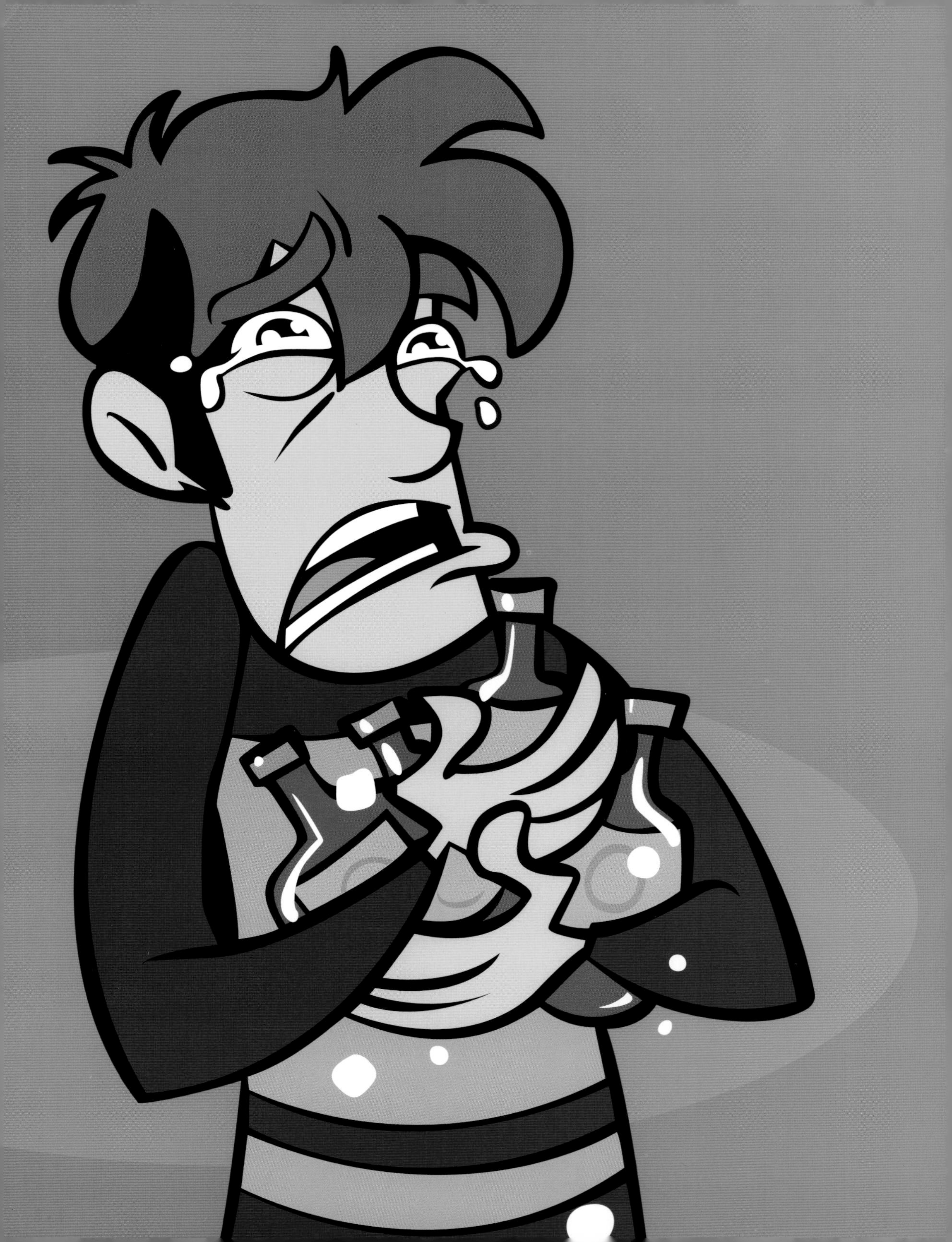

A LITTLE OFF THE TOP

Doodles from the Penny Arcade convention attendances

We attend a few conventions each year, and as a kind of ritual we started to shear the top layer of the tables off at the end of each show. They just staple it on there before the show, it's not really part of the table, and by the end of the long weekend it's usually covered with weird pictures, drawings from readers, and raw ideas.

You'll see notes for a couple strips we ended up doing, and in a couple cases you'll even see the strips themselves. Near the end, you'll find a truly remarkable goat. A couple projects even started on con tables—you'll see the beginning of the Elemenstor Saga, and a couple other secret ones in their primordial form. Remember that Gabe typically sits on the right. I'm not sure why, but that will give you some help with the context—you'll see his DJ table over on that side, complete with his private rave. You'll also see me experimenting over the course of several shows with a powerful, futuristic new signature.

It seemed like something you might find it interesting. Hopefully I was right.

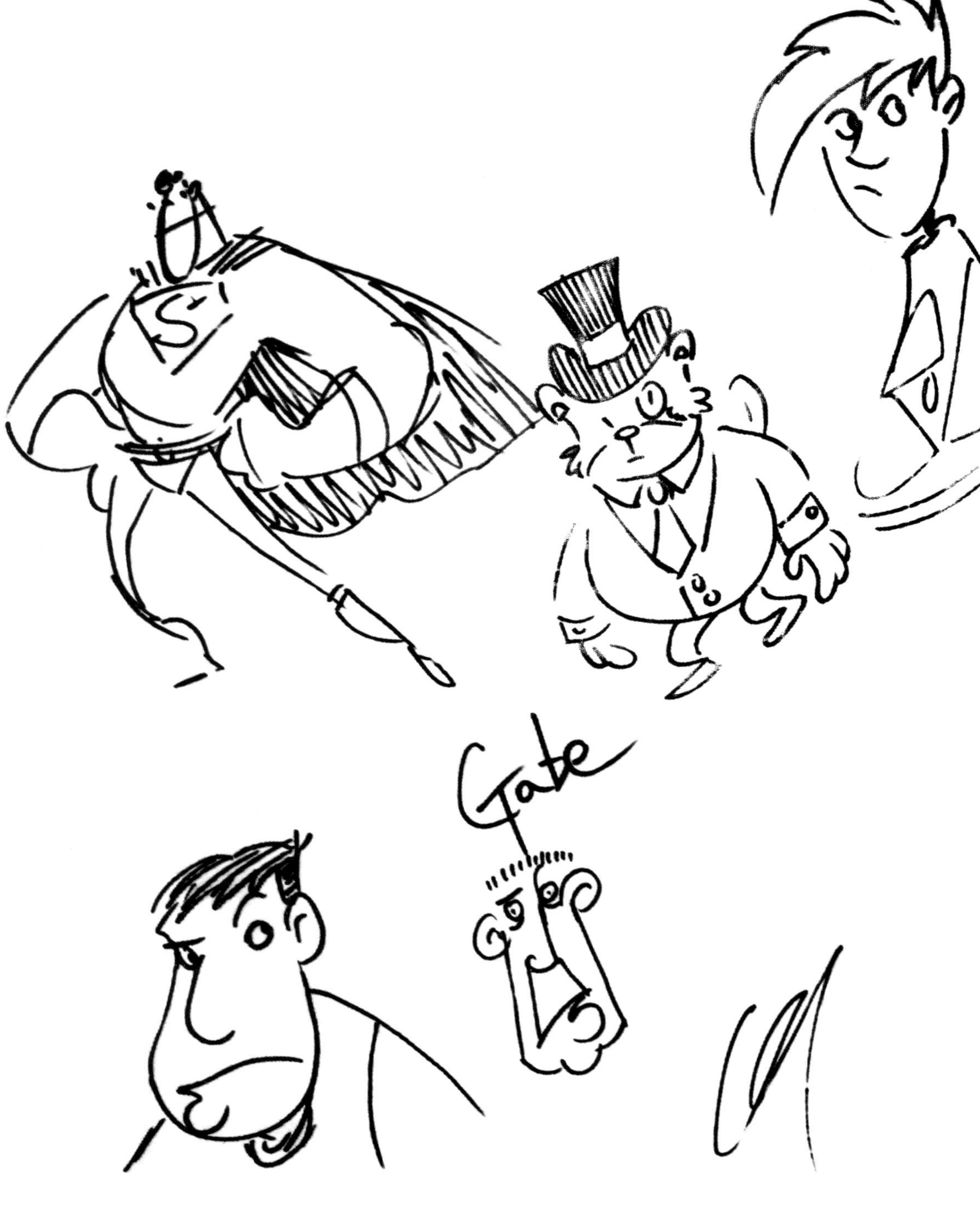
Gate

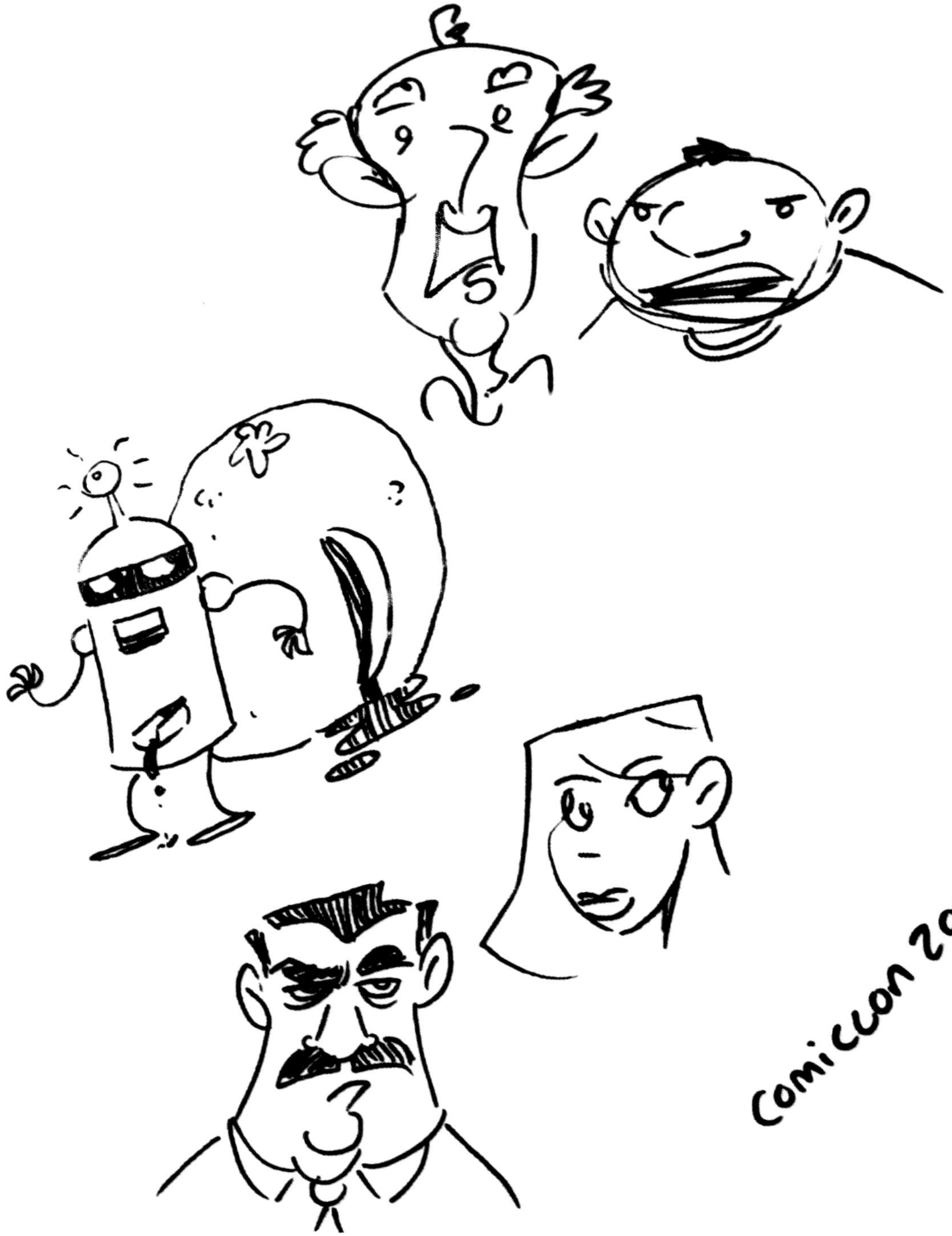
ComiCCon 2005

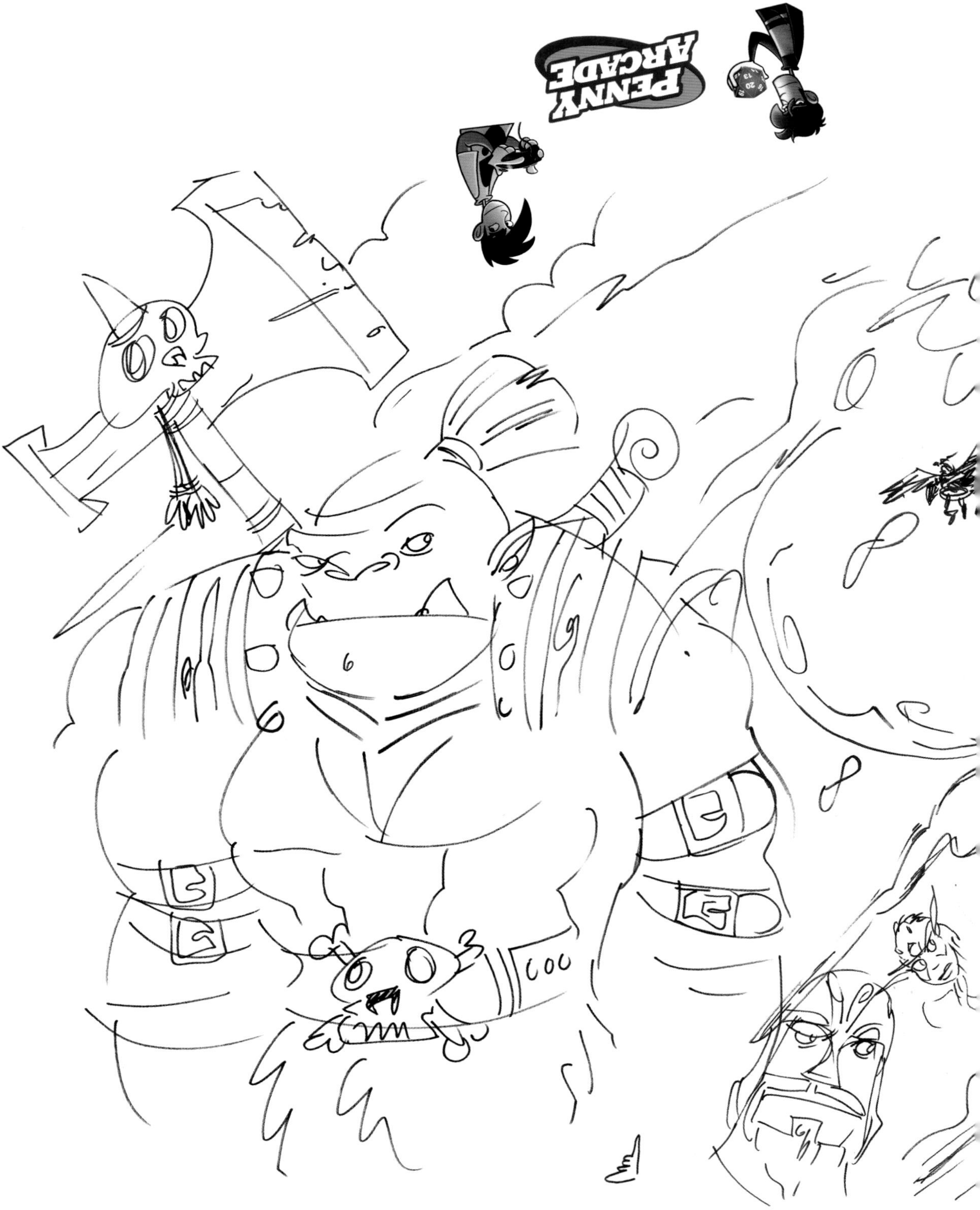
PENNY
ARCADE

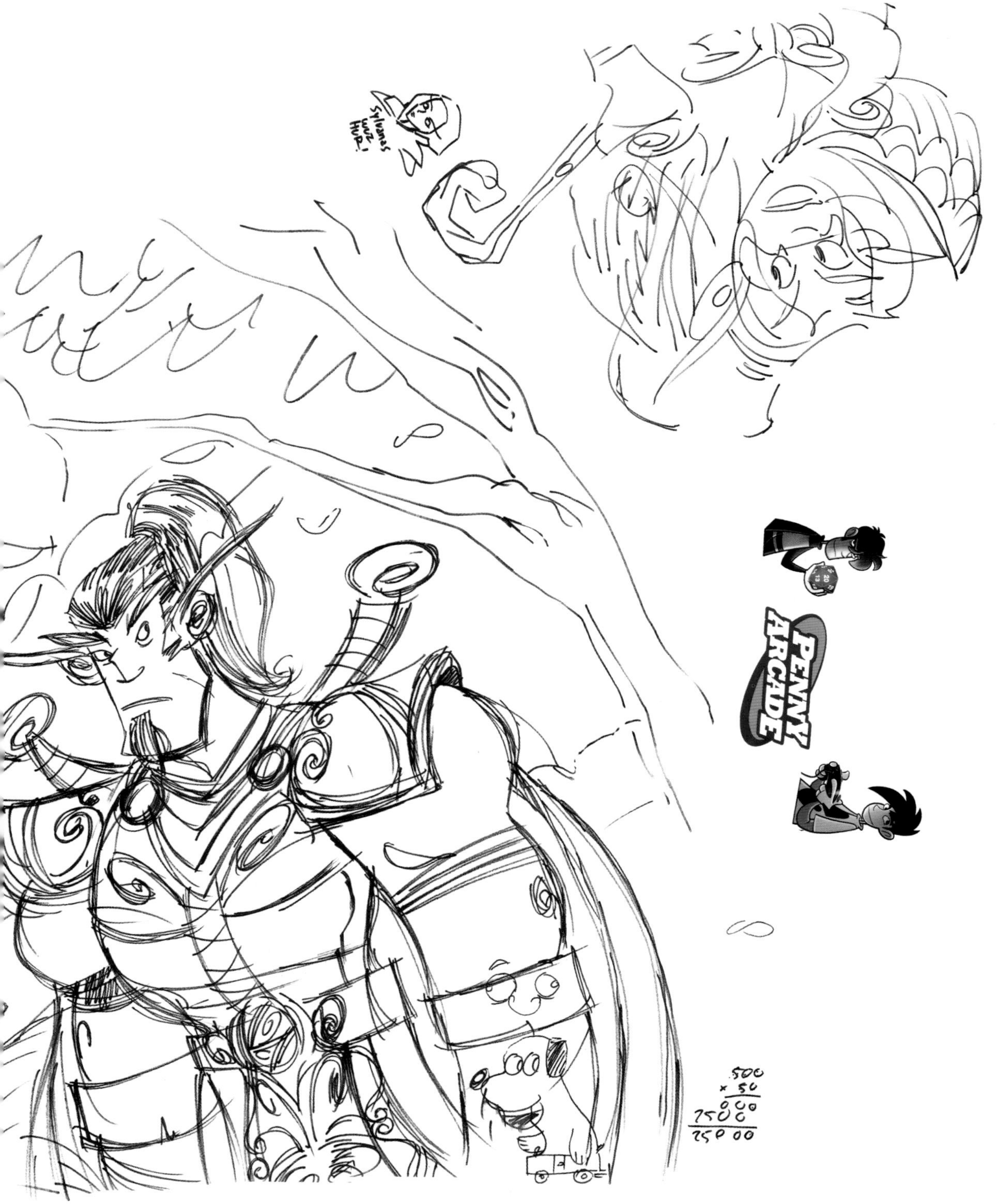
Sylvanas wuz HUR!
PENNY ARCADE

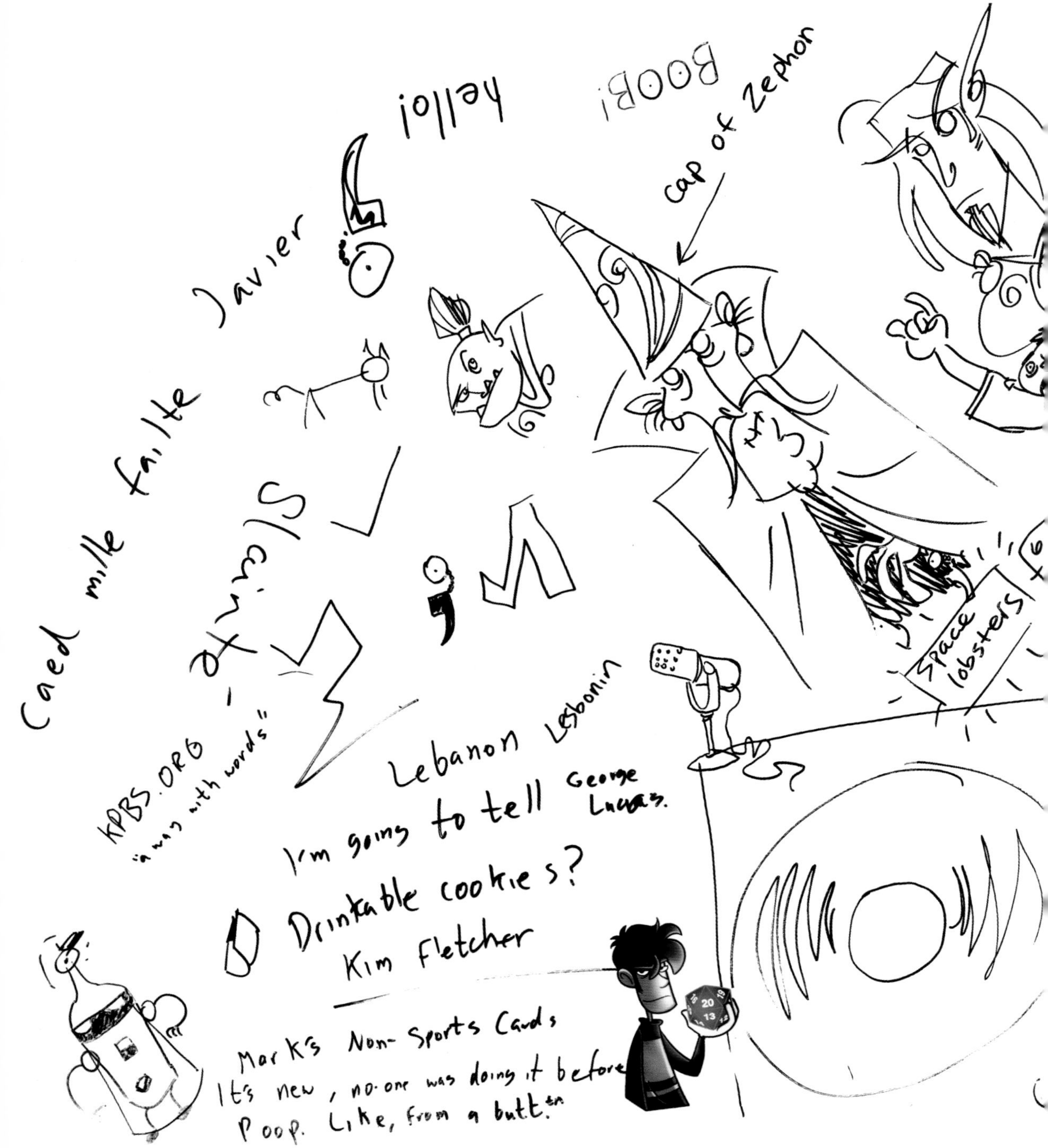
Caed mille failte
Javier
hello!
BOOB!
cap of Zephon
Space lobsters
KPBS.ORG
"in a way with words"
Lebanon Lesbonin
I'm going to tell George Lucas.
Drinkable cookies?
Kim Fletcher
Mark's Non-Sports Cards
It's new, no one was doing it before
Poop. Like, from a butt.

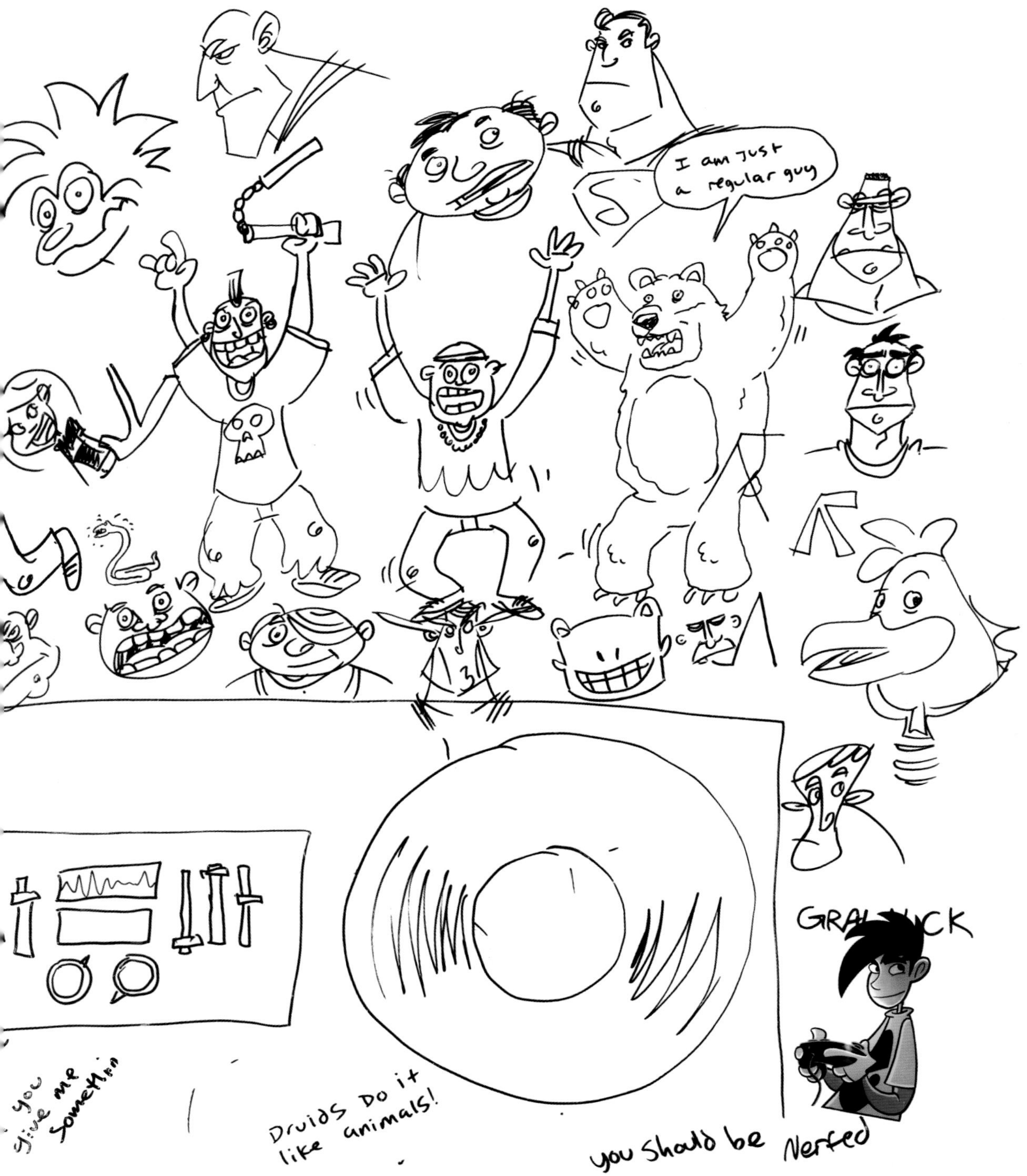
I am just a regular guy
you give me somethin
Druids Do it like animals!
You Should be Nerfed

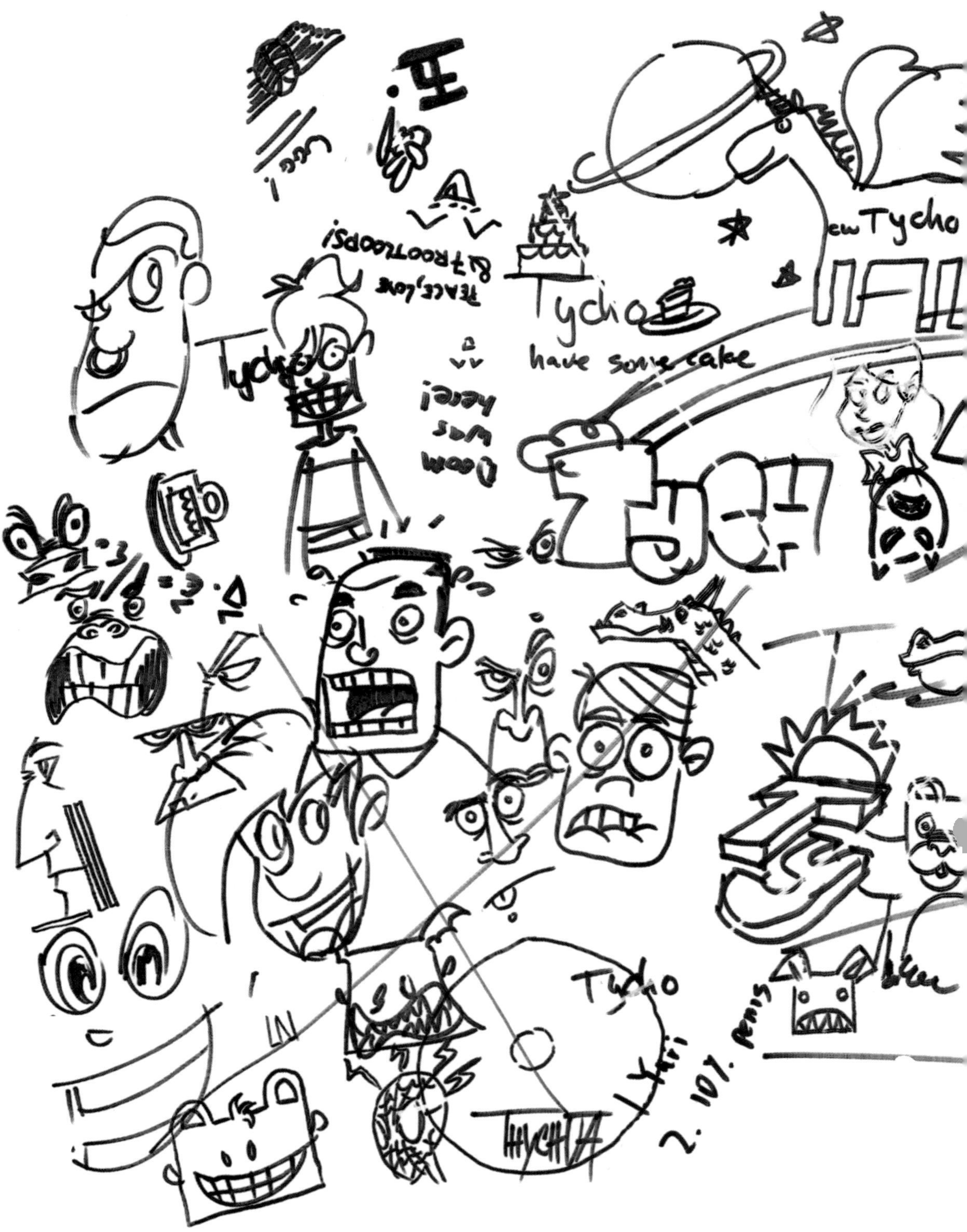
Tycho
have some cake
Tycho
Tycho
Doom was here!

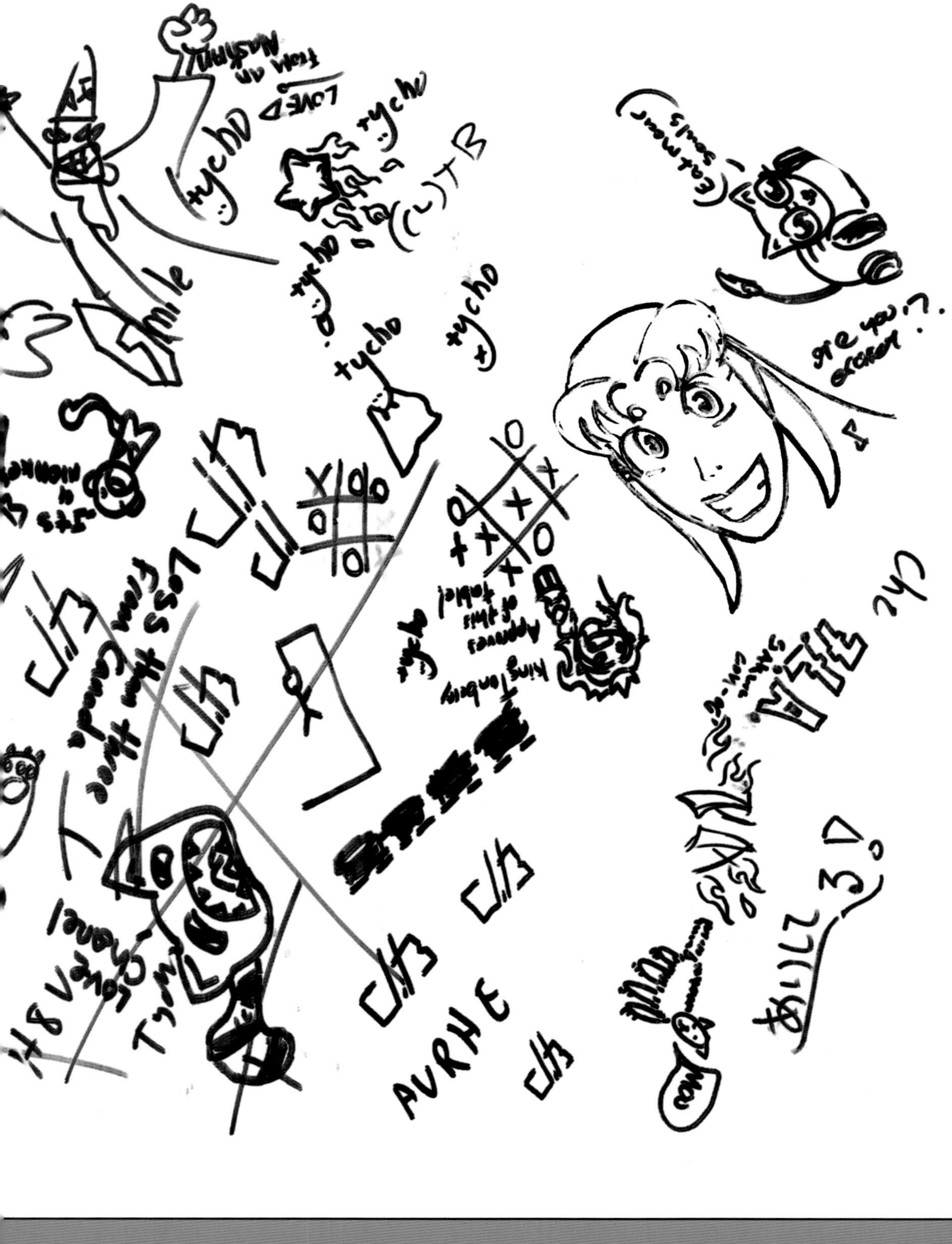
tycho
smile
king tonberry

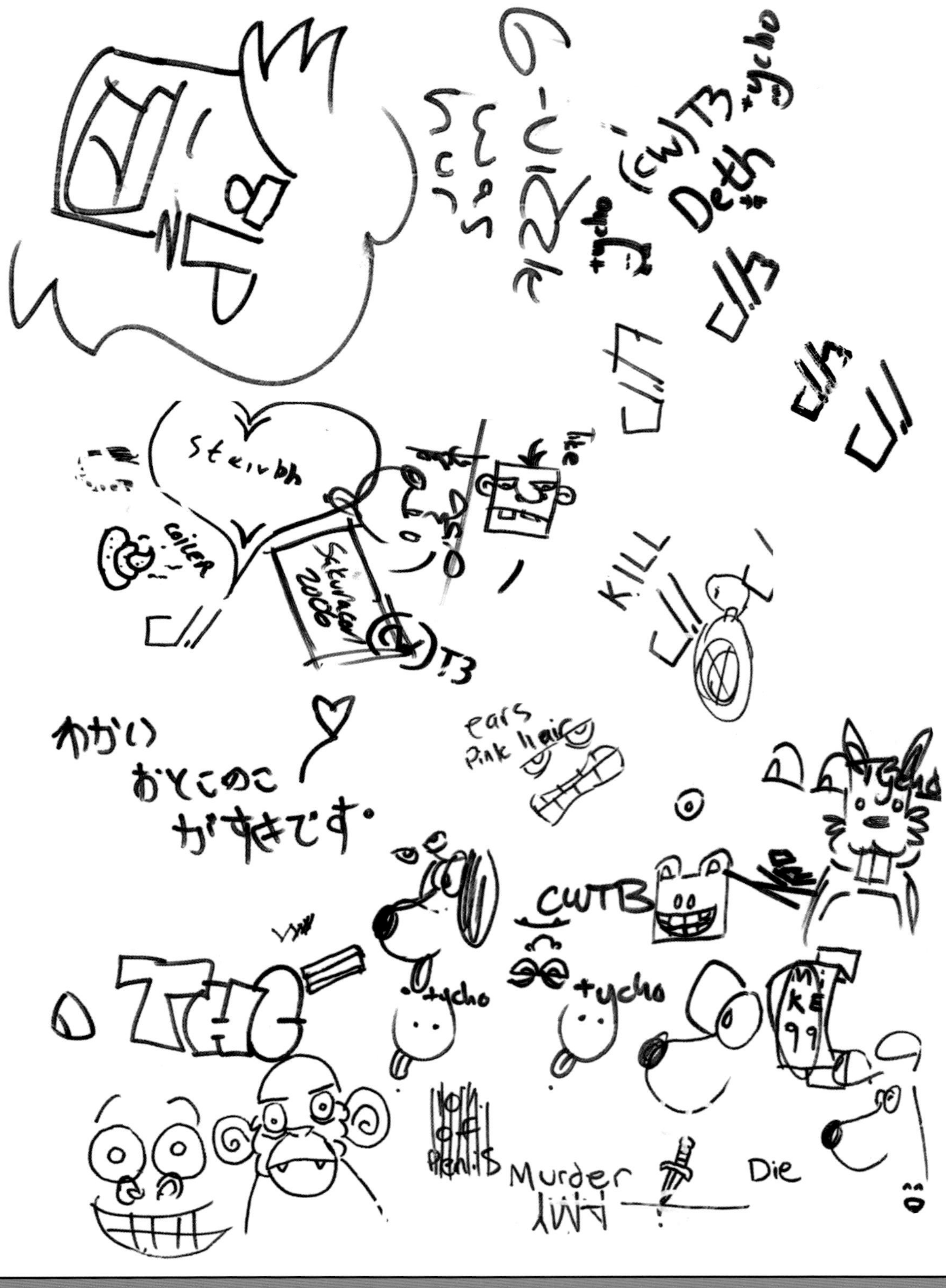

Deth
(cw)T3
KILL
Sakura-Con 2006
ears
Pink hair
かわいい
おとこのこ
がすきです。
CWTB
tycho
tycho
Murder
Die

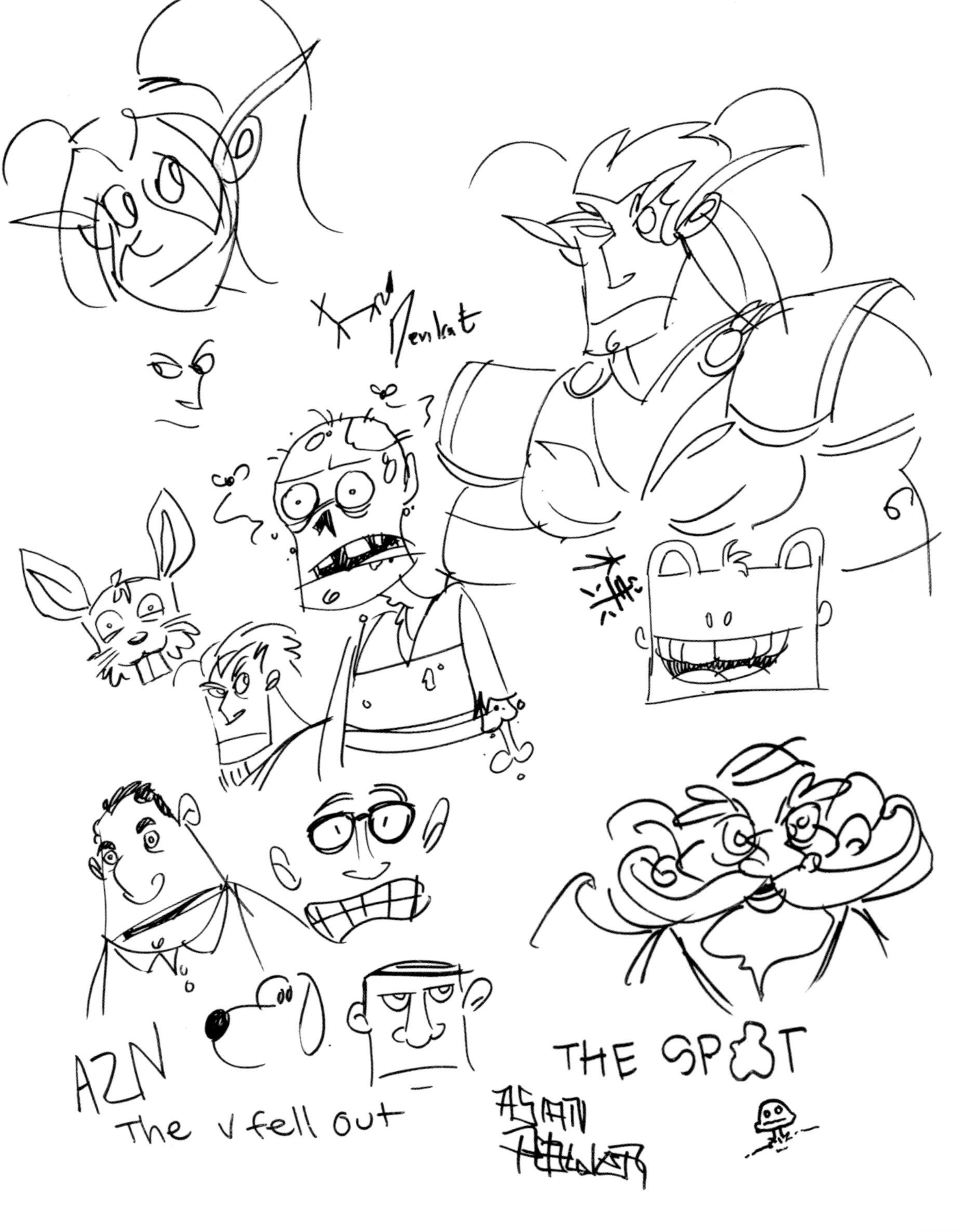
AZN
The v fell out

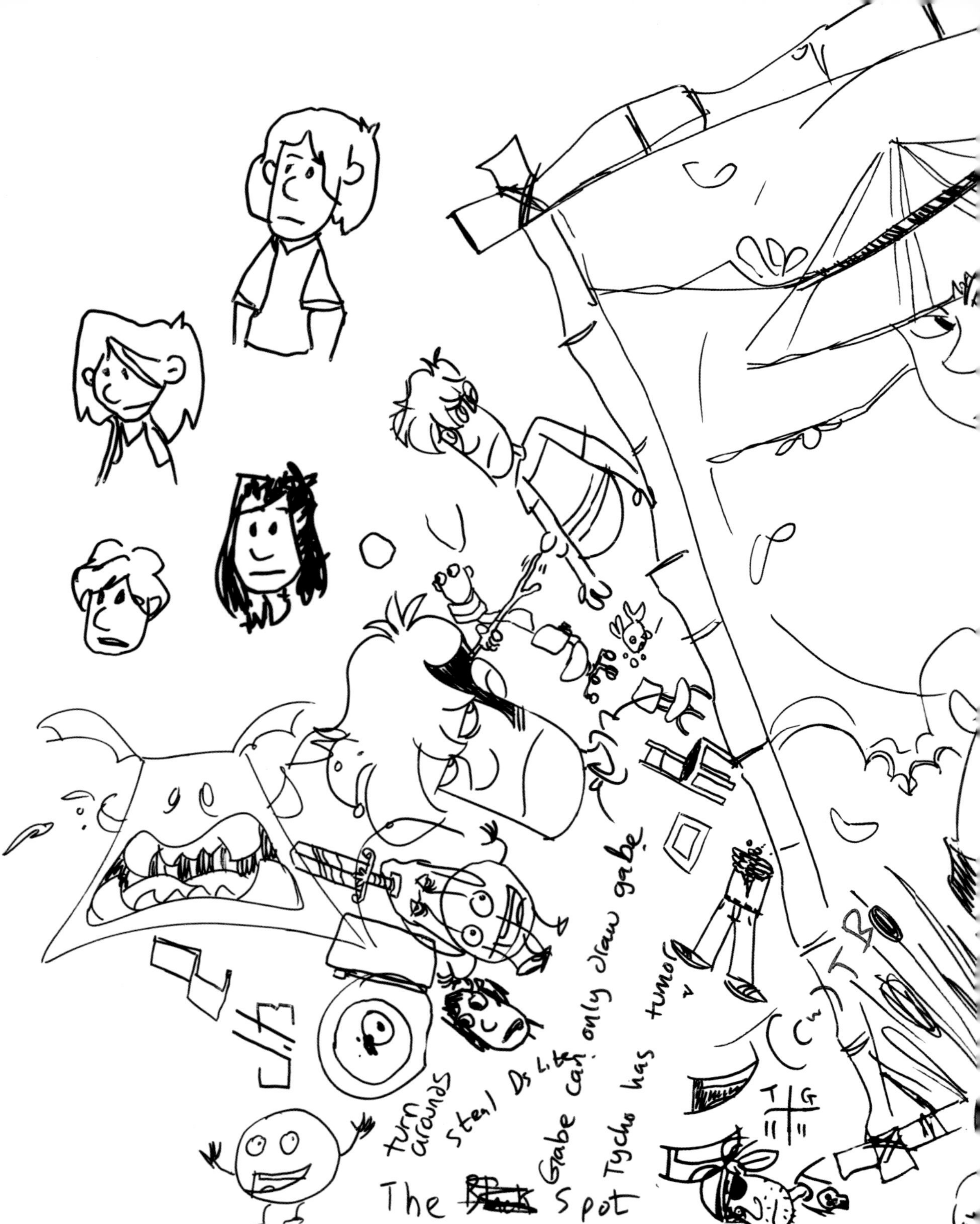
turn arounds
steal Ds Lite
Gabe can only draw gabe
Tycho has tumor
The Black Spot

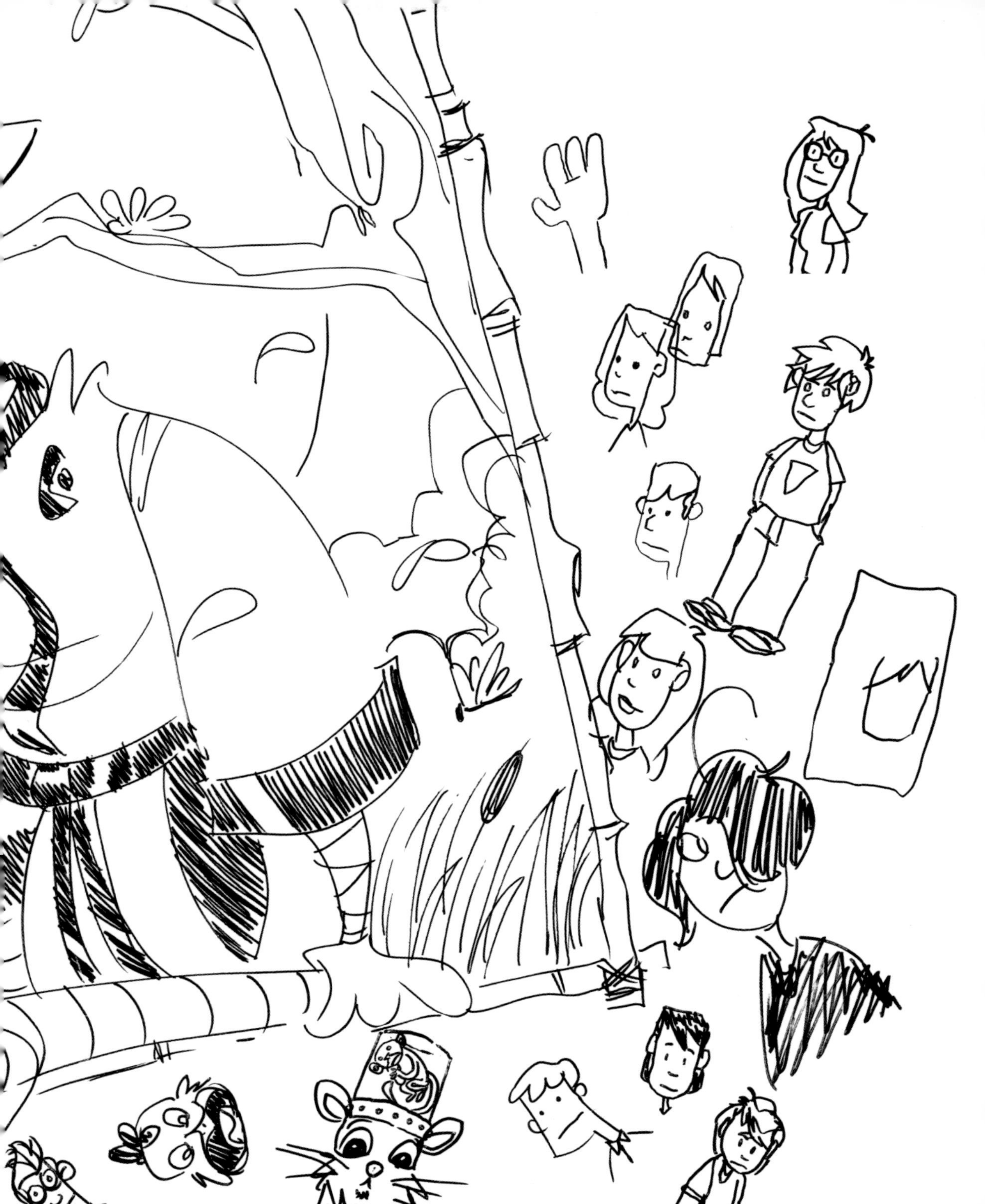

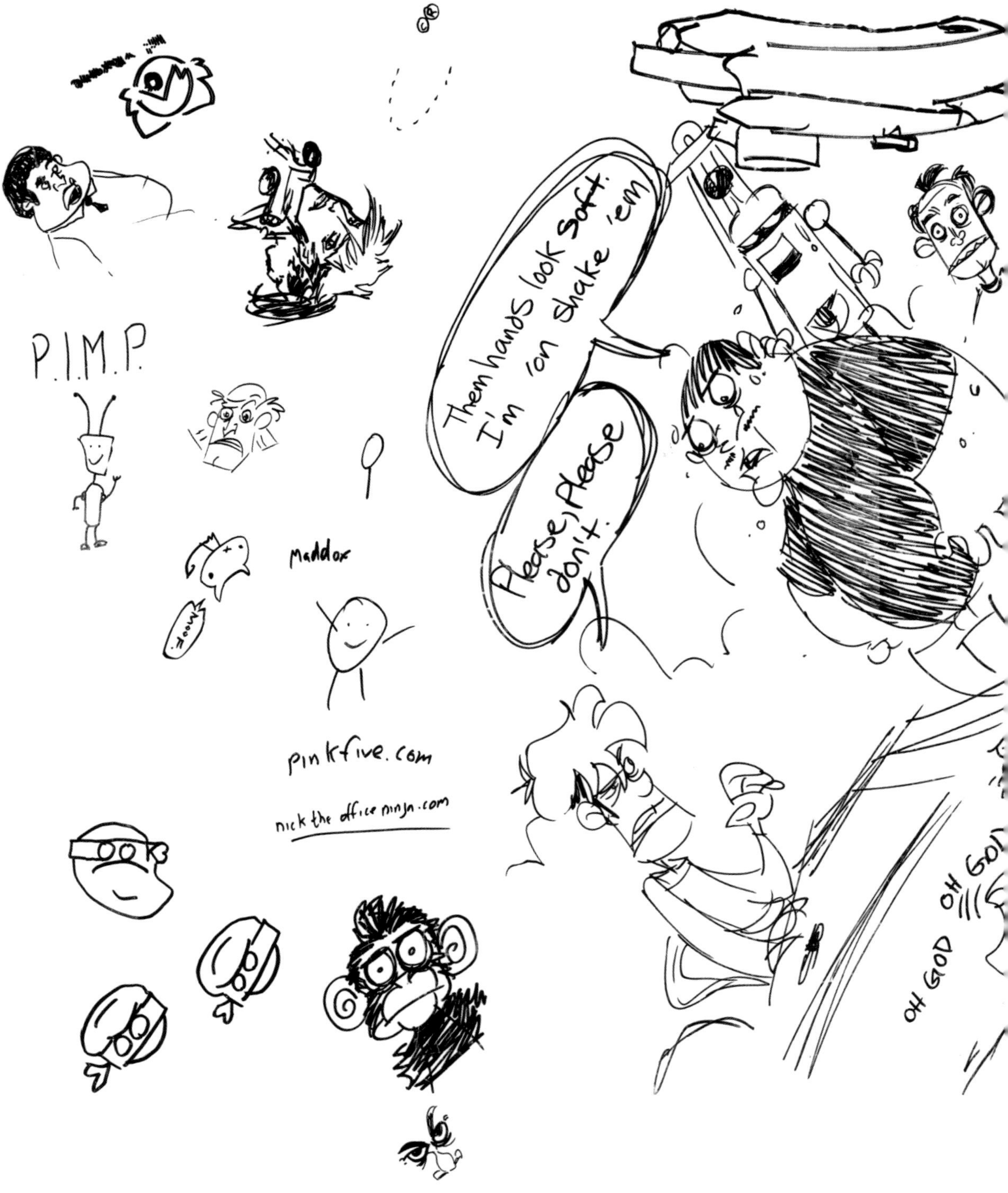
P.I.M.P.
Maddox
pinkfive.com
nick the office ninja.com
Them hands look soft. I'm ion shake 'em
Please, Please don't.
OH GOD OH GOD

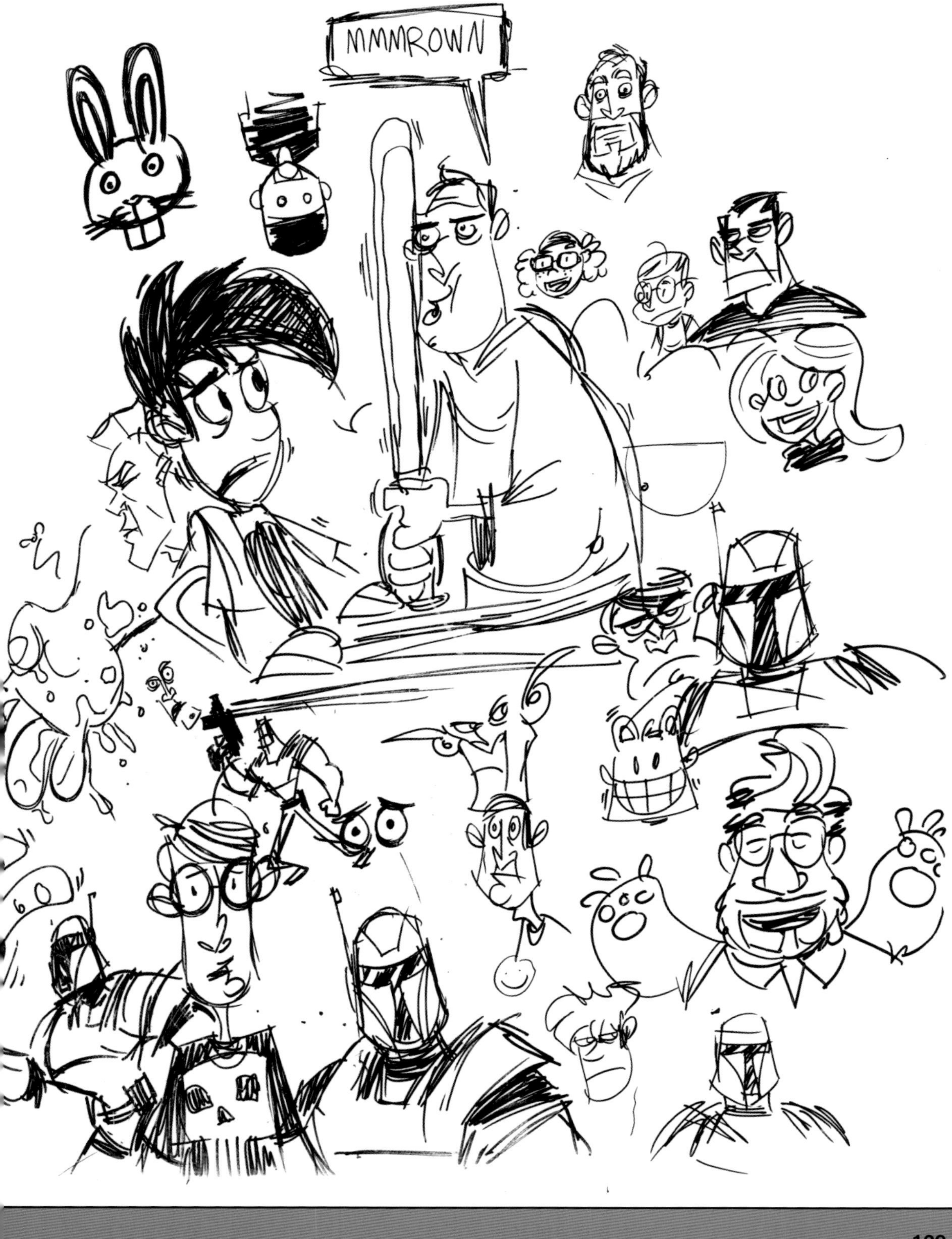
MMMROWN

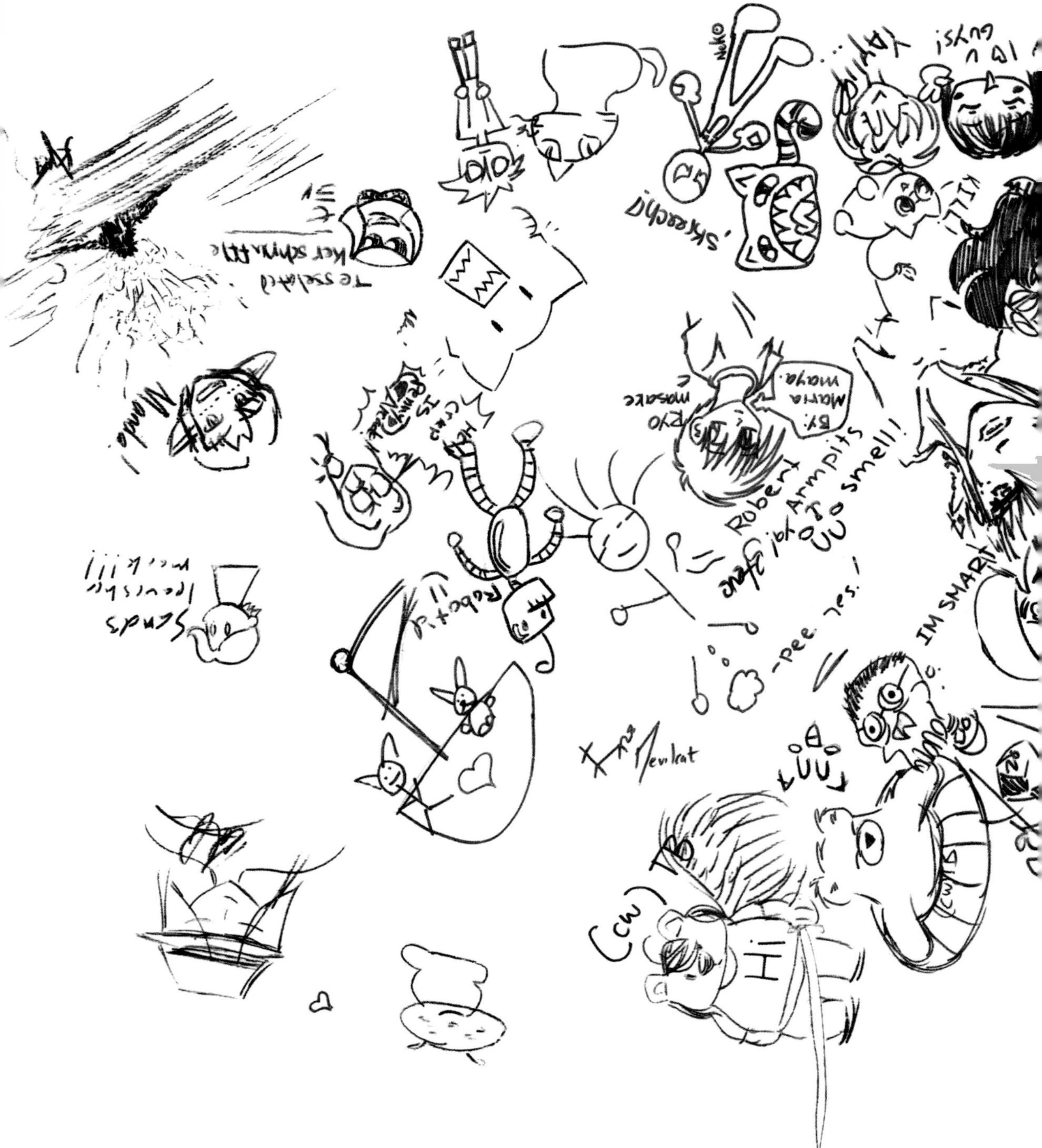
Robert Armpits
you smell!!
IM SMART
-pee. yes!
Hi
(cw)

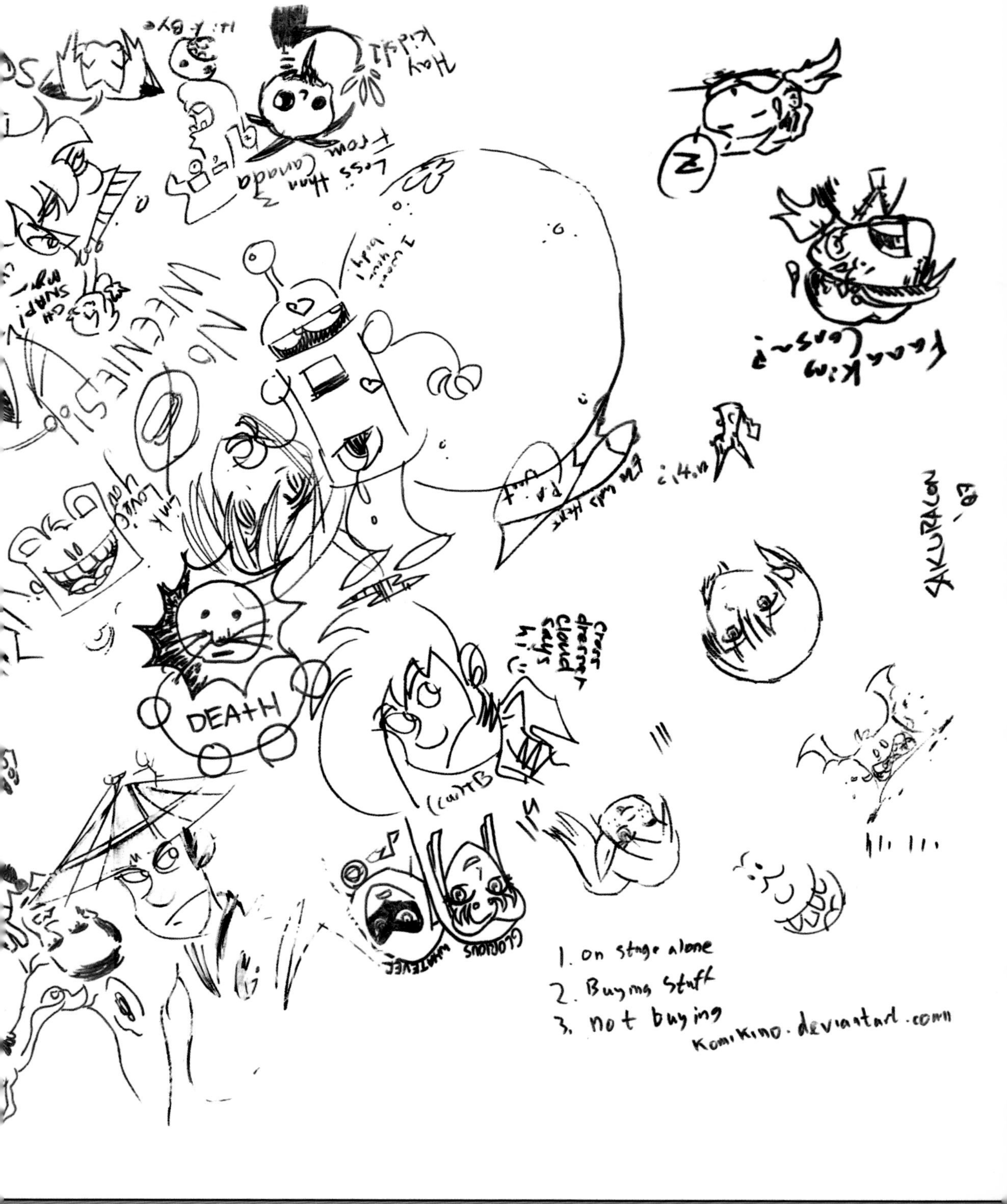

Hey kids!!
Less than 3 from Canada
DEATH
SAKURACON '07
Cross dressed cloud says hi
GLORIOUS WHATEVER
1. on stage alone
2. Buying Stuff
3. not buying
Komikino.deviantart.com

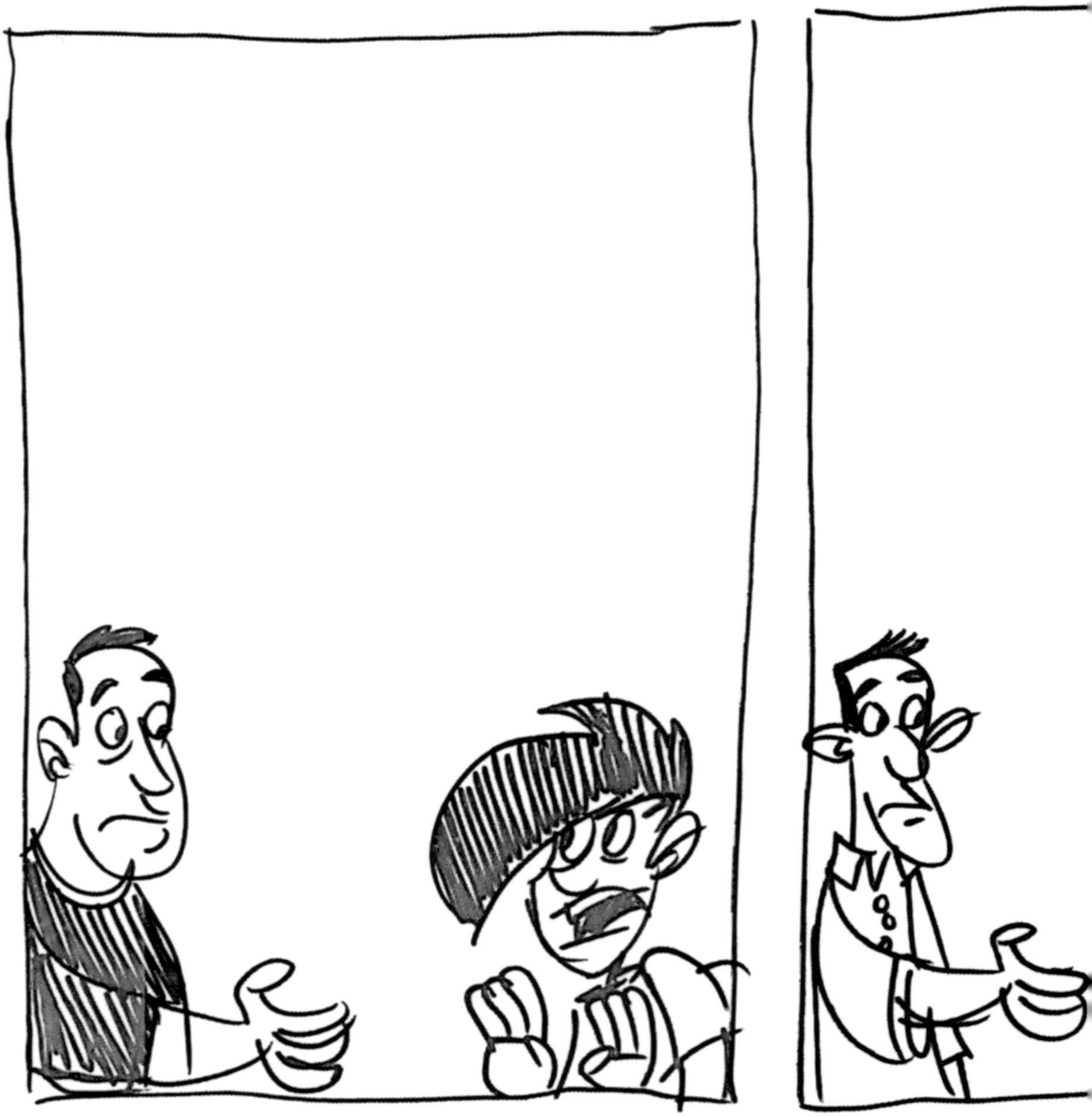

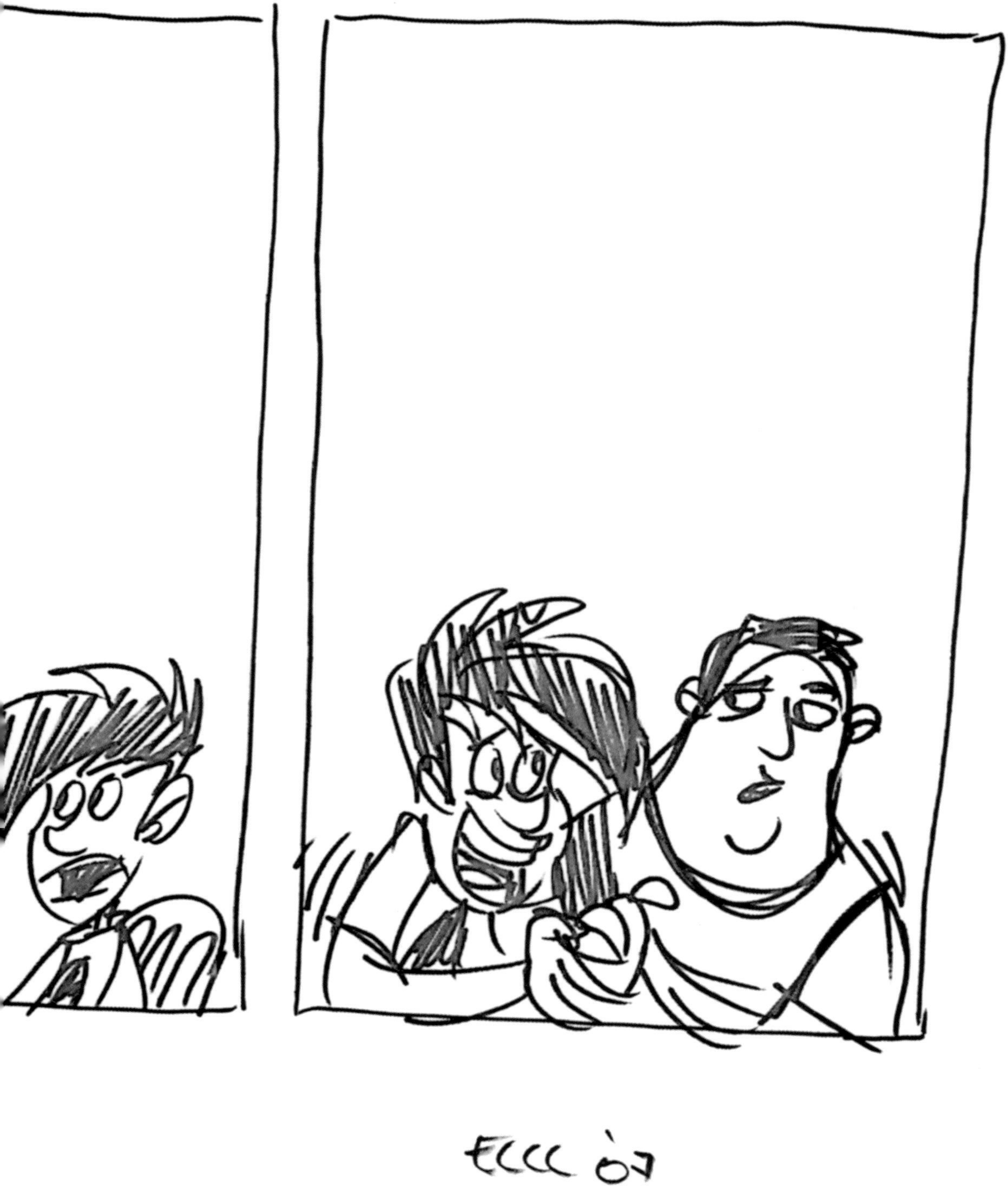
ECCC 07

CLAN WALRUS

EXIT ROOM

@cooki F;

CON!
About a nice

COOKI F;
wuz here?

Δ i hop to be a great day :)

Hi!
:D !

(˘ᵕ˘) TB

Lindon's
CANVAS

1: I'm super sick, man.
You don't want to shake
my hand.

2: No, seriously. You don't
want this. It's like
double A.I.D.S.

3. Steve Kurtz! I love your
work

5: My name is Scott
Kurtz.

6: Is it? that's
great.

(˘ᵕ˘) TB

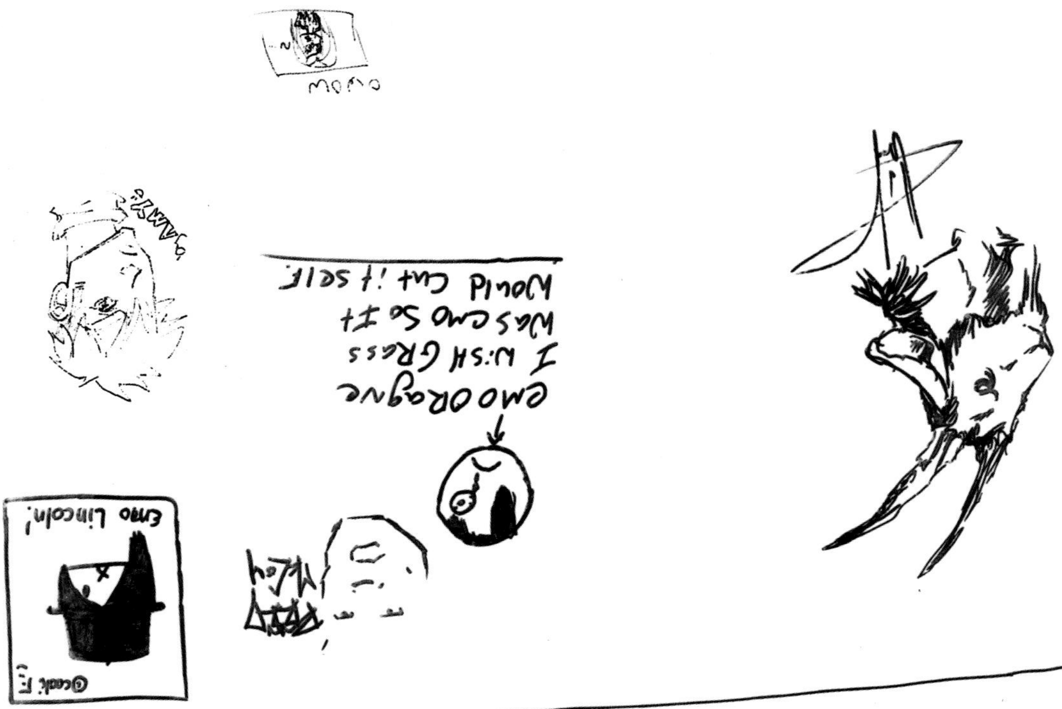
emoRagne
I wish Grass
Was emo So It
Would Cut itself
Emo Lincoln!

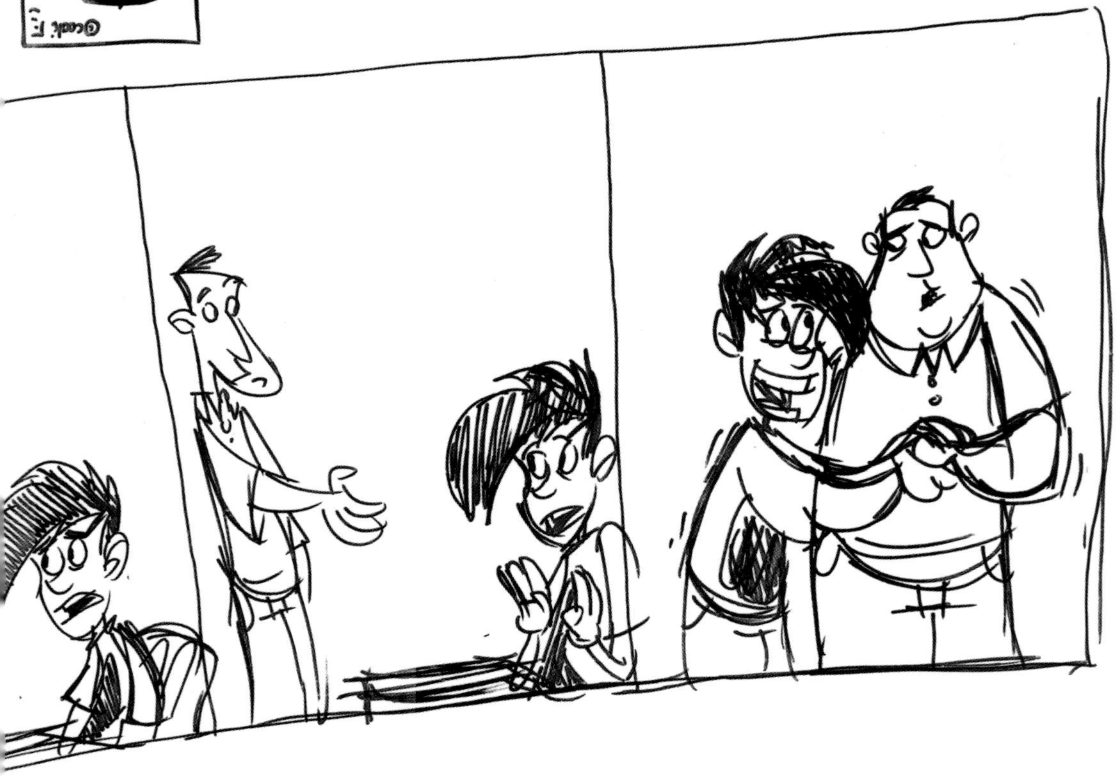

ECCL '07

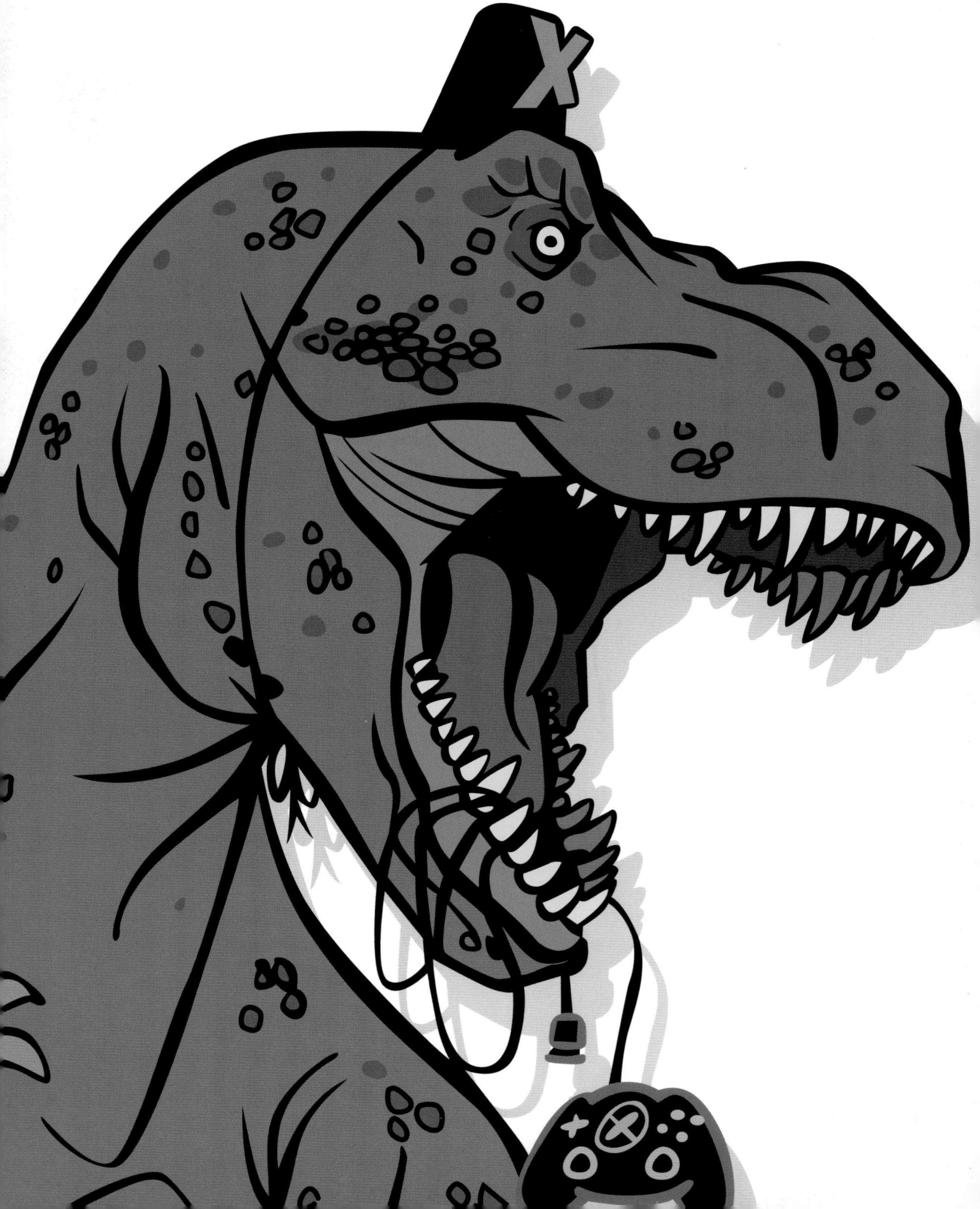